Kudos

"I was a bible-slinging hell defender for many years. My decision to read *Raising Hell* was solely to criticize it. It turned out to be the best decision of my entire life! Tears flowed as all those difficult questions I struggled with were finally answered. Now I understand those famous words, 'I came that they may have life.' No longer am I wasting my life walking on eggshells of religion." –Randy Serrano, NY

"I'm a former pastor and my joy knows no end after encountering this book! Oh the amazing peace! Finally, a clear, logical, and loving picture of a sovereign God. God is gloriously good!" –Lazar Sretenovic, Australia

"At first, I wasn't too interested in reading *Raising Hell*. The author is not a noted theologian or famous pastor. Julie Ferwerda is, however, a gifted author. I read the entire book in one sitting. She is basically a Bible-loving person who wants the whole world to experience the love and grace of God by stepping outside the box and exploring what the Bible *really* teaches about the subject of hell. Not everyone will agree with her conclusions, but if you read with an open heart and mind, you will not be able to walk away from this book without feeling that her conclusions just might be right." –William Nieporte (www.nieporte.name), VA

"I'm at a place in my life where the character and nature of God is being investigated from every angle, *honestly*, for the first time. Instead of trusting Orthodoxy, I'm challenging the double mindedness of my bible college and seminary education that now stands out to me like a sore thumb, wondering how I could have been so blind. *Raising Hell* is the third book I have read on the doctrine of hell, and I want to commend Ferwerda on the painstaking detail, broad foundation, careful scholarship, and the respect and honor in which she conveys the issues. It is a great work and will have a far-reaching, liberating effect." –Mike Glenn, CA

"If you've ever felt an inner conflict with what the theologians and pastors of orthodox Christianity teach about hell vs. what you feel in your heart about God's love...read this book! Let go of the notion that only pastors or scholars have the key to answer your faith questions. The Bible was written for everyone to study and discern its meaning. You have nothing to lose by reading and deciding for yourself whether or not 'the king is naked.'" –Barb Riley, IL

"This book is an easy read, and will challenge you to your core. Whether you are willing to accept that we've all been lied to or not, at least take the challenge. If you are a preacher who holds to this doctrine, you might want to avoid this book unless you're willing to accept the possibility that you were lied to in your seminaries. Julie is very convincing, and I see the truth to be on her side." –Phil Thompson, AZ

"*Raising Hell* has left a deep and lasting impact on me. Julie Ferwerda has articulated the message of freedom and inclusion—the gospel as it was intended—better than any other writer or theologian I have read to date. Others have expressed the same or similar message in writing but, in my opinion, Julie's is the sweetest and most gentle voice—I cannot thank her enough. If your heart is hungry for the gospel of love for all humanity, if you cannot reconcile a God of 'love' with eternal hell fire, then this is the book for you." –David Dellman, MDiv, Baltimore, MD

"Ferwerda's book makes me want to stop strangers in the street and say, 'Hey, man. Did you know...?' The things she explains not only make sense, but answer questions she isn't even asking! It's an enjoyable read—I can't recommend it highly enough!" –David Mclaughlin, Great Britain

"I'm a pastor and am very impressed by the logic and the obvious amount of time spent in research of this book. It's interesting and compelling, and helped me a great deal in my own search." –Neal Johnson, ME

"The message of *Raising Hell* isn't wishful thinking or one of those 'hell just can't be real because it would be so mean' books. Each argument is laid out with evidence and a lot of research. I had doubts about hell for years and was looking for a book that could be used as a resource with others. I have found that book. Everything from the 'lake of fire' to the word 'everlasting' is thoughtfully explained in an easy and understandable manner. I highly recommend this book for anyone looking for scriptural proof that God will save all of humanity." –Tony

"I must say that *this is one of the greatest love stories ever written*. I love Ferwerda's theory on the Jewish Feasts and Harvests. I know many of you may be instantly outraged if I were to ask, but would you please lay down your defense weapons and read this book?" –Tim Richmond, OH

"Things are changing; people are being set free from the great deception. Finally the teaching of everlasting torment is being seen for what it really is: the assassination of God's loving and just character! Thank you, Julie—history will remember you!" –Todd Lange

"Rob Bell's, *Love Wins*, was more about asking great questions; *Raising Hell* is more about great answers." –Tyler B.

"Hell (a.k.a. Dante's Inferno) is a non-biblical, mythological scare tactic that was invented by the early church. Julie does an excellent job at displaying the facts, showing the literary failures used by some of the most common translations. Using wit and good ole fashion charm to keep the reader engaged, she masterfully weaves the history and the origins of this ignorant and oppressive invention of the church. Finally a smart Christian woman who is not afraid to reveal the truth—even if it shakes the foundation of the church to its very core." –Nelson Rose, FL

"As someone who came to Christ later in life, I encountered a lot of difficulties in understanding the Bible, the biggest one being the concept of 'eternal torture' as the punishment for not knowing and believing in Jesus. My frustration grew to the point of my entertaining agnosticism and atheism. However, by God's grace, I 'stumbled' onto this book that introduced me to a completely different perspective on God's love and purpose for humanity. It was truly eye opening. Maybe I have been naive for not knowing about the Universalism viewpoint prior to reading this book, but nobody in my church and bible study has ever mentioned this Christian perspective. This book should be read by every Christian who is struggling with the orthodox view on hell." –Peter Utama, NY

"I have been studying this subject for more than 40 years and have read a lot of books. *Raising Hell* is the best of the best." –Walt Childs, FL

"I had read many academic articles and blogs about the different theories of the afterlife, and had come away an annihilationist. However, I desperately wanted to believe in universalism, especially after having a vivid dream about it, but I could not find the support. Finally, I landed on this book with all its incredible support and overwhelming evidence for the reality of universal reconciliation. By page 60, the book had sealed the deal for me. Ferwerda is witty, intelligent, bold, unapologetic, and very well studied. She takes you through a labyrinth of Hebrew perspectives and obscure truths that the present church is clueless about. She asks questions that stick in your mind, demand your attention, and demand a response that will not allow you to go back to the ignorance of the traditional view. *Raising Hell* will open your eyes to what the Scriptures actually teach about heaven, hell, the afterlife, God, and humanity. It will take you to a place of no return." –Michael Dise, Wake Forest Divinity, NC

"Ferwerda sure finished knocking me off the 'calf path' and helped me go public with the "Good News" in my pulpit." Pastor Don Hendricks, AZ

"*Raising Hell* is the best book I've read on this subject. It's thorough yet easy to read, liberating, and joyful! The manipulative and destructive doctrines that are considered orthodox have warped the world's vision of Christ. Embrace the real Good News." –Rebecca Cabildo, NM

"My warped view of God was destroying me. Deep down I wondered, 'Is God Evil?' Day and night I prayed for God to love the people I loved, crying my eyes out and pleading so that nobody I knew would ever have to spend millions and millions of years in excruciating pain and torment. Then one day I asked for prayer in my church: 'Please pray for me, I don't believe God is good.' My prayers were finally answered — *Raising Hell* was a really big part of that answer." –Laura Di Mare, Costa Rica

"I just knew it! God's mercy extends far past traditional teaching. Such a *heavy, heavy* burden has been lifted." –Lydia Foster, PA

"After Bible College, I had a few persistent questions—the kind that get people into trouble. *Raising Hell* does an excellent job of opening up the scriptures to answer those questions. In the end, we are left with a truer picture of Father God and His heart for His children. Jesus goes from being a wonderful person who gives his best efforts to rescue the few, to being King of Kings, Lord of lords and the Savior of the World!" –Jim Folsom, IL

"This book provides such a refreshing view on a subject that to me had become stale and repetitive. Written in a style that makes it a joy to read, Julie Ferwerda steps out with courage and zeal to bring great news to all who will listen." –Randy Wright, KY

"*Raising Hell* confirmed my belief in a God who is love, and who sent His son for all His children. I hope it goes viral, freeing millions who are tormented by fear, who spend more time in this life trying to avoid Hell than to embrace the Kingdom of God. This book is a celebration of God's love, and will only enhance your gratitude." –Lisa, Petersburg, VA

"Whatever your religious leanings or views on the afterlife, I strongly recommend *Raising Hell*. Not only is it intelligently written, it's also a pleasure to read, following a spiritual intellectual's journey of discovery. Not everyone will agree with her argument, but it's hard to fault her reasoning or her honesty as she makes a powerful case for re-examining some of the oldest traditions of the Church." –Michael Mulloy, TX

"Take the leap! I'd like to encourage people who are thinking about reading this book but may be nervous about 'heretical' writings or what your pastor or even friends may say about the subject matter. *Raising Hell* is a heart-stirring, interesting, informative, and enlightening read that lays the groundwork for a great deal of questioning—something that I think should be encouraged rather than discouraged as we seek the truth about God, life, love, and the future. The Good News is for everybody." –Sarah Elizabeth Jones, FL

"Occasionally you read a book that opens the door to your heart for an amazing revelation from God. Julie Ferwerda has been given an abundant revelation and it changes everything. She leaves almost no stone unturned. Her presentation is very persuasive that not only is the doctrine of hell harmful (and easily refuted), but it is the antithesis of God's plan for eternity. If you long to be able to believe that God's love is much better than we all were taught and you long to be able to believe it with confidence, this book just might be 'the one' that God uses to reveal His beauty to you. This book is revolutionary and sure to one day become a classic." –Emerald Gardevoir, NY

"*Raising Hell* stirred in me a wide range of feelings, from horror at what I've been taught my whole life, to absolute and utter tear-jerking relief and joy at realizing that *there really is no hell!* There isn't! Be free!" –Andy, OR

INDEX

To order additional copies of *Raising Hell* and for discounted bulk orders, please visit:

RaisingHellBook.com

Visit

RaisingHellBook.com

Where you'll find:

- Additional answers to your questions
- More resources and links to great websites
- An opportunity to provide feedback and engage in a discussion about God's inclusive love.

"I had come to a place of near insanity at the horrible thought of such a place as eternal torture actually existing. How could I love a God like that—one who would torture my mother, grandmother, brother, sister, or even my beautiful daughter forever? God would have to destroy every ounce of compassion and caring He instilled in me in order to get me to be capable of doing so. This sick caricature of God is not what the Bible speaks of but is only a position reached by faulty translation, poor hermeneutics, and the tendency of man to impose their views on the biblical text. Julie's book will take its place among other fine texts in providing a beacon of hope and light to a world suffering under the fear and torment of fundamentalism. If you have been haunted by the teaching that says your loved ones are heading to a hopeless, painful eternity, take the time to read this well written and documented treatise on the issue, and spend some time on your knees thanking God that He truly is love. I cannot recommend this book highly enough." –Leonard Curtis, UT

"I've been a pastor for 50 years, swimming in all the murky stuff that Julie's book describes. What a winner of a book!" –Pastor Bob Lee, IL

"*Raising Hell* has the capacity to wholly change and reshape your worldview concerning questions that may have plagued your weary heart for years, answering with integrity and prowess questions that have given Christianity a black eye for centuries. Ferwerda's style is that of a highly competent, investigative journalist, putting precise words to my analytical queries regarding the seeming hypocrisy of God and his apparent hell invention. Every page unearthed and overturned my assumptions, which were founded on the sinking sand of illogical indoctrination. It truly has the ability to capsize your presuppositions and set your heart ablaze as you embrace a God of unfathomable love, kindness, and purpose. Bravo, Julie! This ex-pastor gives you a hundred thumbs up for your scholarship, research, passion and probing heart. I am a huge advocate of this book—it's probably on my top five books of all time." –Terre Woodhead, WA

"I heartily recommend *Raising Hell* as one of the best books I've read on the subject. It's well-researched, convincing, and gracefully communicated. There are many books out there, but I can think of no better place to start than here. Be prepared to have your faith challenged, your paradigms shattered, and your heart filled with joy and wonderment at the vastness of God's great love!" –Ken Eckerty, FL

"As someone raised in troubling and contradictory fundamental Christian beliefs, I could not put this book down. It put into words all my similar thoughts, feelings, and questions. It shows beyond a doubt—to those who really want to know the truth—that the doctrine of eternal torment is not to be found in the Bible. It will leave you with a whole new perspective about God's awesome love for humanity." –Don Griffin, NC

"Ten years ago, I would have called anyone who agreed with what Ferwerda believes a 'heretic.' Now I'm beginning to wonder if maybe the orthodox view of hell is actually the real heresy. To believe in the doctrine of eternal torment in light of the character of God, revealed in His Son Jesus, is difficult. To believe in it in light of what the Scriptures actually say, is impossible. My hope is that this historical work will receive the widest readership possible. It's time for people to discover that the Good News may actually be better than we thought." –Dave Lilligren, MN

"I grew up fearing God to the point of misery and soul sickness. I was taught that God was a fierce and punishing deity. In the next breath, 'God so loved the world.' It never made sense to me! How could God love all of us so much and want us all to be with him, but then punish and send some to hell only because they didn't pray the 'sinners prayer'? *Raising Hell* gave me a firm platform on which to base what I believe God has already been telling me, that He is indeed a God of love and mercy!" –B.W.

"I've spent years and years intensely researching the doctrine of hell, and Julie Ferwerda has done the most comprehensive, outstanding job at breaking down this false doctrine and exposing it for what it really is – a complete falsity, kept up only by tradition. Even if you believe fully in the concept of eternal hell, I would recommend this book as a way to test your beliefs. What do you have to lose? I wish I had hundreds of copies to send to everyone I know! What an outstanding book!" –Steffany Johnson, CA

"*Raising Hell* is a beautifully written book of deliverance from the oppressive torments of theological hell. You are about to joyfully discover that critical theological teachings are wrong. Julie handles the original language and ancient history better than many a veteran biblical scholar, encouraging lay people to take an honest look at the text, and take victory over the distortions and dogmas we have inherited from eons of 'well established precedent.' How exciting to find that the Creator of the Universe really turns out to be far more loving, all-powerful and life-giving than we ever hoped or imagined! He is All in All!" –Kelly Shepherd

"Best book I have read in a long time! If Rob Bell's *Love Wins* opened the door, Julie Ferwerda welcomes you into the house, sits you at the Father's table and brings out some warm cookies and cold milk for you to enjoy as you get to know the Father you always wished He could be (but were told otherwise). Every pastor, teacher, and Christian around the world should read this book – it's life changing!" –Shawn Wilson, LA

"I absolutely love this book! Julie takes your hand and leads you through her own personal journey in finding out what 'hell' is exactly and why we have come to believe what we believe. I love the open and honest discussion of all the hard questions she allowed in herself about hell and then how she proceeds to work through each and every one! *Raising Hell* confirms what my heart has always truly felt!" –Rebecca Ersfeld, IL

Raising Hell

Christianity's Most Controversial
Doctrine Put Under Fire

Julie Ferwerda

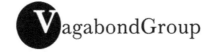

Dedicated to you, my beloved Christian brother or sister
whose questions have outgrown your teachers
you who remain hopeful yet dissatisfied,
believing that God has somehow been
tragically misrepresented and misunderstood.
May God's Good News renew your joy
and empower you in *The Life* like never before.

CONTENTS

SETTING THE STAGE...

There's a childhood fairytale by Hans Christian Anderson about a vain Emperor who had a fetish for extravagant clothing. Two opportunistic scoundrels in the kingdom decided to take advantage of the King's vanity. "Your royal majesty, we are two accomplished and sought after tailors and, after many years of research, we have invented an extraordinary method to weave a cloth so light and fine that it feels practically weightless against your skin. As a matter of fact, it's invisible to anyone who is too incompetent and unworthy to appreciate its quality."

The Emperor envisioned the luxurious nature of such an innovative fabric in his royal collection. Unable to resist the prestige of owning the latest and greatest, he thought it would be money well spent to hire such accomplished men. Not only would he acquire a new, extraordinary suit, he would also discover which of his subjects were incompetent and unworthy of their positions in his kingdom.

Upon finishing the new suit, the tricksters brought the Emperor into his private dressing chambers so they could make final alterations, ensuring the fit was perfect. As it turns out, the Emperor didn't see a stitch. Such a dreadful and disappointing outcome caused him immeasurable inner turmoil. If he admitted to seeing only his nakedness, the others in his kingdom would discover that he was unfit and incompetent for his royal position. Quickly covering his fear and embarrassment he said to the men, "Yes, this is a fine suit and it looks very good on me. You've done a magnificent job." He paid them extravagantly for their goods and services.

Next, the men suggested the King parade in front of his kingdom to show off the new suit. All subjects were "educated" ahead of time that only the worthy and intelligent individuals would be able to see his new clothes. Everyone else would be sniffed out and exposed as unfit for their jobs and positions in the community.

As soon as the parade began and the King proudly flashed in front of them, everyone nervously tried to hide their shock and embarrassment, though many convincingly declared their approval.

"Look at the Emperor's new clothes — they're stunning!"

"Look at the color of that exquisite fabric!"

"I've never seen anything like it in my life!"

From the least to the greatest, everyone behaved perfectly to keep up the uh, fabrication, just as the two scoundrels had predicted. Everyone, that is, except the one who had no important job, no position in the kingdom, and nothing to lose. A child approached the Emperor's carriage and shouted with honest assessment, "What's going on here? Why is everyone ignoring the fact that the Emperor is *naked*?"

The boy's father reprimanded him, but it was too late. The damage had been done. Whispers could be heard circling throughout the crowd until some of the braver bystanders finally cried out, "The boy is right! The Emperor *is* naked!"

What a precarious position for the Emperor. With the evidence as plain as his naked butt, he realized that he had been duped, but he could not—would not—admit to it. He thought it better to continue the procession under the illusion rather than admit to his colossal, gullible mistake. For the remainder of the parade route he continued, proudly as possible, standing upon his carriage.

While it's easy for us to recognize and even make fun of the naïve gullibility of the Emperor, the reality is that all of us have, at one time or another, fallen for wives' tales, urban legends, fables, and even downright deceptions—it's just part of being human. Even our religious, theological, and doctrinal beliefs are not immune to distortions and deceptions.

As I think back over my lifetime, I notice how many of my beliefs have evolved. Many things I believed as a child or even a young adult are no longer things I believe now. Why not? Because somewhere along the line, I learned that what I had been taught was misguided or false, and I no longer subscribed to that belief after learning things that made more sense or were more provably correct later in my learned experiences.

Essentially, we are all on a spiritual journey seeking "truth," though our truths of yesterday may not look so true today. Even the "truths" I wholeheartedly believe may not be true to you, or vice versa. As we grow and mature, we realize that developing our sense of truth is a lot more of a thoughtful, intentional, and open-minded journey than we once realized. But what of those historical, essential doctrines and *orthodox* teachings of the Christian faith? Surely we can have utmost confidence in our orthodox doctrines being true...or can we?

Dare to Question

I was born asking questions—it's part of my makeup. I'm especially one to ask questions when I come across things that don't add up. And in recent years, I've noticed more and more things that don't add up—things I've come across that challenge some of the core beliefs I've accepted and professed all my life. Many of these couldn't be ignored, so I set about trying to find answers.

If you too are inclined to ask difficult questions and to put your core beliefs to the test, a fair word of warning. There is risk involved. I've noticed that often, when people like myself begin to raise honest questions about things we see that appear to contradict what we've been told or that go against "orthodoxy," others become suspicious about our "spiritual condition" and we are put on watch. And when people do attempt to answer our questions, they often give pat answers like, "some things aren't meant to be understood now," or "we just have to take that on faith." Eventually, ignored, intimidated or shamed into silence, we keep our questions to ourselves. Or worse, we stop asking.

If our questioning is particularly contrary or persistent, or if we begin looking "outside the box" for answers, we may be scoffed at, ridiculed, and marginalized. People may label us as unintelligent, liberal, heretical, and perhaps downright cultish. You can see this type of conformity and peer pressure at work today in many churches, Christian peer groups of all kinds, as well as online in blogs and forums. Such labels seek to end the discussion and ultimately to prevent people from learning to think for themselves or from attempting meaningful dialog. In short, we lose the childlike freedom and inhibition to ask honest questions, and are expected to be more like the "competent and worthy subjects" who don't dare challenge the status quo or state the obvious.

I wonder how many critics of those of us who dare to question actually take the time to listen to us or to take a thoughtful, honest look to see if we might have some legitimate and more accurate perspectives. I agree that there is a time and a place to defend what one believes to be "truth," but even when we disagree, it must be done in a loving, civil manner, while at the same time maintaining an open mind to the ways we might be the ones who are misled.

If there's one lesson we can glean from the Emperor's story, it's that questioning without fear is the way of the child. It is only *the childlike*—the one with nothing to gain and nothing to lose in honest assessment—who is the most willing to ask uninhibited questions, and to acknowledge and proclaim the simple, apparent truth, despite the dissenting majority.

Who Am I to Challenge?

I realize that the premise of this book for some is radical, unsettling, and may initially ignite suspicion or even feelings of antagonism towards me, but please keep reading and give me a fair chance to build my case. I'm not asking you to go to South America to drink Kool-Aid, or to wear a toga and sell flowers at the airport, or even to send money. Lay your natural defenses down long enough to read one little book from a perspective that's likely much different than what you've always been taught or believed. When natural, reasonable objections come up as you continue reading, jot them down and let them rest until you are finished. I bet you'll find that I address each of your major questions and objections as we go, so there's no reason to agonize with frustration prematurely. You have nothing to lose by being open-minded and, in my opinion, a staggering, life-transforming amount to gain.

You may ask, is it safe to challenge over 1,500 years of traditional theology-in-the-making on matters such as whether or not there's validity to the doctrine of hell? You may also be wondering what difference does it make whether or not we believe in hell if we all agree that salvation only comes through Jesus. I'll tell you why we must question the teaching of hell. *The very name, character, and purposes of God are at stake!* What if, by not questioning and not taking the time to get to the bottom of these matters, we are guilty of completely misrepresenting God's character and intentions to the world? In my opinion, it's not safe to NOT question. Living at the forefront of the information age, I believe we have both the crucial responsibility and the unique opportunity, unlike at any other time in Church history, to make an informed determination of what we believe and why we believe it. We have been offered a prime peek into the looking glass of history.

You might also be asking, who am I to question or doubt the majority of today's mainstream Bible translators, theologians, MDivs, and pastors? I've certainly thought about that, but then I've also thought about what kind of people Jesus gave insight and understanding to. Was it the educated, religious hierarchy in the form of theologians, scribes, and leaders of His day? Or was it the simple, uneducated, illiterate fishermen, tax collectors, and prostitutes, all of whom could easily offer a spiritual parallel to today's folks who haven't been to seminary and who are overlooked, disregarded, or despised by those more knowledgeable?

It was to the *childlike* that Jesus promised to reveal the hidden treasures of the Kingdom. Besides, if I'm going to leave matters of critical scriptural interpretation as to the character and authority of God fully up to the scholars, theologians, and pastors to decide for me, which ones should I listen to? Depending on which ones I talk to, these learned men adhere to opposing views (Calvinism and Arminianism) on what I consider to be two of the most important foundational doctrines of the Christian faith—who Jesus died for, and whose will prevails in the end—man's or God's. Can I afford to take a risk like that?

Arminianism declares that God desires but is unable to save all people because He cannot infringe upon the "free will" of people, even that of uninformed, infinitely inferior, fatally wounded from birth, inherently self-destructive beings. *Calvinism* declares that God is unwilling—does not desire—to save all of His children because He has only "elected" a few for salvation. This theological sway says that God purposely created most of His own children to be damned forever, perhaps merely to provide a contrast to those whom He created to love forever.

These two diametrically opposed views, held and taught by brilliant, studious, devoted, well-trained theologians, pastors, and Bible teachers, comprise nearly 100% of today's evangelical Christian beliefs regarding salvation. Depending on which doctrine you side with, the Kingdom of God appears to be either an anarchy or a dictatorship, yet they can't both be right. Shouldn't there be solid, conclusive evidence for one position or the other on so important a matter? Is there a chance they could *both* be wrong?

I know it's easy to want to rely on the strength of numbers for our beliefs, but of all the multitudes of people He encountered, including well-trained, religious leaders and teachers of His day, Jesus had only a handful of simple, unscholarly followers who were willing to hear, follow, and even die for a different message than the orthodox teachings of His day. I believe Jesus' true message, as we'll fully explore, was that *He came to save all people with the assistance of a chosen people, in a purposeful plan that extends long past this mortal lifetime.* Jesus died for ALL (1 Peter 3:18), and His Father's unrelenting will that "none should perish" prevails in the end (2 Peter 3:9).

Throughout the last 2,000 years, this belief, embraced by a significant segment of Christianity, has been referred to as: Universal Reconciliation or Restoration, Universal Salvation, the Blessed Hope, Christian Universalism, Irresistible Grace, and a host of other names. It is not the same as the New Age belief that there are "many ways to God," or that living a life of sin is of no consequence. Universal Reconciliation is the belief that all people for all time will eventually be reconciled to God — that this lifetime is not the "only chance" to be saved — but that there is only one way to God, through Jesus Christ.

Through a very intentional plan that reaches into future ages, I believe the true Gospel is that all people for all time will be willingly and joyfully drawn by the unconditional, irresistible, compelling love of a Father into a relationship with Him through His Son. In the end, every knee will have bowed, and every tongue will have confessed Jesus as Lord, giving praise to God (see Rom 14:11, Philippians 2:10).

To see and believe such a beautiful truth requires nothing more than the simple faith of a child. "I thank You, Father, Lord of heaven and earth, that You have concealed these things from the wise and understanding and learned, and revealed them to babes (the childish, unskilled, and untaught). Yes, Father, for such was Your gracious will and choice and good pleasure" (Luke 10:21, AMP).

Bring the Child Along

What child in the world would ever believe (without adult influence) that a loving parent would create a fearful place of torment, and then endlessly abandon most of his or her children there, punishing them for a limited duration of unbelief or rebellion, or for choices made from ignorance, distortions, deceptions, or bad influences? My educated, reasoned belief is zero.

In the coming pages, I'm inviting your inner child to take a journey. Drop the fear of being rejected or labeled, unshackle yourself from the desire to conform, and allow yourself to ask (or be presented with) some honest, valid questions in order to follow where the evidence leads you.

I'm certainly not suggesting the evidence will necessarily lead you to the same conclusions as it did me, but at least allow yourself to weigh the options and make an informed decision. Dare to question what you've been taught, retesting all against the full counsel of Scripture, according to 1 Thess. 5:21: "But examine everything carefully; hold fast to that which is good."

Without a doubt, this book will likely challenge many core orthodox teachings you've been taught in church, yet my hope is that your Bible will be illuminated like never before, offering a much more sensical and cohesive story about God's amazing and largely forgotten plan for humankind. No longer will you have to ignore seemingly contradictory passages or do painful contortions to make the pieces fit. My desire is that, through the pages of this book, your God will become more unlimited, more powerful, and more loving than you ever dreamed possible. Of course, He is the same today as He was yesterday; what will change, with perspective, is you.

One important point I wish to mention is that I have received a few criticisms for my use of Wikipedia as one of my sources in this book. *Raising Hell* is intended to be the starting place, the opening of a most important conversation that I hope continues well beyond this book. One of my goals within these pages is to teach the reader how to do their own research by using a large variety of scholarly, historical, and informative resources that are easily accessed by anyone and everyone.

Wikipedia has been shown to be equally (or more) credible to other encyclopedia sources. It is easy to understand and streamlines a lot of information in one place. But regardless, I don't use it heavily, and I include a plethora of other scholarly resources for backup. In short, if you don't appreciate its value as I do, enjoy the other resources that offer plenty of supportive evidence.

I wrote this book to share my journey of learning and discovery. My journey didn't just leave me cautiously hopeful, but *proved* to me that the doctrine of hell is nothing more than a human invention—a "tradition of men." The alternative perspective I'm about to share with you has totally transformed my views of life, God, people, and has given me complete peace about the destination of loved ones who have yet to embrace Christ as their Savior. No longer do I worry about evil gaining the upper hand, no longer do I wonder just how much control God has over His creation, or question His limits on mercy and love. Since this transformation, my life has blossomed with joy, hope, purpose, and excitement like never before. How I long to share it with you.

Again, I don't expect that everyone who follows my journey will embrace it or come to the same conclusions. These are my beliefs, based on the evidences that I have uncovered. But you should also know that, despite mainstream Christianity's attempts to marginalize these beliefs, there has always been a significant number of Christians throughout history who have embraced the same beliefs (news to me!), and there are a rapidly growing number of studious, thoughtful Christ-followers worldwide today who also believe the same.

Ultimately, everyone must decide for themselves what is "truth." If you are comfortable with your current orthodox Christian theology and you don't wrestle with significant theological questions, this book may not speak to you. But if you've ever questioned the doctrines of heaven, hell, election, free will, and evil, or ever wondered why so many scholarly and educated people can't agree on many theological pillars of the faith, then this book will likely speak to you as nothing you have encountered before.

Lastly, perhaps you're relatively happy with your flavor of Christianity, but have never known what questions to ask. I hope this book will challenge and nurture your questions and faith, whether you embrace the message or just listen to the evidence presented.

Dare to ask. Dare to question. Dare to open your mind to the possibilities of a bigger God than you've ever heard about before. It could be the greatest decision of your life! Perhaps you'll find, just as I did, that it's time for all hell to break loose.

Let me take you on my journey…

Part 1
Hell: Fact or Fiction?

The Calf Path

by Sam Walter Foss (1858–1911)

One day, through the primeval wood,
A calf walked home, as good calves should;
But made a trail all bent askew,
A crooked trail, as all calves do.

Since then three hundred years have fled,
And, I infer, the calf is dead.
But still he left behind his trail,
And thereby hangs my moral tale.

The trail was taken up next day
By a lone dog that passed that way;
And then a wise bellwether sheep
Pursued the trail o'er vale and steep,
And drew the flock behind him, too,
As good bellwethers always do.

And from that day, o'er hill and glade,
Through those old woods a path was made,
And many men wound in and out,
And dodged and turned and bent about,
And uttered words of righteous wrath
Because 'twas such a crooked path;
But still they followed — do not laugh —
The first migrations of that calf,
And through this winding wood-way stalked
Because he wobbled when he walked.

This forest path became a lane,
That bent, and turned, and turned again.
This crooked lane became a road,
Where many a poor horse with his load
Toiled on beneath the burning sun,
And traveled some three miles in one.
And thus a century and a half
They trod the footsteps of that calf.

The years passed on in swiftness fleet.
The road became a village street,
And this, before men were aware,
A city's crowded thoroughfare,
And soon the central street was this
Of a renowned metropolis;
And men two centuries and a half
Trod in the footsteps of that calf.

Each day a hundred thousand rout
Followed that zigzag calf about,
And o'er his crooked journey went
The traffic of a continent.
A hundred thousand men were led
By one calf near three centuries dead.
They follow still his crooked way,
And lose one hundred years a day,
For thus such reverence is lent
To well-established precedent.

A moral lesson this might teach
Were I ordained and called to preach;
For men are prone to go it blind
Along the calf-paths of the mind,
And work away from sun to sun
To do what other men have done.
They follow in the beaten track,
And out and in, and forth and back,
And still their devious course pursue,
To keep the path that others do.

They keep the path a sacred groove,
Along which all their lives they move;
But how the wise old wood-gods laugh,
Who saw the first primeval calf!
Ah, many things this tale might teach —
But I am not ordained to preach.

CHAPTER ONE

LOST AND FOUND

I must have read the parable of the prodigal son in Luke chapter fifteen a hundred times, before I noticed the most important, defining detail.

Perhaps you remember the story. One of two sons asks his father for his portion of the inheritance, and then leaves home to squander it on fast living. Far away from home and with no money to his name, a severe famine takes place. He lands a job tending pigs, longing to fill up his stomach with what the pigs are eating, which is better than nothing. But even then, his luck has run out and no one offers him anything to eat. It is then, in his recognition of deepest need and end of self-reliance, that the son remembers the generosity and merciful nature of his father back home. As the realization of the error of his ways sinks in, he makes up his mind to go back to his father to humbly admit his sin and failure, and to ask if he might be taken in, if only as a hired hand. Even if he is no longer regarded as a son, at least he will have something to eat.

Look what happens next:

> But *while he was still a long way off*, his father saw him and felt compassion for him, and ran and embraced him and kissed him.

Did you see that? Before the young man could utter a word of remorse, before he had a chance to admit what a screw-up he'd been, the father had been scanning the distant horizon for his son's form and ran to meet him with open arms. We can't help but feel a bit of the father's joy when he recounts to the older brother what this moment meant to him:

> …We had to celebrate and rejoice, for this brother of yours was dead and has begun to live, and was lost and has been found (Luke 15:32).

What does this parable reveal to us about God's heart toward His children—even the rebellious, ungrateful, unbelieving, completely lost ones who are as good as dead to Him at the moment? Is this offer of reconciliation being promised to all, or only to a few? Is it limited to this lifetime or does the offer continue into the next, for as long as necessary? Is there ever a limit or deadline to God's love and patience in waiting for His children to come home?

It was only recently I noticed that the parable of the prodigal son is the third in a series of parables, all revealing the same crucial point: Something of great value has been lost—a sheep, a coin, and a boy—and that which is lost is helpless to rescue itself from its circumstances and must be sought after diligently, *until* it is found and restored to where it belongs. The owner or father is not satisfied as long as even one—one sheep, one coin, or one son—remains lost.

Twice in this series, Jesus conveys the heart of heaven: "In the same way there will be more rejoicing in heaven over one sinner who repents than over ninety-nine righteous persons who do not need to repent" (vs. 7, 10). Doesn't that imply it is necessary that we repent? Of course, but did the son have to repent before he was received into welcome arms? Did he have a choice about whether his father watched for him, found him, and never gave up on him? Did the straying sheep ultimately have the choice not to rejoin the flock? Did the misplaced coin have a choice not to be swept up and put safely into the purse? Do sinners and unbelievers have a choice when it comes to ultimately being reconciled to their heavenly Father? Might the point be, in any case, that the move to "come home" will eventually and always be agreed upon as desirable by the one lost?

In the parable of the lost sheep, it is the shepherd who goes searching for his missing sheep. He does not wait for the animal to find its way home; he searches it out, puts it on his shoulders, and carries it back to the flock. Similarly the woman from the parable of the lost coin searches by lamplight for her missing coin. She does not wait to happen upon it, or consider it hopelessly lost unless fate brings it to her.

These lessons seem to stand in contrast to how most of us are taught that God relates to His children. In our Bible study groups and from the pulpit, we hear time and again that the Lord is our Shepherd, but ultimately this Shepherd waits passively for his flock to come to Him—to choose Him. We learn that He does not search for helpless stragglers and carry them home on His shoulders. Instead He watches over only those sheep that remain in His sight while damning those who wander away or do not know how to find their way home.

The lost sheep, the missing coin, and the prodigal son are really parables about each of us—every person ever born. We have all either inadvertently gotten lost or willfully left home for the illusion of something better. "All of us like sheep have gone astray, each of us has turned to his own way; But the LORD has caused the iniquity of us *all* to fall on Him" (Isaiah 53:6). Paul's words also come to mind, echoing the message of the parables: "For *while we were still helpless,* at the right time Christ died for the ungodly. …But God demonstrates His own love toward us, in that *while we were yet sinners, Christ died for us*" (Romans 5:6–8).

The word "sin" means to "miss the mark." In ancient times, this idea was about getting off the right path—getting lost. We have all been qualified as ungodly, helpless sinners and path-missers who wandered off the right path, following our own way. Yet isn't this exactly who Paul says Jesus died for? Was His death for most in vain?

Throughout this book, we are going to explore how understanding the message of these parables and learning the heart of the Father will deliver the fatal blow to any such notion of an everlasting hell, or even the more palatable version of "eternal separation from God." As we piece together a remarkable story, we'll find that it can't be possible that He would turn away even one son or daughter, and that every person, given enough time to "starve among the swine," will come to the realization that home is where they belong. Even before they can round the bend for home, they will be welcomed with the happy reassurance that the eyes of their true Father never stopped searching the horizon, ready to run to them with loving, open arms. If Jesus' words are to be our instruction in the matters of life, then we can have assurance that love is the healer of all things. Our Father will ultimately never give up on nor ever reject—ever!

Wait! What about hell?

The Bible mentions hell repeatedly, doesn't it? Yet hell doesn't seem consistent with the theme of Luke 15. It doesn't seem consistent with the Pauline gospels, and it doesn't seem consistent with many of the words of Jesus. The doctrine of hell tells us that for most of mankind, there will be no fattened calf waiting when they realize the error of their ways and are ready to come home. That, unlike the good fate of the lost son, there will ultimately be no open arms for most of the sons and daughters who have ever lived.

Many of us resist such things intuitively. When you question any loving Christian, they will admit that they desire for everyone to be saved and they cannot truly make sense of the alternative. But pick up almost any Bible translation and there it is—hell, with its fire and brimstone, its everlasting torture and torment.

So if hell appears to be inconsistent in many ways with the character of God—a God who asks us to forgive all our enemies as many times as necessary, and who tells us that "love does not fail"—could there be a better way to interpret Scripture? If we are free to ask questions like a child, might some of our questions include the following?

- Could there be a reason that some authoritative Bible translations don't even use the word "hell" or convey any kind of "everlasting destruction" throughout?

- Could it be possible, over the course of two thousand years, that mainstream Christianity has been misguided into believing lies about the character and intent of our loving heavenly Father to the point that it became reflected in Bible translations over time?

- Is there historically and scripturally a viable Christian theological position that doesn't teach a literal, eternal hell?

- Is hell a necessary component of the Gospel message or the Christian faith?

- Is it possible that the hundreds of years of Church doctrine formation and traditional teachings could have veered off course?

These and many more controversial yet intriguing questions will be discussed and answered in the coming chapters. These will not be answers that merely prey upon emotions, or that sacrifice reason to wishful thinking, but will offer perspectives that are scripturally and historically sound. As we begin to chart new territory, all you have to do is maintain an open mind and concede that there might be a context that differs from the one you accept as orthodox truth now. If you can take that leap, if you can allow yourself to put to the test things that have been foundational to your Christian faith, then let us continue.

I want to start by telling you my story of how I got to the place where I began questioning. Every journey starts with a single step, so let's start at the beginning.

CHAPTER TWO

QUESTIONING HELL

I'd been waiting with great anticipation for a couple of weeks to make this phone call. When my eighteen-year-old daughter answered her cell phone, I didn't waste any time. "Dani, I've been dying to tell you the exciting news for a few weeks now. I've made some amazing discoveries in my studies lately and, well, you were right all along — *there is no hell!*"

"I knew it!" My daughter shrieked into my ear, not missing a beat. She didn't ask me what I was talking about, or question the insanity of what I was saying to her now, even without any apparent logical context. From the time she was a young child, it was Dani who first doubted the veracity of this oft-reinforced teaching from her traditional Christian upbringing. It was the child who innately believed in the benevolent character of God.

When I finally revealed my findings to my daughter, she didn't know that I'd been immersed in nonstop study for over two months, trying to sort out history and Scripture, after the prompting of some eye-opening discoveries. I didn't dare get her hopes up prematurely, until I was absolutely sure.

Throughout my oldest daughter's childhood, she often questioned Sunday school teachers, youth leaders, and especially me about the logic of eternal torment. Certainly she has a very compassionate heart for people, but it was deeper and more profound than that. She couldn't accept the seeming contradiction of God's character that professed unconditional, sacrificial love for all people on one hand, but on the other hand declared an end to that love as soon as a person died without professing faith in Jesus Christ. She couldn't accept the injustice that billions of people would be punished and separated from God eternally because of a limited period of rebellion or unbelief during their mortal lives, especially when most of those people had no way of knowing about or entering into a relationship with Jesus or the Christian God.

As she entered her teen years, she began going on overseas mission trips, where her inner wrestling over the notion of hell only intensified. She witnessed the utter desolation and despondency of multitudes of people who had the deck stacked against them since birth—people who had virtually no chance or "choice" of encountering the Savior of Christianity in their squalor and misery. This led to her frequent questions, inner torment, and eventually disbelief.

In my mother-knows-best reasoning mode, I patiently yet uncompromisingly explained to her, each time I sensed her rejection of such a cornerstone tenet of our faith, what I had been ingrained to believe over a lifetime: "God deeply loves every person He ever created, but in that love, He had to give them a choice to love and accept Him or to reject His free gift of salvation. God doesn't send anyone to hell, people choose to go to hell by rejecting Him."

"But Mom, not everyone has the same opportunity to choose God or to love Him back. Either they don't ever get the chance to hear because they don't live in a Christian country, or they can't hear because of so many factors outside their control."

"Dani, we have to believe that in God's sovereignty and power, He makes sure everyone gets a fair chance to choose. If they haven't heard, He will reveal Himself to them somehow over the course of their lives and they will be without excuse. Again, God doesn't *want* them to go to hell— it's their choice to go there because He won't force anyone to accept Him."

I have to admit, when your own child is challenging your beliefs like this, the answers often sound pretty lame to your own ears. I gave her the best of what I could with what I knew at the time, but even to me, my rationale had serious flaws. I too had been to places like India and Haiti, witnessing the same lack of opportunity people had by not growing up in a loving Christian family or hearing the Gospel. It bothered me too, but I squelched my own dissonance with blind, unquestioning "faith," assuming that the Christianity I grew up with and the people I looked up to for spiritual guidance couldn't be wrong. This is all I'd ever known. I had never heard or read anywhere that there's a historically and scripturally sound alternative to the doctrine of eternal torment—an alternative that many scholars and historians agree was the predominant view of Christians for the first several centuries after Christ.

Before that day of sharing the truly Good News with my daughter, no matter how hard I tried, my pat answers and misguided attempts at reasoning out the doctrine of eternal torment did not make sense to her or bring her comfort. Before the day of that phone call, I often worried while watching her struggle to believe in the loving character of God, and hoped she wouldn't lose faith until she was able to accept such a core tenet of modern Christianity.

Confronted with Evidence

If you are a conservative Christian, your views on the teachings of the Bible are likely not much different than the views I held until a few years ago. I grew up in an evangelical, hell-preaching, hell-believing church, and continued that course unquestioningly in various church experiences for most of my adult life. I have been actively involved in a gamut of evangelical denominations and ministries—Nazarene, Baptist, Evangelical Free, Navigators (college), Christian and Missionary Alliance, and non-denominational Bible churches. In short, I have always believed in hell (eternal torment and separation from God) as the "due punishment" for those who do not accept Jesus as Savior in this mortal lifetime, regardless of when and where they were born, and whether or not they ever heard the Gospel of Jesus Christ. All my life, I unquestioningly rationalized that hell was somehow compatible with God's "perfectly loving and perfectly just" nature. Since I saw the word "hell" used numerous times in my Bible, and since I had heard about it in many a sermon in church, and since missionaries have been traipsing the globe for centuries to try to rescue people from hell "before it's too late," I assumed that hell must be real.

Since college, I've been deeply involved in various ministry leadership positions—youth, young adult, women, and singles—usually teaching the Bible, my greatest passion, either in classrooms or through my writing. I don't say any of this to impress, but only to provide the backdrop of my beliefs and experiences that you might better understand my journey and the great care and thoughtfulness that went into arriving at these conclusions.

I've read through the Bible numerous times, but have always had the sense that significant meaning was hidden from view, locked up beneath the surface. When reading the Old Testament (OT), it always felt like there were so many disconnected ideas and unrelated stories that didn't really make sense for us today. I often thought, shouldn't the "inspired Word of God" be more meaningful and relevant for us today and tie together more fluidly? For instance, what does a neighbor's ox falling into a landowner's pit (Ex. 21:33), or a warrior's dream about a barley loaf destroying an enemy camp (Judges 7:13), or a bunch of Israelites celebrating the end of the harvest of grains and grapes (Deut. 16:13–14) have to do with *anything*? I often asked God to open my heart to understanding, as He promises. Even so, I did not intentionally set out to find any of what I am about to share with you, but I'd say, "it found me."

In the summer of 2008, my Bible-crazed friend Darcy and I began studying the Bible with a Messianic Jewish woman, Maxine. Maxine introduced us to insightful Messianic Hebrew teachers online, and it seemed a whole world of understanding began to open up in our Bibles, particularly in the Old Testament (OT). We marveled at the beauty and complexity of the Hebrew language, and how *one verse* in the Torah (Genesis–Deuteronomy) can contain a whole book's worth of meaning through the many layers of the rich Hebrew language.* Many Hebrew scholars even claim that there are as many as seventy layers of meaning in every verse of the Torah, referred to as "The Seventy Faces of Torah."†

Suddenly, previously obscure passages began to unlock and tie together in profound ways, and I began to realize that, without this critical view of the Scriptures, it is almost impossible to decipher the meaning of so many significant OT concepts and themes—themes that carry over to the New Testament (NT). I became painfully aware of how a lifetime of studying the Scriptures without the correct lenses, whether at home or in church, left my understanding far short of the original framework and intent.

At this time, through the encouragement of the Hebrew teachers, I learned the illuminating joy of studying the Scriptures in the original languages. There is a wealth of free online resources available today and, with some time and effort, anyone can learn to dig deeper into the richer meanings of the Hebrew and Greek Scriptures with tools like a Concordance and an Interlinear Bible. ‡

---

* One example, *Creation's Heartbeat: The Bible's Entry Code in Genesis 1:1*, by Dr. Y. Fass (2009) is a fascinating full-length book devoted to the underlying, layered meanings in Genesis 1:1 from the Hebrew language.

† Learn more: hebrew4christians.com/Articles/Seventy_Faces/seventy_faces.html.

‡ An Interlinear Bible is a word-for-word Greek (or Hebrew) to English. Locate an Interlinear online at: scripture4all.org/OnlineInterlinear/Greek_Index.htm. We will cover more about studying from and using these resources later.

And for me (along with Darcy and my husband, Steve), that's where all the "trouble" began.

It actually started with the discovery of what appeared to be a significant translation error of a Bible verse. This created a giant problem. For one thing, I had often gotten into big arguments with my husband when he occasionally questioned the inerrancy of Scripture. I defended it to the point of heated argument insisting that, in God's sovereignty, He had preserved the inerrancy of His Word, despite the lengthy span of time and fallibility of countless human scribes and translators involved. But in this particular case, the translation error stuck out to the three of us as plain as the Emperor's naked butt.

That set the ball rolling and soon we were exploring the translation accuracy of many well-known passages. By then, we were getting comfortable with checking out the Greek and Hebrew ourselves, and were often able to study out and get an idea of where things went wrong. Needless to say, my belief in the "inerrancy of my modern Bible translation" was soon shot. The more we questioned and studied, the more inconsistencies and translation errors we found—errors in the NASB, the KJV, the NIV, and especially the NLT (my previous favorite)!

Now, I expect there will be some Bible students and pastor types reading along right now who will think it naïve of me to have ever believed that the KJV, NIV, NLT, NASB, and other modern translations are "inerrant," since many of them learn about translation errors in their formal training. While this is all well and good, the fact remains that most church statements of faith specifically state that "the Bible is the infallible, inerrant Word of God," and as such, most lay people do not differentiate the original language manuscripts from the modern translations they read from. Recently, I've noticed some statements of faith being modified to say that the Bible in its "original form" (which no longer exists) is inerrant, but that is the exception rather than the rule. Sadly, out of fear of the backlash, very few pastors and churches feel the liberty to discuss and work through these issues with their congregations.

It wasn't just the translation errors that caught our attention, though. We also found curious inconsistencies between translations, and what appeared to us to be arbitrary or slanted renderings of passages that are foundational to certain Christian orthodox doctrines. Up until this time, I had always been told that any existing errors or inconsistencies were sparse and decidedly insignificant to central doctrines of the orthodox Christian faith.

Some people have questioned our ability to discern errors ourselves, and have suggested that we need a trained pastor or theologian to help us decipher what we are reading. But many of the errors and inconsistencies we've encountered are so elementary that even a third grader would be able to see them. Take Hebrews 1:2 for example. Let's compare five different versions of just one little phrase out of this verse:

NIV: "...but in these last days he has spoken to us by his Son, whom he appointed heir of all things, and through whom *he made the universe*."

NASB: "...through whom also *He made the world*."

KJV: "...by whom also *he made the worlds*."

BBE: "...through whom *he made the order of the generations*."

YLT: "...through whom also *He did make the ages*."

Is there any way we can say these versions convey the same meaning? No. Yet they're all translated from the same Greek text.*

Ironically, what initially encouraged me that we were not getting off-base in discovering so many translation errors and, at times, even suspecting foul play or agenda, was a verse I happened upon in Jeremiah:

> "But My people do not know the ordinance of the LORD. How can you say, 'We are wise, and the law of the LORD is with us'? But behold, the lying pen of the scribes has made it into a lie. The wise men are put to shame, they are dismayed and caught; Behold, they have rejected the word of the LORD, and what kind of wisdom do they have" (8:7–9)?

Right there, in black and white, Jeremiah confirmed that the scribes had inserted lies into the OT writings, many centuries before a Bible was ever published or canonized.†

---

* There are two different Greek texts from which our modern translations are derived — the Textus Receptus and the Nestle Aland. It wouldn't matter which text these translations used because they both agree in this particular verse. The more correct translation is Young's Literal, "through whom also He did make the ages."

† *Biblical canon* is a list of books considered to be authoritative as Scripture by a particular religious community. The standard Bible that we read today was not canonized until at least the middle of the fourth century A.D., and it should be noted that the Protestant Bible contains a slightly different set of books than the Catholic or Eastern Orthodox versions. See Wikipedia for a description: http://en.wikipedia.org/wiki/Biblical_canon.

I'm not suggesting that all translation errors are intentional, but somewhere along the line, people with the authority to influence the theology of billions, made some serious alterations. Perhaps they tried to improve what they thought was meant by the original writer or scribe, or they didn't know the meanings of certain words they translated from languages that were not their mother tongue (our modern Bibles evolved through five very different languages—Hebrew, Aramaic, Greek, Latin, and English). Others who followed them, knowingly or unknowingly continued in the same course, not correcting what was done before. We arrive today with several thousand years' Scriptures-in-the-making, communicated from one generation to the next (for many centuries via oral tradition or hand copied), over four to five language changes, and hundreds, if not thousands, of scribes and translators, who were basically the only literates of entire societies (read: major lack of accountability). It's not a stretch to imagine that "stuff happened." As a result, the Bible we open today often reads very differently than it did 1,500 years ago.

In recent days, I've discovered that even the Jews do not believe in the inerrancy of Scriptures, but teach that they are inspired writings in varying degrees, to be interpreted within the whole. Quoting from, *The Seventy Faces of Torah: The Jewish Way of Reading the Sacred Scriptures,*

> Even if the Torah contains fairly accurate historical memories, it is likely that these memories were reworked and retold to fit the needs of later times. This should not surprise us. The history of the American Civil War, for example, needs to be retold in every American generation as our understanding of race relations, the relationships between the various regions of our country, and our sense of the meaning of the American Constitution and American history evolve with the times.[1]

Surely this doesn't mean that errors dominate the Scriptures, or that truth isn't there to be found, or that we need to throw out everything we've held to. But what I have realized is that getting to the fuller, truer picture of the Scriptures is going take a lot more thoughtful and personal study—more digging and searching—than most of us have ever done before, and it's going to be a lot like searching for buried treasure.

A Bigger Story

One day, in the midst of our probing and researching, Darcy called me to say she'd come across a website that led her to believe we needed to question the doctrine of hell. I was out of town, taking care of a sick friend for several days, and Darcy's unexpected suggestion immediately threw me into a tizzy. Having had a close family member wander into a cult-like following several years before, I cautioned Darcy strongly.

"Darcy, now you're scaring me! Remember that when we started down this road of questioning, we agreed that, number one, we wouldn't place our trust in any one teacher or group (there had to be a significant number of people from different walks of life throughout Church history who believed the same) and, two, in the case of any foundational doctrinal question, we must fully study it out together, making sure we come to agreement that any new perspectives are not leading us away from truth."

Now, I realize that none of what we agreed to is foolproof, and that one man's truth is another man's heresy, but this is what I told her. I made Darcy promise that she would stop studying this crazy, radical idea until I got home and we could look into the matter together.

When I did get settled back at home, she sent me to a website, Savior-of-all.com, asking me to read the article, "The Work of the Cross." She also sent me a list of verses she'd looked up (most of which are located in the Resources section of this book), and something struck a chord within me. How had I never noticed *all those verses* before—verses that seemed to express a much more inclusive Gospel than what I had always believed? There was certainly enough scriptural evidence to warrant further investigation. I also knew that I should honor what I had always taught my children: If you believe you have the truth, you shouldn't be afraid to read or question anything—let the truth defend itself.

When we located a plethora of *Christian* websites and information on the topic of hell being a false tradition of men—a huge surprise in itself—I told Steve and Darcy that if this new view of the Scriptures had any merit, it needed to answer every single one of our significant objections. If it was true that hell does not exist and the Bible doesn't actually support the concept, there should be solid, overwhelming evidence. In addition, this new understanding of Scripture should help to answer other theological questions, not just those about hell. Let me tell you, I had lots of questions and objections—similar to the ones I'm frequently confronted with by fellow Christians now:

- If there is no hell, what did Jesus die for and exactly what then am I saved from?

- What about all the Scriptures that mention hell and eternal punishment?

- Does everyone get off scot-free, no matter how they live their lives? Why not live however we want if we're going to be saved regardless?

- Why evangelize or tell people about Jesus at all?

- How could millions of devout Christians over many centuries have been duped, especially intelligent people who have devoted their lives to Bible scholarship?

- Isn't this some New Age teaching in an attempt to make God more palatable to the lost?

- How could this satisfy God's demand for justice?

- Isn't the Bible clear that people only get one chance to accept Jesus in this lifetime, before they die?

- Doesn't the New Testament mention hell more often than heaven?

These difficult questions—questions we will be exploring together—as well as my previous "rock solid" beliefs, were why I was more than skeptical that my belief in hell could be overturned satisfactorily.

It took loads of time, patience, intense research, debate, and study, but we *were* able to find solid, convincing answers to every one of our substantial questions and objections. We found many more satisfying answers, in fact, than our old belief system offered; not just answers about hell, but about God's largely unrecognized and forgotten plan for humanity taught from Genesis to Revelation.

What was particularly remarkable and awe-inspiring was that everything we learned corresponded perfectly with our recently formed Hebrew perspectives as well. Most importantly, we found plenty of evidence in Greek and Hebrew texts, in OT teachings, from early Church history for several centuries after Christ, and even from Paul's writings, all pointing directly to the teaching of God's plan to save and reconcile all people through a plan of ages, and to eternally damn none.

What we came to realize is that this mortal life is merely the introductory chapters in a lengthy Story—a concept that is beautifully revealed in Scripture when one knows what one is reading. As you are soon about to learn, Scriptures offer a much more sublime and glorious purpose to our future than the modern church acknowledges. The goal of this life, and ultimately the sacrifice of our Savior, is so much more profound than just living in preparation for an eternal vacation in the cosmos.

For the rest of this section and before moving on to the bigger story, we're going to find out where the notion of hell came from and explore what the Scriptures actually teach in regard to it. Hopefully, I can prove to you, not just why our modern grasp of hell is suspect, but ultimately why hell can't be true. Are you ready?

CHAPTER THREE

WHO IS GOING TO HELL?

Let's assume for now that orthodox Christianity is right – our Bibles are translated correctly and must be taken literally and unquestioningly on the subject of hell. Let's assume that hell does exist for all the really bad people, like Adolph Hitler and Osama Bin Laden, for all the cold-hearted atheists like Bertrand Russell and Richard Dawkins, and even for lots of nice, loving people who don't say "the sinner's prayer" before they die. If we are going to give equal weight to all passages and not disregard the ones that don't fit in with our orthodox belief system, a lot more people must actually be going to hell than those we just mentioned.

Masses. Have you ever noticed that when Jesus spoke to the crowds, He always set up mental obstacles? "All these things Jesus spoke to the crowds in parables, and He did not speak to them without a parable" (Matt. 13:34). The disciples, His closest companions, were always complaining that the parables were hard (if not impossible) to understand and asking for explanations (Matt. 13:10; 13:36; 15:15; 16:5-12; Mark 4:13; 7:17-18).

Assuming that those masses of people were headed to hell (by default, as Christianity teaches), why would He make the truth so obscure, I wondered? Then I found Jesus's answer in Mark 4:10-12.

> As soon as He was alone, His followers, along with the twelve, began asking Him about the parables. And He was saying to them, "To you (disciples) has been given the mystery of the kingdom of God, but those who are outside get everything in parables, so that while seeing, they may see and not perceive, and while hearing, they may hear and not understand, otherwise they might return and be forgiven."

Hmmm. You have to admit, it's kind of upsetting to find out that Jesus actually hid the truth about how to stay out of hell from the crowds – crowds who got the chance to hear from the "Savior" himself. Apparently He intentionally doomed those large crowds of people forever without a decent chance at belief. If you look into it, Jesus never even spoke to the crowds about "hell" (that we read about), only privately and in smaller contexts to His disciples and the Pharisees — religious people — and only, at the most, on three or four unique occasions.

Depending on how we interpret what Jesus was doing, we might actually make a case for the Calvinist doctrine of *election* where only a small, privileged few are predestined — chosen ahead of time — for salvation while everybody else is chosen ahead of time for everlasting punishment and separation from God. However, the thought has always seemed pretty weird to me that God would go to the trouble of creating billions of people in His image, knowing ahead of time that He would endlessly reject and torture them. Not only does it fail to correspond with the forgiving and loving nature of God as revealed in Scripture, but also it sounds sort of Voodoo pin dollish.

In questioning Calvinists about the seeming unfairness of such a doctrine, they often quote Romans 9:14-24, explaining that God hardens most people who ever lived, forming them with no choice of their own into "vessels of wrath prepared for destruction." Of course they assume this passage implies "everlasting" destruction, which it does not, nor does it imply "destruction" in the way we imagine, but we will cover that later.

Such reasoning causes me to wonder how a Calvinist would hold up under the scrutiny of the Scriptures on the topic of "who's going to hell," according to modern Christian lenses? If we are to consistently read and apply all the teachings of the New Testament (NT), it appears that there are a lot more people going to hell than just the crowds who heard parables and the rest of the unbelieving billions in the world since.

Wise and learned (scholarly folks). Jesus, primarily speaking about the orthodox scholarly teachers and religious leaders of His day, also hid truth from these wise and intelligent types.

> At that very time [Jesus] rejoiced greatly in the Holy Spirit, and said, "I praise You, O Father, Lord of heaven and earth, that You have hidden these things from the wise and intelligent and have revealed them to infants. Yes, Father, for this way was well-pleasing in Your sight." ...Turning to the disciples, He said privately, "Blessed are the eyes which see the things you see, for I say to you, that many prophets and kings [wise, important, and scholarly people] wished to see the things which you see, and did not see them, and to hear the things

which you hear, and did not hear them [because they were hidden from them]" (Luke 10:21–24).

If Jesus "rejoiced" about God hiding truth from educated and intelligent people of his own religious heritage, does that mean He was glad they were going to hell? Could there be educated and intelligent folks today for whom the truth is hidden — perhaps even Calvinists?

Disobedient people. Jesus frequently made statements like: "Not everyone who says to Me, 'Lord, Lord,' will enter the kingdom of heaven, but he who does the will of My Father who is in heaven will enter" (Matt. 7:21). Paul, the apostle to the Gentiles made many similar statements to both Jews and Gentiles alike. "Therefore, let us fear if, while a promise remains of entering His rest, any one of you may seem to have come short of it. ...Therefore let us be diligent to enter that rest, so that no one will fall, through following the same example of disobedience" (Heb. 4:1, 11). Does this mean all disobedient people are going to hell? Would this not include many Calvinists, as well as many Christians in every denomination?

Rich people. I wonder if there are any rich Calvinists in America. I'm certain that there are plenty of rich Christians in general. I recently heard that there's a new mega-church opening every two days in the U.S.[2] One recently went up in Dallas for 120 million dollars. Now that's really impressive. I've read statistics that only two percent of American church budgets go to overseas missions and humanitarian aid, while more than thirty percent or more go to building projects.[3] Yet when I read the Bible, it would appear that rich followers of Christ who amass wealth in the "last days" (since the days of Christ) are in for some big surprises:

> Come now, you rich, weep and howl for your miseries which are coming upon you. Your riches have rotted and your garments have become moth-eaten. Your gold and your silver have rusted; and their rust will be a witness against you and will consume your flesh like fire. It is in the last days that you have stored up your treasure! ...You have lived luxuriously on the earth and led a life of wanton pleasure; you have fattened your hearts in a day of slaughter (James 5:1–5).*

The book of James is written to *believers*, not the unbelieving world. We should certainly take stock of which believers James is warning "in the last

---

* See also Matt. 19:23–24; Luke 4:18; 1 Timothy 6:6–19.

days." I suggest that American Christians in general, the wealthiest in the world by far, fit this description better than anyone. And what exactly is he warning them of? If hell is a real place and James is warning wealthy Christians about going there, this should be a little unnerving to many in the Church today.

Did you know that if Evangelical America put just their church building funds toward feeding the poor that they could drastically reduce, if not eradicate, world hunger? Each and every one of us could certainly bring this lesson even closer to home when we consider how we spend our own money on, or save up for, ourselves. Though difficult for us to accept according to the way most of us have been raised to cherish the American Dream, Jesus made this message pretty clear during His ministry. "If you wish to be complete, go and sell your possessions and give to the poor, and you will have treasure in heaven; and come, follow Me" (Matt. 19:21).*

If we are to literally and consistently apply all the passages in our Bibles, and if such a place as hell truly exists (according to orthodox Christian theology), doesn't our list of people going there seem to be growing by leaps and bounds? I sincerely hope somebody is left for the Kingdom of Heaven before we get through the rest of the NT warnings.

Gentiles. In the days of Jesus, it appears that all the Gentiles (non-Jews) went to hell. I realize this changed when Paul came on the scene, but before Paul, I guess all Gentiles were pretty much doomed: "These twelve Jesus sent out after instructing them: 'Do not go in the way of the Gentiles, and do not enter any city of the Samaritans; but rather go to the lost sheep of the house of Israel'" (Matt. 10:5-6; 15:22-24). This has always bothered me a great deal. If Jesus knew the Gentiles of His day were going to hell — the worst fate a person could possibly imagine or experience — how could He ignore all of them? How could He ignore *any* of them?

Jews. After the days of Jesus, when the Gentiles finally got included in the plan of salvation, it appears that there was a big shift and all the unbelieving Jews started going to hell. Quoting from Romans 11:7-10,

> What Israel is seeking, it has not obtained, but those who were chosen obtained it, and the rest were hardened; just as it is written, "God gave them a spirit of stupor, eyes to see not and ears to hear not, down to this very day." And David says, "Let their table become a

---

* See also Matt. 25:31-46; Luke 6:2-21; 14:7-14.

snare and a trap, and a stumbling block and a retribution to them. Let their eyes be darkened to see not, and bend their backs forever."

If we are to consider and apply all passages equally and fairly from our modern Bible translations, the Kingdom of Heaven sounds more and more like some ultra-exclusive club, with a very limited membership. Even the Calvinists should be feeling pretty insecure, as should those in the Arminian (free will) camp.

So now who is left for the Kingdom? Maybe a few missionaries who gave up everything to follow Jesus? Mother Teresa, assuming she actually said the sinner's prayer before she died? Perhaps children who have not yet reached "the age of accountability," and the unborn? Unless there's an alternative to what we've always been taught and believed, the odds don't look good for most of the rest of us.

CHAPTER FOUR

WHO'S RESPONSIBLE FOR LOST SOULS?

If hell is real, who is ultimately responsible for spreading the word and preventing billions of people from going there? The Calvinists (somewhere between ten and thirty percent of American Christians[4]) are probably off the hook for the moment, since they believe those who will be in "heaven" are chosen for it ahead of time. They basically believe that no pre-appointed believer will miss out on their get-out-of-hell-free pass, even if their Christian neighbor slacks in sharing Jesus with them. God will simply send somebody else to show them the way.

But for the majority of Evangelical America, those who believe one's "free will" decides their eternal fate (a.k.a. Arminianism), they've really dropped the ball in keeping as many people as possible out of hell. How can a person exercise his or her "free will" to believe in a God and Savior of whom they have never heard? Don't those who do know about Jesus and who believe in hell possess a grave responsibility to make sure everyone is offered an informed choice about their eternal destiny?

I have heard a few Christians back down at this point and say that those who have never heard will be given a "fair" chance to believe later, at the Judgment. If that's the case and those people will have a chance later to profess Jesus while being dangled over the lake of fire in the presence of God—a situation that will take no faith at all—then wouldn't it make more sense to stop sending missionaries to them? Maybe we are *sending* people to hell by giving them a choice now, in a world where they have to choose by faith. But would this be fair to the rest of us who did encounter the responsibility of hearing now and who had to choose by faith or potentially be doomed forever because of it?

As to the orthodox majority who do believe that anyone who doesn't profess Christ in this lifetime goes to hell, I guess what bothers me most is this: If they (and this should have been a question for my old hell-believing self as well) really believe that most of those people they know and care about—next door neighbors, "lost" family members, beloved friends, people of their community, and destitute multitudes of people like the 147 million orphans of this world—are going to a never-ending, terrifying, fiery hellhole of torture where there is "weeping and gnashing of teeth," why are they not out 24/7, sharing the love of Jesus with the lost multitudes...or at least trying out a few parables on them? Why are they going about life as usual, attending soccer games, church socials, Super Bowl parties, luxury Christian cruises, shopping sprees, beach vacations, beauty appointments, and even expensive Holy Land tours? If they really believe that hell is real, why are they not expending every penny and every spare minute they have to snatch as many people as possible from "the lake of fire" before it's too late? Why are they only tithing ten or even twenty percent of their income when they could be sacrificing so much more to support more missionaries in order to win more souls? Why are they not volunteering every week for the street evangelism team or down at the local hospitals and nursing homes, trying to save those who are about to go off to an eternity of conscious terror?

For those of us who have adhered to the notion of salvation by free will, how many people over the course of our lives have we been responsible for sending to a never-ending BBQ, just because we were too lazy, or too scared, or too preoccupied to help them find their way? Why does the thought of hell not deeply affect most of us, changing the way we live our everyday lives? Sure, it's up to God to convict and transform a person's heart, but isn't it up to those who are convinced hell is real to plant the seeds and spread awareness?

Motivation or Manipulation?

I like dissecting themes in Scripture to see what I can learn about usage and intent. The first thing I notice about the word "gospel" is that it actually means "good news." The next question I want answered is, for whom is it good news? In Luke 2:10 the angel says, "Do not be afraid; for behold, I bring you good news of great joy *which will be for all the people...*"

Have you ever wondered how the Gospel can be "good news" for *all people* if most people will not benefit from it? If most of the people who have ever lived are going to hell, wouldn't the "good news" actually be really bad news for multiple billions? Perhaps if hell is true the angel should have said, "I bring you good news of great joy for only the people who receive it and believe it."

Once I looked up "good news" in all the places it occurs in the NT Greek. It appears fifty-two times as an action, "bringing good news," and seventy-three times in noun form, "good news." I could not find one instance where it was used in the same context with hell or everlasting torment or even judgment—like the way we use it when we share the gospel today. In other words, the NT writers didn't share it as "*The good news or else! Turn or burn!*" When did this change?

Acts records NT believers sharing the Good News with Jews and non-Jews alike. The lengthy message in Acts 2:14-3:26 is the perfect opportunity for Peter to tell the unbelieving men of Israel that if they don't shape up and accept the message, they're going straight to hell. Yet Peter fails to seize such an opportunity. "Therefore repent and return, so that your sins may be wiped away, in order that times of refreshing may come from the presence of the Lord; and that He may send Jesus, the Christ appointed for you, whom heaven must receive *until the period of restoration of all things* about which God spoke by the mouth of His holy prophets from ancient time" (Acts 3:19-20).

Paul, the apostle to the Gentiles, also blows his opportunity in Acts 17:30-31 when he delivers a gracious and inclusive message to the learned men of Athens, who were non-believing, idol-worshiping, pagan Greeks: "Therefore having overlooked the times of ignorance, God is now declaring to all people that everyone everywhere should repent, because He has fixed a day in which He is about to be judging the inhabited world in righteousness through a Man whom He has appointed, *furnishing belief* to all* by raising Him from the dead" (MLT†).

This Scripture is clear on two things: God has set a day to judge the world in justice AND belief will be furnished to all humans. But it is

---

* NASB uses the word "proof," but the word in Greek, "pistis," is consistently translated as "belief" or "faith," 241 out of 243 times in the NT. In this case, translators concealed the important concept of God "furnishing belief to all humans." From the volumes of Koine Greek papyri discovered near the turn of the century, "pistis" was determined to more literally translate as, "obedient trust." See definition of pistis in, *The Vocabulary of the Greek New Testament: Illustrated from the papyri and other non-literary sources*, Hodder and Stoughton, 1914-1929, pg. 515. Available on Google Books.

† MLT stands for "More Literal Translation." In verses where modern translations have changed or watered down words, I have gone to the Greek or Hebrew and printed the more literal translation. Be sure to check passages yourself in the Interlinear Bible at: scripture4all.org/OnlineInterlinear/Greek_Index.htm.

important to understand that God's judgments do not inherently indicate an everlasting hell sentence. Isaiah 26:9, to which Paul very well could have been referring, explains the purpose of God's judgments: "For when the earth experiences Your judgments the inhabitants of the world *learn righteousness.*"

Here's my experience. If you even suggest to people these days that they should leave hell out of it when they share the Good News about Jesus with others (like Paul and Peter did), the first thing they ask is, "Well, if I leave out hell — what's left? What do I tell people they're being saved from?"

My response? First of all, if you have to use the fear of hell to get people into the Kingdom, then what does that say about your gospel? What does it say about your God? If hell is the most powerful motivating factor for getting people saved, then they are only being manipulated into something out of fear and coercion, not out of love and desire. I daresay that those people are not really saved after all! This is the very kind of "faith" Jesus criticized when He quoted Isaiah, "These people honor me with their lips, but their hearts are far from me" (Matt. 15:8).

I've had people say to me, "If I found out there's no such place as hell, I'm afraid I would get complacent in sharing my faith. I mean, what would motivate me to try to love people and to share the Gospel with them if they're not being saved from hell?"

The purpose of heaven's Good News is relationship with our Father through Christ, not fear of Him. Receiving the Good News brings abundant life *now* to people who are suffering in loneliness, emptiness, purposelessness, and lovelessness. The true Gospel brings about healing and reconciliation right now between God and His children, and ultimately among His children. It's not about being saved from hell, but about every person who ever lived being saved from the gloom and despair of all forms of death — the curse of Adam — and made ready for a very special Kingdom where all enemies of the Father will ultimately be overcome by love and brought to joyful agreement under the dominion of the Most High King. Perhaps that is why we are told in 1 John 4:18, "There is no fear in love; but perfect love casts out fear, because fear involves punishment, and the one who fears is not perfected in love."

If God is love, and if there is no fear in love, how has the primary doctrine of the most widespread religion on our planet become all about fear? How could such a fearful place as hell truly exist?

As we'll soon discover, understanding the *true Gospel* will release us from the frantic bondage of feeling like we only have X number of days during our mortal lives to save the world (even though most of us aren't trying all that hard to do it anyhow). Remember that even Jesus lived an unhurried pace. He was calmly intentional, investing in relatively few individuals, ignoring many, and speaking in riddles to most. Only those "with ears to hear" could understand Him and believe. But understand, ears to hear and eyes to see do not originate with people:

Deut. 29:4: "Yet to this day the LORD has not given you a heart to know, nor eyes to see, nor ears to hear."

Proverbs 20:12: "Ears that hear and eyes that see — the LORD has made them both" (NIV).

Rom. 11:8: "God gave them a spirit of stupor, eyes to see not and ears to hear not, down to this very day."

With verses like these and the lifestyle of Jesus in mind, let's be honest. If a place like hell exists, Jesus would be the most unfair and unloving "savior" that the world could have encountered. Add to that, if you're not a Calvinist and you're not doing everything you possibly can to keep people from hell, then you are personally responsible for many a lost soul. On the other hand, if the Good News is really just that — *good news* — then perhaps your job description has marvelously changed!

But wait a minute. If that's true and if there's ultimately no bad news, and if we have a new job description in the way we share the Good News, then we must figure out what to do with all the teaching and propaganda we've heard all our lives about hell.

That should be pretty easy. For starters, hell isn't even found in the Scriptures!

CHAPTER FIVE

THE MISSING HELL

In my experience, it never occurs to most Christians to research what evidence there actually is for the doctrine of hell, as taught in church. It seems like a given—the sky is blue, winter is cold, socks get lost in the washer and…there is a hell. Sure, the word "hell" is found in most modern Bible versions, but is there any concrete evidence to support such a teaching as eternal torment or separation from God?

Bible scholar types are big about interpreting Scripture in context. So let's consider the context of the entire Bible, beginning with Genesis. If I were going to defend my position on hell, Genesis would be the first obvious stop. I should think that if God wanted to present the ramifications of the most crucial choice and potentially fearsome destiny for mankind—the price for sin—*in the beginning* is where He should lay it all out, not waiting until the middle or the end. So what does God say?

> The LORD God commanded the man, saying, "From any tree of the garden you may eat freely; but from the tree of the knowledge of good and evil you shall not eat, for in the day that you eat from it *you will surely die*" (Gen. 2:16–17).

Nowhere in this passage does it say they will "die forever," or they will go to a place of eternal suffering. It just says they will die, as in stop breathing, or kick the bucket. Obviously, Adam and Eve didn't die the same day they ate. That's because the Hebrew text offers more of a progressive sense of entering into the death process. Young's Literal renders the translation, "dying thou dost die," and the Greek Septuagint* says, "to death you shall die."

---

* The Septuagint (LXX) is the Greek translation of the Hebrew Scriptures (OT), produced in the 300-200 BC era for Greek speaking Jews who had been exiled into the Greek empire and could no longer read or speak Hebrew. Though not used in modern Bibles, it appears to be credible and somewhat authoritative since it is the version used by NT writers when quoting the OT. The Septuagint is of importance to critics because it is translated from texts now lost. No copy of the original translation exists.

The apostle Paul referred to this first act of disobedience and the ensuing implications for all people. "Therefore, just as through one man sin entered into the world, and death through sin, and so death spread to all people, because all sinned" (Rom. 5:12). Through Adam, everyone inherited sin and sin's consequence—dying. Mortality. All people are born dying. And as far as I can tell, everyone dies.

After looking for evidence of the dire outcome in Genesis, the next place I would look for clear warnings would be throughout the OT. Were people properly warned of hell's disastrous consequences throughout? Were the people in Noah's day warned before they were destroyed? Did the prophets declare that the people should repent or they would go to hell? If not, wouldn't this be infinitely irresponsible and unfair?

The notion of hell is suspiciously missing from the OT as the destiny for most of mankind, unless you read the KJV or TM (The Message), both of which include the word *hell* over thirty times. Do KJV and TM know something others don't? Why the inconsistency?

Let's consider the Hebrew word that KJV translates as hell; it is the Hebrew word *Sheol*. * Sheol is more accurately translated as *grave, place of the dead,* or the *unseen,* (similar to the NT Greek counterpart, *Hades*). Throughout the OT, both good and bad people end up in Sheol at death. Rather than a literal grave (in the sense of a hole in the ground or tomb, which has a different Hebrew word), Sheol is the concept people devised in ancient times to imagine and describe the afterlife experience that they had no knowledge about. In ancient cultures, such as Babylonian, Egyptian, and Greek, you see numerous mythologies and imaginations about this afterlife, each culture influencing and building upon later thought. So the word translated as "hell" by KJV and TM is actually this word, Sheol.

As to why KJV would use hell where most other translations do not, see if you can spot any kind of agenda, as revealed in the first two verses and compared to the second two verses:

---

* NLT and The Message translate an additional Hebrew word, rapha, as hell in the OT. None of the other versions translate this word as such, not even KJV. Strong's translates rapha as "spirits of the dead" or "dead," but this is strange because rapha is usually associated with the word for "healing" in other passages. NLT also translates Abaddon as hell one time.

Psalm 9:17 (KJV): "The *wicked shall be turned into hell* (Sheol), and all the nations that forget God."

Psalm 55:15 (KJV): "Let death seize upon them, and *let [the wicked] go down quick into hell* (Sheol)."

Psalm 89:48 (KJV): "What man is he that liveth, and shall not see death? Shall he deliver his soul from the hand of *the grave* (Sheol)?"

Job 14:13 (KJV): "O that thou wouldest hide me in the *grave* (Sheol), That thou wouldest keep me secret, until thy wrath be past..."

KJV translates Sheol as *hell* whenever they want to convey it as the particular destination of the wicked. However, when portraying the fate of the righteous, they translate it *grave*. Hmmm. Obviously, the translators would have had a major problem if they had consistently translated Sheol as hell in all these verses. The third example would convey that every person would go to hell, and the fourth that Job asked to go to hell!*

In the rest of the popular modern versions, the literal translations, and the Hebrew and Greek texts, there are NO references to hell in the OT, or of the concept of everlasting tormenting flames—not one. Sure, some theologians will try to find a connection between a few obscure passages, but most reputable scholars have admitted that the OT doesn't provide any clear references.

Wait! Hell Actually Does Occur in Daniel

I believe there is one reference in the OT to our modern teaching of the doctrine of hell—chapter 3 of Daniel, verse 15. Check out King Nebuchadnezzar's command to Shadrach, Meshach, and Abednego:

"Now if you are ready...to fall down and worship the image that I have made, very well. *But if you do not worship, you will immediately be cast into the midst of a furnace of blazing fire...*"

King Neb (for short), ruler of Babylon† erected a 60 X 6 cubit‡ golden statue in the image of a man that he required everyone in his kingdom to

---

* Interesting translation statistic: KJV translates Sheol thirty-one times as "grave," thirty-one times as "hell," and three times as "pit" in the OT.

† Babylon in Revelation is considered by many to correspond to the last days' image of the unfaithful, idolatrous Church.

‡ In Hebrew the number for man is 6, as in 666. Though regarded by those in Babylon as a deity worthy of worship, this statue has been made by man, in the image of man.

worship. If they did not, they would be thrown into blazing fire. The three captives who revered the true God, esteeming His name and character, wouldn't bow down to the statue and were not afraid of the threat of fire, so Neb had them thrown into it. Well guess what? The young men weren't burned and they didn't even smell like smoke.* *Why not*, one might ask? I believe it's because the threat of the fearsome, destructive, fiery destiny devised by men for their enemies (and their idea of God's enemies), is merely a myth created in the image of faithless men. It's not real.

Daniel is a prophetic book about future kingdoms and unfolding events. It could well portray a picture of the last days' Church with its teaching of a god made in the image of man (60X6) who would throw away most of his creation into everlasting, tormenting flames. The true God is described as a "consuming fire" of purification and not utter destruction. Jesus said, "You have heard that it was said, 'You shall love your neighbor and hate your enemy. But I say to you, love your enemies and pray for those who persecute you, so that you may be sons of your Father who is in heaven…'" (Matthew 5:43–45).

So I guess we struck out in the Old Testament as far as finding evidence of hell or of any kind of everlasting torment to support our doctrine. Maybe we'll have better luck in the New Testament.

New Testament Hell

When defending hell, you'll often hear pastors and other teachers make statements like, "Hell is absolutely taught in the Bible and in fact, Jesus Himself mentions hell more than anyone—even more than heaven." Does Jesus really talk about hell, or could that be a misleading word and concept that translators opted to insert for whatever reasons? Let's look more closely.

Red flag alert. There are essentially *three different* Greek words that translators inconsistently pick and choose to translate as "hell"—*Hades*, *Gehenna*, and *Tartaroo*, but not one conveys hell as we know it and teach it today. We've already discussed *Hades* (The NT equivalent to the Hebrew word, Sheol) as the unknown or unseen place of the dead. *Tartaroo* is only mentioned once (2 Pet. 2:4) and appears to be a temporary confinement for

---

* The verse indicating that the King's men died when throwing the three young men into the fire (3:22) does not occur in the Greek Septuagint.

certain spirits until Judgment. "For if God did not spare angels when they sinned, but cast them into hell (Tartaroo) and committed them to pits of darkness, reserved for judgment." What is interesting about this word is that Tartaroo is a *verb* meaning, "to cast down," yet it's used in 2 Peter as a noun (a *place* called hell). An accurate translation should read, "but cast them down and committed them to pits..."

The word most often translated as hell in the NT is the word *Gehenna*, found only twelve times—once in James and the rest occurring in the Gospels. In the Gospels, Jesus warned about Gehenna on only four unique occasions *at most*. I say at most, because Matthew is the only Gospel that uses it on four separate occasions. Mark and Luke only use it in one passage (repeating Matthew), and John doesn't use it at all.

Gehenna (or Gehinnom) is a literal valley near Jerusalem. In the OT Hebrew it was called, "the valley of Ben-Hinnom" or "Topheth." This valley, still in existence today, is located just outside Jerusalem and was notoriously a place where extreme forms of idolatry were practiced, resulting national, collective judgment for Israel. In this valley, some Israelite parents sacrificed their children in real fire to their false god Molech (Hebrew: "king"), an act that God referred to as "evil, detestable, and an abomination" (Jeremiah 7:30–31). Ironic, huh? Because the Israelites did such a thing—a thing that God says "never even entered His mind to do or to command"—they are reported by their own prophets to have come under severe judgment in this very valley.*

By the times of the NT, most scholars today acknowledge that this valley had turned into a garbage dump outside the city gates of Jerusalem, where fires were always burning to consume trash and dead bodies; where worms and maggots roamed freely throughout the refuse. Lepers and criminals were sent to live there in shame, away from the rest of society. Here is the definition and screen capture (next page) from Biblestudytools.org (notice how the less ominous definition has been somewhat influenced by seemingly enthusiastic hell proponents):

---

* See Jeremiah 7:32 and 19:6–15.

Geenna

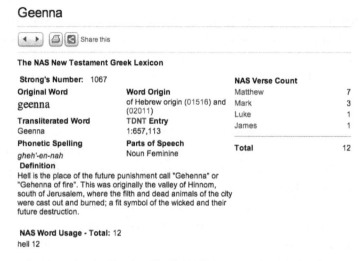

The NAS New Testament Greek Lexicon

Strong's Number: 1067		**NAS Verse Count**	
Original Word	**Word Origin**	Matthew	7
geenna	of Hebrew origin (01516) and (02011)	Mark	3
		Luke	1
Transliterated Word	**TDNT Entry**	James	1
Geenna	1:657,113		
Phonetic Spelling	**Parts of Speech**	**Total**	**12**
gheh'-en-nah	Noun Feminine		

Definition
Hell is the place of the future punishment call "Gehenna" or "Gehenna of fire". This was originally the valley of Hinnom, south of Jerusalem, where the filth and dead animals of the city were cast out and burned; a fit symbol of the wicked and their future destruction.

NAS Word Usage - Total: 12
hell 12

Greek lexicon based on Thayer's and Smith's Bible Dictionary plus others; this is keyed to the large Kittel and the "Theological Dictionary of the New Testament." These files are public domain.

One should wonder why Jesus would refer to a literal valley that the Jews were familiar with just outside their city gates, and expect them to infer that it really meant a place of eternal torment. Why would "hell" not have its own conceptual word and associations carried over from the OT? At the very least, if Gehenna truly equates with the notion of hell, Bible translators should have been more consistent, using the word "hell" in the OT whenever the Valley of Ben Hinnom or Topheth occurs.

Gehenna, if it truly represents hell, is dangerously infrequent in the NT as a place to describe where most of mankind is headed. If people are only given one chance in this mortal lifetime to get it right, shouldn't hell litter the entire NT...in fact, the entire Bible?

Wouldn't it be totally wrong and irresponsible of someone like the Apostle John, and especially the Apostle Paul, not to include any mention of hell or eternal torment in their books? And even moreso in the book of Acts, where the Good News is being proclaimed to Jew and Gentile alike?

We should also be asking how and why Gehenna suddenly was renamed hell and nobody at least explained that to us in church. I've spent a lot of time trying to sort out in my mind how translators and those who study and teach Scriptures made the conceptual leap from Gehenna to hell. Perhaps it is because the Promised Land in the OT has been assumed by Christianity to symbolize a future place of eternal rewards or eternal life (which it does not, but we'll cover that later), they may have made a connection in their minds that Gehenna must symbolically represent the opposite—a place of everlasting punishment and separation from God. However, if this is how they arrived at such a notion, it was simply because they didn't realize that both Gehenna and the Promised Land symbolize temporary, cyclical conditions of judgments and rewards in Jewish thought, not eternal destinies (again, we will look at this more in depth). I'm sure that the passage of time and certain traditions aided the degradation process, as we read about in the New World Encyclopedia:

> The rabbinic tradition draws a distinction between Sheol and Gehenna or "Gehinnom." Originally, Judaism described life after death as a bleak underworld named Sheol, which was known as the common pit or grave of humanity. However, with the influence of Persian thought and the passing of time, the notion of 'hell' crept into Jewish tradition and became associated with the biblical word Gehinnom or Gei Hinnom, the valley of Hinnom (Joshua 15:8, 18:16; II Kings 23:10; Jeremiah 7:31; Nehemiah 11:30). This view of hell was allegedly imported into Judaism from Zoroastrianism, and it appears to have supplanted the earlier concept of Sheol (mentioned in Isaiah 38:18, Psalms 6:5 and Job 7:7-10).

> Jews who embraced this view of hell included the group known as the Pharisees. The larger, dogmatically conservative Sadducees maintained their belief in Sheol. While it was the Sadducees that represented the Jewish religious majority it was the Pharisees who best weathered Roman occupation, and *their belief in Zoroaster's heaven and hell was passed on to both Christianity and Islam.*

> In subsequent centuries, rabbinic literature expounded on Gehenna as a place (or state) where the wicked are temporarily punished after death. The godly, meanwhile, await Judgment Day in the bosom of Abraham. "Gehenna" is sometimes translated as "hell," *but the Christian view of hell differs from the Jewish view of Gehenna.*[5]

When Jesus warned His disciples and the religious leaders of the fires of Gehenna, He wasn't warning them of eternal hell. I believe He warned them of the impending real world consequences for their nation's blatant transgressions of the timeless teachings of the Torah, which all involved acts of injustice (i.e. ignoring the needs of the poor and violent takeover of land). Some people call it "karma." It has been suggested that Jesus referred to the impending Roman siege against Jerusalem in 70 A.D,* about forty years later. In this siege more than a million Jews were killed inside the city (either starved or put to the sword) and their dead bodies were reportedly taken outside the city and burned in the garbage dump of Gehenna ("hell"), where the worms and maggots infested any remains. The siege was so severe, contemporary historians recount that some citizens even killed their children and ate them, all happenings that closely resemble a prophecy in Jeremiah 19:4-9:

> "Because they have forsaken Me and have made this an alien place and have burned sacrifices in it to other gods, that neither they nor their forefathers nor the kings of Judah had ever known, and because they have filled this place with the blood of the innocent and have built the high places of Baal to burn their sons in the fire as burnt offerings to Baal,† a thing which I never commanded or spoke of, nor did it ever enter My mind; therefore, behold, days are coming…when this place will no longer be called Topheth or the valley of Ben-hinnom, but rather the valley of Slaughter. …I will cause them to fall by the sword before their enemies and by the hand of those who seek their life; and I will give over their carcasses as food for the birds of the sky and the beasts of the earth. I will also make this city a desolation and an object of hissing; everyone who passes by it will be astonished and hiss because of all its disasters. I will make them eat the flesh of their sons and the flesh of their daughters, and they will eat one another's flesh in the siege and in the distress with which their enemies and those who seek their life will distress them."

It's certainly quite possible that Jesus' warning about Gehenna may apply in the future at a more symbolic (relational or spiritual) level when He sets up His Kingdom on earth (see Isaiah 66:23-24). I suspect it would then be more of a condition of internal sorrow and remorse over one's

---

* Read more about the 70 A.D. Jerusalem siege at
http://en.wikipedia.org/wiki/Siege_of_Jerusalem_(70). You can also find an in depth article on the history of Gehenna at http://gospelthemes.com/hell.htm.
† Many commentaries assert that Baal and Molech is the same god, called "Baal-Molech."

previous actions that caused harm to others. Both in the referenced Isaiah passage and Mark 9 (referring to Isaiah), it says, "...Gehenna...the fire unquenchable where their worm does not die and their fire is not extinguished." This is not because Gehenna is a state of eternal burning and torture for individuals. I believe the point is that, as long as there is something that reeks of impurity, death, and destruction in us, we will be subject the Refiners fire, a concept we will continue to explore.

For the moment, let's entertain the idea that Jesus was referring to hell as we know it—some kind of never-ending conscious torment after death. Most Jews of that day would have been completely perplexed since there had been no warnings of such a place in the Torah and the Prophets. The warnings against serious offenses throughout the Hebrew Scriptures, like murder (a life for a life), declared physical death or mortal (temporary) destruction. The very few verses that seem to imply "everlasting" destruction (there aren't as many as you might think) are translated from the word "olam," a word decidedly associated with duration of time, not eternity.* Even the first definition of olam (#5769) in Strong's Concordance† is "long duration." Early Jews would have known that "olam destruction" did not imply everlasting destruction.

When I have researched Gehenna on many Jewish websites today, they still refer to it as a historical place of mortal, national judgment for the Jews living in Israel. However, a few more prominent Jewish sites do have some connection between Gehenna and the afterlife. Earlier we saw a quote in the New World Encyclopedia about how this happened over time because of Persian influence. On both JewFaq.org and MyJewishLearning.com, two authoritative orthodox Jewish websites, we read a minor variation of the following:

> Some views see Gehinnom (Gehenna) as one of severe punishment, a bit like the Christian hell of fire and brimstone. Other

---

* A substantial list of well-known, respected scholars and Bible translators who have acknowledged that the concept of eternity does not appear in the Scriptures is located in the resource section.

† *Strong's Exhaustive Concordance*, one of the most widely used Bible reference tools of our day, describes itself as, "the most complete, easy-to-use, and understandable concordance for studying the original languages of the Bible." In my experience, it is a vital and excellent tool in personal studies but does contain some questionable definitions influenced by translators and traditions. As you learn to study things out, problematic definitions become more obvious.

sources merely see it as a time when we can see the actions of our lives objectively, see the harm that we have done and the opportunities we missed, and experience remorse for our actions. *The period of time in Gehinnom does not exceed 12 months,* and then [a person] ascends to take his place in Olam Ha-Ba [afterlife].[6]

As you can see, even most of today's Jews who may associate Gehenna with punishment in the afterlife still believe it's temporary. Shouldn't those to whom it was addressed as a warning be most familiar with what it represents? On the other hand, if Gehenna actually represented eternal hell when Jesus came along, wouldn't it have been pretty troubling to the Jews if somehow God changed the stakes and suddenly sent Jesus to warn them about a place of everlasting conscious torment when they had never heard of such a place before? It bears mentioning again that if hell is real, and God really doesn't want anyone to go there, He would have taken great pains to explain it in repetitive detail through Moses and the prophets.

As mentioned, Gehenna was likely a reminder to unjust, violent people (Jews) that their physical death might come sooner because they knew the right way to live but didn't. On the Wikipedia page, *The Problem of Hell*[7], I found a couple of enlightening quotes:

> In the Abrahamic religions, *except for Judaism, which does not have the concept [of hell],* hell has traditionally been regarded as a punishment for wrongdoing or sin in this life, as a manifestation of divine justice. Nonetheless, the extreme severity or infinite duration of the punishment might be seen as incompatible with justice. ...*In some ancient Eastern Orthodox* traditions, hell and heaven are distinguished not spatially, but by the relation of a person to God's love.*

> "...I also maintain that those who are punished in Gehenna, are scourged by the scourge of love. Nay, what is so bitter and vehement as the torment of love? ...It would be improper for a man to think that sinners in Gehenna are deprived of the love of God...it torments sinners...Thus I say that this is the torment of Gehenna: bitter regret."
> —St. Isaac of Syria (7th Century), Ascetical Homilies 28, Page 141.[8]

---

* The Eastern Church was the Church established by the apostles and early Christian converts following Christ.

I have personally asked several orthodox Jewish friends about their concept of hell, and they had none because, as stated, it has never been a part of their traditional teachings (though certainly some Jews in the modern world have adopted the notion from Western Christianity, especially Messianic Jews).

Eternal Fire, Punishment, and Destruction

So what about all of the NT references to things like "eternal fire" and destruction? Perhaps the writers *meant* hell even though they didn't use the actual word. I looked up all the places in the NASB New Testament that refer to anything that might be construed as everlasting destruction or that might imply our traditional view of hell. Out of 120 references to "eternal" in the NT, I came up with a total of ten instances that could possibly imply a negative destiny, the rest being favorable connotations associated with the word *eternal* (eternal life, etc.). We are going to completely dissect and disarm these verses later, but for now, giving the benefit of the doubt to hell proponents, it is significant to me there are only ten potential references to everlasting destruction (in addition to the four occasions Jesus spoke of Gehenna) in twenty-seven books of the latest and reportedly most authoritative message from God to humans.

One other crucial understanding addressed by a whole later chapter is that, in addition to the Israelites and Jews not subscribing to a concept of an afterworld of torturous, burning flames, they also held no concept of "eternity." In Scripture-writing history, people thought in long periods of time called *eons* or *ages*. Even today if you ask most devout Jews about their take on "eternity," they will tell you that they do not entertain such a concept. Their focus is on *this life*—the here and now. JewFaq.org says:

> Traditional Judaism firmly believes that death is not the end of human existence. However, *because Judaism is primarily focused on life here and now rather than on the afterlife,* Judaism does not have much dogma about the afterlife, and leaves a great deal of room for personal opinion.[9]

Most Jews even find it laughable that the Christians describe God as "eternal," because to the Jews, God is outside the realm of time, space, and human description. They do not label God and they think it's ridiculous that we Christians try to pin human adjectives and concepts on Him.

At more than 13,000 articles, the Jewish Virtual Library (JVL) describes itself as: "The most comprehensive online Jewish encyclopedia in the world, covering everything from anti-Semitism to Zionism." What does the JVL say about the hereafter?

> Jewish teachings on the subject of afterlife are sparse: The Torah, the most important Jewish text, has no clear reference to afterlife at all.[10]

What About the Apostle Paul?

So the OT never mentions hell, but only Sheol (the unknown hereafter). Jesus mentions Gehenna—a geographical place the Jews were familiar with—on four occasions. As Gentiles (non-Jewish persons), our last remaining hope and best bet for finding out about hell would have to fall on the Apostle Paul. Unlike Jews, the NT Gentiles were new converts and had no history with the God of Abraham, and therefore needed a thorough education. It would only be prudent for their primary teacher, Paul, to catch them up to speed about the impending consequences of endless doom for unbelief, right? Anything less would be horribly inexcusable. Well, guess what? Paul never mentions Gehenna. Paul never mentions hell. Only *one place* he mentions being taken away from the face of the Lord for *eonian (pertaining to an age) destruction* (2 Thess. 1:9), but the translators erroneously rendered it, "eternal destruction."

The Greek word used for destruction in this verse is "olethros," and Strong's Concordance #3639 defines it as: "For the *destruction of the flesh*, said of the external ills and troubles by which the lusts of the flesh are subdued and destroyed." Does that sound like utter and final destruction to you?

Even if, by some stretch, Paul did mean to convey everlasting fiery hell in this passage, don't you think it's unconscionable that, as the NT's most prolific writer, he would only mention it once in all his writings? And that he wouldn't take the opportunity to elaborate on it to anyone?

In 1 Cor. 3:11–15, Paul does teach that our works will be tested with fire, and he certainly mentions a corrective process for sin, but he never claims anybody is going to burn forever. "If any man's work is burned up, he will suffer loss; but he himself will be saved, yet so as through fire."*

Perhaps you are now asking, "You've made some good points, but how is this possible? Christians have been teaching hell, preaching hell, and sending out missionaries to save people from hell for hundreds of years, and now you're saying *it's not true*? It's been one of the most influential doctrines of the Church and has impacted practically the entire world. If it's not true, how did it get started?"

When I set out to research this question, I was completely surprised at what I discovered!

---

* The concept and purpose of fire will be discussed at length in chapter 7.

CHAPTER SIX

WHEN HELL BECAME "GOSPEL TRUTH"

If you study a bit about Church history since about the second century, the term "orthodox Christianity" really becomes an oxymoron. Merriam Webster defines *orthodox* as, "conforming to established doctrine, especially in religion."[11] You might also hear it defined as "right doctrine." Orthodox suggests that there are certain truths and doctrines that have always been peacefully and consensually agreed upon, accepted by the majority of "people like us" throughout all the centuries, and those who entertain opposing ideas or who question too persistently are usually labeled as liberal or heretical. In fact, these are the assumptions I grew up with in church, and I never heard anyone challenge them. It's as if mainstream Christianity wants you to think there has always been this harmonious consensus, and if you are to question, you will be singlehandedly going against 2,000 years of what "those who are in the right and who are following the Spirit of God" believe and accept as truth.

While I do believe that tradition and orthodoxy can have their place in preserving certain truths, much of Western Christian Orthodoxy has been preserved and strongly implemented out of fear and control, as a way to "protect one's turf" and to suppress valid questions and ideas. What's particularly ironic is that the modern Evangelical Church tries hard to distance itself from the teachings of the Roman Catholic Church, yet much of today's orthodox theology comes directly out of the councils, doctrines, and creeds established by the early Roman Catholic and Latin Church.

Since the very beginning, Church history has been rife with unrest, conflict, and even bloodshed—primarily over matters of establishing orthodoxy. While you might think that such unrest was primarily a European and Mediterranean phenomenon, the Church in American history is far from excluded, which you can easily learn more about in history books, on websites, and through some great documentaries like the six part series, "God in America," available on Netflix. I've also included a list of some others in the Resources section of this book.

Being armed today with more ready access to Church history, it's time for us churchgoers to rethink the *myth of orthodoxy*, particularly when so firmly imposed on us as having "always been this way."

For instance, many Christians insist that if you question hell, you are rejecting what has always been agreed upon by the Church, yet the doctrine of eternal torment was not a widely held view for the first *five centuries* after Christ, particularly in the early *Eastern* Church, the Church of the early apostles and Church fathers such as Paul, Clement of Alexandria, St. Gregory of Nyssa, Origen, and others.

This important discovery led me to many others, like the fact that the expansion and proliferation of pagan myths about the afterlife, repackaged as eternal, fiery torment, originated in the Western (Catholic) Church, namely by Latin theologians and Church leaders from Rome, most likely because of political expediency and as a means to control the masses with fear. Later pop culture added fuel to the fire (pun intended) through imaginative works like *Dante's Inferno*.

For the rest of this section, we will look at a very brief and condensed history of how the teaching of eternal* torment originated, as well as some historical evidence for the early Eastern Church's teaching on the assured and eventual salvation of all people. For starters, three particular men of great power and influence were primarily responsible for the inception of eternal torment theology.

Dr. Ken Vincent, retired psychology professor from Houston Community College, and author of over one hundred books in the fields of psychology and religion, notes:

> The first person to write about "eternal hell" was the Latin (West) North African Tertullian (160–220 A.D.), who is considered the Father of the Latin Church. As most people reason, hell is a place for people you don't like! Tertullian fantasized that not only the wicked would be in hell but also every philosopher and theologian who ever argued with him! He envisioned a time when he would look down from heaven at those people in hell and laugh with glee! [12]

---

* For a fantastic history on how and when "eternal" anything got inserted into Scriptures, read the in-depth article, "Whence Eternity? How Eternity Slipped In," (http://thetencommandmentsministry.us/ministry/free_bible/whence_eternity).

Out of the six theological schools in Tertullian's day and beyond (170–430 A.D.), the only school that taught the doctrine of eternal hell to its students was the Latin (Roman) school in Carthage, Africa. Four of the other five taught that, through the death and resurrection of Christ, all people would be saved through restorative judgment and reconciliation in a plan of ages.[13] As earlier mentioned, this teaching was called, "Universal Salvation" or "Universal Reconciliation." Dr. Vincent says,

> By far, the main person responsible for making hell eternal in the Western Church was St. Augustine (354–430 CE). Augustine...was made Bishop of Hippo in North Africa. He did not know Greek, had tried to study it, but stated that he hated it. Sadly, it is his misunderstanding of Greek that cemented the concept of eternal hell in the Western Church. Augustine not only said that hell was eternal for the wicked, but also for anyone who wasn't a Christian. So complete was his concept of God's exclusion of non-Christians that he considered un-baptized babies as damned. When these babies died, Augustine softened slightly to declare that they would be sent to the "upper level" of hell. Augustine is also the inventor of the concept of "hell Lite," also known as *Purgatory*, which he developed to accommodate some of the universalist verses in the Bible. Augustine acknowledged the Universalists, whom he called "tender-hearted," and included them among the "orthodox."[14]

Not only was Augustine somewhat the champion of the hell doctrine in the Western Church, he also had a major influence on the onset of religious bigotry and hate campaigns in the following centuries.

In the 1907 book, *Lives of the Fathers: Sketches of Church History in Biography,* by Frederick D. Farrar, who was Chaplain in Ordinary to the Queen of England, we read about Augustine:

> The advocacy of hell came primarily on the scene with Augustine: In no other respect did Augustine differ more widely from Origen and the Alexandrians [Eastern Church] than in his intolerant spirit. Even Tertullian conceded to all the right of opinion.

> [Augustine] was the first in the long line of Christian persecutors, and illustrates the character of the theology that swayed him in the wicked spirit that impelled him to advocate the right to persecute

Christians who differ from those in power. The dark pages that bear the record of subsequent centuries are a damning witness to the cruel spirit that actuated Christians, and the cruel theology that impelled it. Augustine was the first and ablest asserter of the principle which led to Albigensian crusades, Spanish armadas, Netherland's butcheries, St. Bartholomew massacres, the accursed infamies of the Inquisition, the vile espionage, the hideous bale fires of Seville and Smithfield, the racks, the gibbets, the thumbscrews, and the subterranean torture-chambers used by churchly torturers.[15]

Samuel Dawson, author of, *The Teaching of Jesus: From Mount Sinai to Gehenna a Faithful Rabbi Urgently Warns Rebellious Israel*, says:

Most of what we believe about hell comes from Catholicism and ignorance of the Old Testament, not from the Bible. I now believe that hell is the invention of Roman Catholicism; and surprisingly, most, if not all, of our popular concepts of hell can be found in the writings of Roman Catholic writers like the Italian poet Dante Alighieri (1265–1321), author of *Dante's Inferno*. The English poet John Milton (1608–1674), author of *Paradise Lost*, set forth the same concepts in a fashion highly acceptable to the Roman Catholic faith. Yet none of our concepts of hell can be found in the teaching of Jesus Christ![16]

Following on the heels of Augustine, the greatest influence on today's hell theology via most modern Bible translations came from Jerome's *Latin Vulgate*. Jerome translated this version of the Scriptures from a very inferior Latin text in the late 4th century. According to Wikipedia:

For over a thousand years (c. AD 400–1530), the Vulgate was the definitive edition of the most influential text in Western European society. Indeed, for most Western Christians, it was the only version of the Bible ever encountered. The Vulgate's influence throughout the Middle Ages and the Renaissance into the Early Modern Period is even greater than that of the King James Version in English; for Christians during these times the phraseology and wording of the Vulgate permeated all areas of the culture.[17]

What was the problem with Jerome's Bible? It was heavily influenced by Latin hell-inventing theologians like Tertullian and Augustine. Many of the words used in the Vulgate, such as eternal, redemption, justification, sanctification, sacrament, perdition, punish, torment, damnation, etc., were coined by Tertullian and his contemporaries and came to be associated with concepts foreign to the original Greek. According to historian Alexander Thomson:

> [The Latin Church's emphasis on fear-based dualism] was reserved for three great Carthaginians, Tertullian, Cyprian, and Augustine, so to influence the Latin Church it deflected and declined into a system of dogmatic hierarchy and spiritual despotism. But Tertullian was the individual who set this current in motion. ...This, then, is the man in the hollow of whose hands lay the clay which was to be molded into concrete Latin dogma. This is the man in whose hands reclined the fate of the word *eternal*.
>
> ...Augustine, who later outdid Tertullian and his doctrines, maintained that the whole human race was "one damned batch and mass of perdition (conspersis damnata, massa perditionis)," out of which a few are elected to salvation, while all the remainder are lost for ever. He beheld evil as a force integral in a universe apart from God, while Origen believed that all is out from God, even evil, which God must undo and banish. One who has no place for eons to come* must look on the future as a shoreless eternity. Having failed to grasp what God had revealed concerning the eons, Tertullian had no alternative but to impart to the Latin word *eternal* that sense which it now bears.[18]

When you realize that the hell doctrine was so late in being adopted by the Church and Scriptures, not to mention the introduction of a host of other vague "churchy" words and concepts, the poorly constructed walls of orthodoxy begin to crumble. It was several hundred years after Jesus and the apostles that men began formulating many new Church doctrines and creeds, many still a part of Evangelical Christian orthodoxy to this day. Had our old English Bibles been translated directly out of the Greek instead of Latin, it's very probable that the doctrine of eternal torment would never have found its way into our modern Bibles and theology at

---

* Since no such concept or expression of eternity was ever included in Scripture by the original writers, periods of time called eons or ages are crucial in understanding God's plan for mankind. This topic is developed in chapter 14, "Eternity vs. Ages."

all. Many of these doctrines were strong-armed into the Church through major dissention and even bloodshed, with intolerant, oppressive Church leaders insisting that they were "led by the Spirit" on such matters.

In a sense, how is the Church adopting such major theological shifts so many years after Christ any different than, say, the Mormons or the Jehovah's Witnesses adopting their objectionable doctrines in more recent times?

Hell Discrepancy

As the centuries went by, the Bible was translated and retranslated into Latin (mainly from Greek), and more than twelve centuries later translated into English (from Greek and Hebrew) with the advent of the original King James in the 1600s.

It's not hard to see how morphing Church beliefs and language changes influenced each Bible version that came along. In his book, *The Bible in English: its history and influence,* David Daniell notes that when King James gave the translators instructions for working on his King James Authorized Version in 1604 (a seven-year project), he intended to make sure that the new version would "conform to the ecclesiology and reflect the episcopal structure of the Church of England and its belief in an ordained clergy."[19]

Since then, it has undergone over 400 more years of translator interventions and theological interpretations. When you think of how many people, opinions, doctrines, misunderstandings, language barriers, as well as political and theological agendas may have worked into the mix in 2,000 years, it's hard to believe (and shouldn't be believed) that the Bible has maintained inerrancy or complete adhesion to the original intent.

In fact, even Scriptures themselves never claim inerrancy. People primarily depend on two verses to build a case for Bible inerrancy. "All Scripture is inspired by God" (lit. "God-breathed," 2 Tim. 3:16), and "For truly I say to you, until heaven and earth pass away, not the smallest letter or stroke shall pass from the Law until all is accomplished" (Matt. 5:18).

As you carefully read these verses, is either of them claiming biblical inerrancy? The Scriptures, as given originally, were inspired; and nothing God has said will pass away until it is fulfilled. We have read too much into those verses. In fact, when 2 Timothy was written, the only Scriptures available were the Torah and the Prophets. A second point is that even if Scriptures were inspired as given, their correct interpretation still depends on the inspired mind of the one reading them. Think about how one verse of the Bible can have a dozen interpretations, depending on who's reading it. This is how more than 30,000 church denominations have been formed. This is how Calvinists and Arminianists are reading the same Bible, yet coming away with completely different impressions of the core teachings.

We will explore several scriptural errors more in depth later, but here's a great visual example on our topic of hell. If our Bibles are truly accurate and reliable, wouldn't you expect all of the major translations to have the same number of hell occurrences? Here is the astonishing incongruency of how many times the word, "hell," occurs in some of the more familiar versions:

The Message=56	Amplified=13
King James=54	New American Standard=13
New King James=32	LXX (Septuagint)=0
New Living Translation=19	Young's *Literal*=0
New Century=15	Concordant *Literal*=0
English Standard=14	Complete Jewish Bible=0
New International=14	World English Bible=0

My whole life, I never even knew that there was such a disparity in the number of occurrences of the word hell in different Bible translations. I assumed everyone was in agreement, since they were taking from the same text. It was really eye opening to make this discovery. After such a discovery, it was like I began to "wake up." I began to see how many beliefs I had that weren't provable and really didn't make rational sense.

For instance, one day the thought occurred that, if hell is really true, and God is actually losing most of His creation to evil and darkness, you could say that good is overcome, and darkness overtakes light. Ultimately, Satan wins the tug-of-war over creation, and God loses. What a terrifying thought—how did I ever get through life with such a fatalistic view?

CHAPTER SEVEN

SATAN WINS, GOD LOSES?

Best selling author, Bart Ehrman, was raised a dyed in the wool evangelical who studied at Moody Bible Institute, graduated from Wheaton College, and later received a PhD from Princeton Theological Seminary. At a very basic level, something happened to turn him into an avowed agnostic who now challenges problematic doctrines of Christianity, both in his books and in the classroom, where he teaches religious studies at the University of North Carolina at Chapel Hill.

In his famously controversial book, *Jesus Interrupted,* Bart discusses his experiences in seminary where he learned of many biblical errors and inconsistencies during his studies and lectures. It was then that he realized a majority (if not all) pastors learn about these biblical problems in seminary, yet fail to teach their congregations. Bart says:

> Perhaps pastors are afraid that if the person in the pew learns what scholars have said about the Bible, it will lead to a crisis of faith, or even the loss of faith. My personal view is that a historical-critical approach to the Bible does not necessarily lead to agnosticism or atheism. It can in fact lead to a more intelligent and thoughtful faith — certainly more intelligent and thoughtful than an approach to the Bible that overlooks all of the problems that historical critics have discovered over the years.[20]

As Bart indicated, it was not the errors, inconsistencies, and contradictions in the Bible that turned him into an agnostic. He says that in spite of those, he could still see a divine finger print of authenticity and could have gone forth in faith beyond the Bible errors alone. But similar to the objections of the renowned Christian-turned-atheist and college friend of Billy Graham, Charles Templeton, Bart's struggle went deeper.

> There came a time when I left the faith. This was not because of what I learned through historical criticisms, but because I could no longer reconcile my faith in God with the state of the world that I saw all around me. There is so much senseless pain and misery in the

world that I came to find it impossible to believe there is a good and loving God who is in control, despite my knowing all the standard rejoiners that people give.[21]

I believe mainly what Bart is getting at is that, in light of most people "going to hell," their suffering in this world makes no sense. He goes on to express his utter contempt of the idea that a God would torture people 30 trillion years for sins they committed over the course of thirty years, referring to a god like that as a "divine Nazi."[22]

Sadly, I think Bart is right. Without realizing it, the "god" we have put our hopes in and portrayed to the world is more like Hitler than Mother Teresa. The god we have unwittingly manufactured has feeble hopes for His own children—hopes that are dependent upon human free will, and confined to the length of His children's brief, mortal lifespans. Along with that, He's either too short-tempered and callous to forgive His enemies and save them, or He's too weak and limited in His power to eventually overcome their stubborn wills and save them. As a result, orthodox Christianity would have you believe that more than 90% of God's own creation is headed for everlasting doom because He's not all that "mighty to save." This sure sounds ultimately like *Satan wins and God loses*. But is this the God revealing Himself to us through original Scriptures? Does this sound like a loving, all-powerful heavenly Father?

Does God Stay Angry Forever?

If people go to an everlasting hell for rejecting God, then that would imply that God will have everlasting enemies. It would seem then that God would have at least a part of Him that remained in a constant state of righteous anger at His enemies—forever. But is this what the Scriptures teach or how God portrays Himself? Does He stay angry and keep a record of wrongdoings forever?*

Psalm 103:8–10: "Pitying and merciful is the Lord; lenient and full of mercy. Not unto the end shall He be provoked to anger, nor into the eon (age) will He cherish wrath. Not according to our lawless deeds did He

---

* Since I contend in this book that the Greek and Hebrew Scriptures do not contain references to "forever," I'm providing the more literal translations that consistently demonstrate the complete dissolution of God's anger and enemies.

deal with us; nor according to our sins did He recompense to us" (Septuagint).

Isaiah 57:16: "I shall not punish you into the eon, nor shall I be provoked to anger with you perpetually" (Septuagint).

Hosea 14:4: "I will heal their apostasy (unbelief), I will love them freely, for My anger has turned away from them."

Romans 11:32: "For God has shut up all in disobedience so that He may show mercy to all."

James 2:13: "Mercy triumphs over judgment."

Though some people may try to make a case that these verses only applied to Israel, why should He show favoritism and forgive some people's lawlessness and heal their apostasy, but not others? Though it may appear to the contrary at times, we are all equally valued to God and He pointedly declares that He doesn't show favoritism (Deut. 10:17, Romans 2:11), but only works through some people sooner in order to bring the same opportunities to all.

In his groundbreaking book, *The Inescapable Love of God*, professor of philosophy, Thomas Talbott says:

> As the Augustinians (the foundational belief system inherited by most of Christianity today) see it, God opposes sin enough to punish it, but not enough to destroy it altogether; instead of destroying sin altogether, he merely confines it to a specially prepared region of his creation, known as hell, where he keeps it alive for an eternity. According to our alternative picture, however, God forgives sin for this very reason: In no other way could he oppose it with his entire being. ...So the opposite of a sinful condition is a state of reconciliation.[23]

Death Swallowed Up For All Time

As we've previously noted, Orthodoxy teaches that billions of people will be in a state of "everlasting spiritual death." So what do the Scriptures teach? In the Bible, we find many elements described as being *spiritual:* thoughts, words, service, law, gifts, songs, wisdom, forces, sacrifices, blessings, future bodies, and food. But not once do you find "spiritual death," at least not in the way it is taught in church today. When it comes to death, the Bible does allude to different forms and types of death, both physical and metaphorical, but nowhere does it teach that any of these is final or eternal. Let's take a look.

The first (physical) death. Everyone experiences the "curse" of Adam, or death of the mortal body. In chapter 5, we read about Adam's death (Gen. 2:17) passing on to all people. Interestingly, in Hebrew, "Adam" means "humanity" or "mankind."

The second (spiritual or metaphorical) death. The second death is obviously not literal, but is the requisite overcoming of the rebellious, self-serving, divisive, "fleshly" nature of each person that is not in agreement with the loving Father's nature and all-inclusive will for His creation. I now believe that this second death is the inward remorse and response that happens when we are awakened to the damage we have caused ourselves and others. Some people voluntarily surrender to this death in this lifetime, while I believe others do so in a future age. Consider these passages:

Matt. 16:24-25: "If anyone wishes to come after Me, he must deny himself, and take up his cross and follow Me. For whoever wishes to save his life will lose it; but whoever loses his life for My sake will find it."

Rom. 8:13: "If you are living according to the flesh, you must die; but if by the Spirit you are putting to death the deeds of the body, you will live."

Gal 2:20: "I have been crucified with Christ; and it is no longer I who live, but Christ lives in me…"

Revelation teaches that the second death for the majority of mankind takes place after this lifetime in "the lake of fire," a concept we will explore in the next section. As we will discover, the second death is both a temporary yet necessary renewal process to be experienced by everyone in order to be conformed to the image of Love through Christ. This is the meaning of John 12:24, "…unless a grain of wheat falls into the earth and dies, it remains alone; but if it dies, it bears much fruit," and 1 Cor. 15:36, "That which you sow does not come to life unless it dies."

Loss of abundant life. I see a third form of death spoken of as a current reality resulting from personal choices. It's no surprise that our choices bring life or death *now* — death of dreams, death of peace, joy, and purpose. Our choices surely can lead to physical death, but frequently they lead to death of the abundant plans God has for us. To live for one's self through a life of treating others unjustly, whether a Christian or not, often leads to hardships and death of dreams; to live by the two greatest commandments—love God and people—leads to a life of blessing by being in communion with God (and others), enjoying His best for life.

Deut. 30:19-20: "I call heaven and earth to witness against you today, that I have set before you life and death, the blessing and the curse. So choose life in order that you may live...by loving the LORD your God, by obeying His voice, and by holding fast to Him..."

John 5:24: "Verily, verily I say to you that the one hearing my word and believing the One who sent me is having eonian life [now] and is not coming into judging but has stepped out of death into life" (MLT).

Rom. 8:6: "For the mind set on the flesh is death, but the mind set on the Spirit is life and peace..."

1 John 3:14: "He who does not love abides in death."

Is there any form of eternal death? Not if you take God at His word. There are several passages where God declares His intent for all forms of death, making no exceptions. Here are three:

Isaiah 25:8: "*He will swallow up death for all time*, and the Lord GOD will wipe tears away from all faces, And He will remove the reproach of the people from all the earth; For the LORD has spoken."

1 Cor. 15:53-55: "For this corruptible must put on incorruption, and this mortal must put on immortality. So when this corruptible shall have put on incorruption, and this mortal shall have put on immortality, then shall be brought to pass the saying that is written, '*Death is swallowed up in victory*. O death, where is thy sting? O grave, where is thy victory'" (KJV)?*

Rev. 20:13-14: "And the sea gave up the dead which were in it, and death and Hades gave up the dead which were in them; and they were judged, every one of them according to their deeds.† *Then death and Hades were thrown into the lake of fire.*"

"Hold on!" you say. "If you keep reading in Revelation, those resurrected people who are not written in the book of life‡ are thrown into the lake of fire. Isn't the lake of fire the same as hell or everlasting death?"

---

* This is a reference to Hosea 13:14.
† Notice that everyone is judged according to deeds and not faith alone! This explains a lot of the warnings throughout the NT, demonstrating that modern theology has gone awry with the teaching that Christians are off the hook for behaviors such as ignoring the needs of the poor, hypocrisy, and oppressing others.
‡ Find more about "the book of life" in the *Questions* section in Resources.

Lake of Fire

I love how most Christians (including many theologians) interpret Revelation. They read about the woman riding on the beast, the red dragon with seven heads, the harlot sitting on many waters, and people standing on the sea of glass mixed with fire, and they all say, "Oh, obviously those are symbolic." But as soon as they get to *the lake of fire*, aack! "That's totally literal!" they say. But at the beginning of the book, John clearly states that all of Revelation is a vision—not to mention that Jewish teachers recognize that all of John's writings are symbolic or "mystical." Keeping that in mind, Revelation is the only place in the entire Bible that even refers to the lake of fire.

Fire is a fascinating concept in Scripture. It's almost always figurative or symbolic with the purpose of purifying, refining, and for accomplishing general *good*. The Greek word for fire, "pur," is the word from which we get all forms of our English word, *pure* and *purify*. When interpreting and gaining an understanding of the symbolism of the lake of fire, it's helpful to check out how the word fire is used throughout Scripture.

- God is "a consuming fire" (Ex. 24:17; Deut. 4:24; Is. 30:27; Heb. 12:29).

- Believers are baptized and anointed with fire (Matt. 3:11; Luke 3:16; Acts 2:3).

- Jesus and His messengers appear in and are described as fire (2 Thess. 1:7; Heb. 1:7; Rev. 10:1).

- God will judge "all flesh" with fire and sword* (Is. 10:17; 66:16; Rev. 19:15).

- Jesus' eyes are described as fire (Rev. 1:14; 2:18; 19:12).

- Fire acts as a testing, refining, and purifying agent, removing the chaff from our lives (chaff is *on* the wheat; it is not the wheat itself (Is. 48:10; Matt. 3:12; Luke 3:17; 1 Pet. 1:7; Rev. 3:18).

- The Israelites were refined in a fiery furnace (Deut. 4:20; 1 Kings 8:51; Is. 31:9; 48:10; Jer. 11:4).

---

* Along with my belief that fire is symbolic for purifying, I also believe that the "sword" that judges all flesh is the "sword of the Spirit," or the Word of God.

- Fire "destroys" enemies,* lawbreakers, hypocrites, those who ignore the needs of the poor, and slackers (Matt. 3:10; Matt. 7:19; Matt. 13:40–43; Matt. 25:31–46; Heb. 10:27).

  - Everyone who separates from Jesus is thrown into fire (John 15:6).

  - Fire is used to reveal the quality of our works (1 Cor. 3:13–15).

  - Everyone must have the experience: "Everyone will be salted with fire" (Mark 9:49).

Let's take a closer look at Revelation 20:10. In this passage it is speaking of the fate of the beast and the false prophet, but if you compare it to Revelation 14:11, it uses similar language to describe the fate of *anyone* who "takes the mark of the beast."

> The devil, who deceived them, was cast into the lake of *fire* (pur) and *brimstone* (theion) where the beast and the false prophet are also. And they will be *tormented* (basanizo) day and night forever and ever (literally, "into the ages of the ages").

As mentioned, *pur* is the Greek word for fire (Strong's #4442). Throughout the Bible it conveys burning away impurities and once again, it's the word from which the English word "pure" and "purify" originate. According to Strong's Concordance #2303, *theion*, the Greek word for *brimstone* is defined as, "divine incense, *because burning brimstone was regarded as having power to purify, and to ward off disease.*" Notice that brimstone (theion) shares the same root word as "God" (Theos).

Next, the Greek word for *torment* in the verse above is *basanizo*. Basanizo (verb) comes from the root noun, "basanos," which is defined by Strong's #931 as:

> A touchstone. Originally, a black, silicon-based stone used as "a touchstone" to test the purity of precious metals (like silver and gold). In the papyri,† basanos also means, "touchstone, test." #931 (basanos)

---

* A case can be made that an enemy is "destroyed" when he or she has become a friend. Hence, fire is often portrayed in the Bible as reforming a person's character to the point that they are no longer enemies of God or others, but friends.

† The papyri are ancient Greek Koine texts discovered around the turn of the 20th century, and were records used in matters of everyday business in ancient Greece. These texts were critical in understanding the use and definition of certain Greek words that had been little understood, guessed at, and mistranslated in Scriptural context for many centuries.

was originally (from oriental origin) a touchstone; a "Lydian stone" used for testing gold because pure gold rubbed on it left a peculiar mark. Then [basanos] was used for examination by torture. Sickness was often regarded as "torture" (WP, 1, 37).[24]

So what exactly is a "touchstone"? Webster defines it as: "A stone by which metals are examined; a black, smooth, glossy stone; any test or criterion by which the qualities of a thing are tried; as money, the touchstone of common honesty."

If you go to strongsnumbers.com/greek/931.htm, you find all the information above about the touchstone, testing purity, and the papyri, and sickness being regarded as torture (perhaps a better word is "testing")—and that's it. But then toward the bottom, you find the final, authoritative, "conclusive definition" by the Strong's people:

A touchstone (a dark stone used in testing metals), *hence examination by torture; torture.*

People, really? Do we not see a bit of spin being added here? And if we put all three of those more literal meanings together (purification, divine incense to ward off spiritual sickness, and testing), throwing out the dubious insertion of torture, we begin to get a distinctly different feel than endless eternal punishment taking place in Revelation. Can you see how things get misconstrued and distorted to the untrained eye? The Greek word that was translated as "tormented," not only has nothing to do with eternal conscious torment like we think of torment today (burning to a crisp in hell for all eternity), but is actually a process that tests purity, true to the beautiful, masked symbolism of Revelation. It seems clear to me that verses like Revelation 20:10 suggest more of a refining and purifying process going on in people's lives.

One thing I have learned in studying the Scriptures is that, if it doesn't make rational sense or fit the overarching, consistent character of a loving and inclusive God, it's probably not true. Like the idea of fire endlessly burning a human body. Literal fire only burns as long as it has something to consume. A flesh and blood person couldn't burn more than a few hours (2–4 according to cremation experts). Frequently throughout Scripture, God compares the purifying process in us to that of silver or gold being refined in fire, burning away the dross and impurities. With regard to people, fire typically is used for the ultimate good of the one being put through it:

Isaiah 48:10: "Behold, I have refined you, but not as silver; I have tested you in the furnace of affliction."

Ps. 66:10-12: "For you tried us O God. You set us on fire as silver is set to the fire...we went through fire and water; but you led us unto respite" (Septuagint).

Zech. 13:9: "And I will bring the third part through the fire, refine them as silver is refined, and test them as gold is tested (note the word "tested" in association with fire and gold — just like the Revelation passage above)."

The more I study, the more I realize Scripture teaches of fire being a purifying agent, not a punishing, utter destroying agent. In both of the following verses where the English word "pure" and "purified" occurs, the Greek (Septuagint) word is "puroo." The Greek definition of puroo is "to burn with fire."

Daniel 11:35: "Some of those who have insight will fall, in order to refine, purge and *make them pure* ('burn with fire') until the end time; because it is still to come at the appointed time."

Daniel 12:10: "Many will be purged, *purified* ('burned with fire') and refined, but the wicked will act wickedly; and none of the wicked will understand, but those who have insight will understand."

Notice how the translators did not convey the more literal translation of "burning with fire," since this was pertaining to godly people. Instead they chose to convey purification. Had it been about unbelievers, I wonder if they would have extended the same benevolence, or if they would have tried to convey fiery damnation, roasting those sinners on a stick like toasted marshmallows?

One of my favorites is from Zephaniah 3:8-9 (when translated correctly), where you see the nations and all the earth devoured by fire. Does God tell us why people are devoured by fire (from the Septuagint)?

"Wait for me," says the Lord, "for the day of my resurrection, for a testimony! For my judgment shall be for gathering of nations, to take kings, to pour out upon them all my passion — the passion of my desire. For all the earth shall be consumed by the fire of my zeal. For then I will transfer upon the peoples one tongue for her generation, for all to call upon the name of the Lord, to serve him under one yoke."

NASB phraseology (see if you can spot anything suspicious):

> "Indeed, My decision is to gather nations, to assemble kingdoms, to pour out on them My indignation, all My burning anger; for all the earth will be devoured by the fire of My zeal. For then I will give to the peoples purified lips, that all of them may call on the name of the Lord, to serve Him shoulder to shoulder."

If Revelation is literal, and the lake of fire is literal, and if such notions of endless torment aren't actually terrible mistranslations of certain words, then one must conclude also from Revelation that our friends and loved ones will be tormented forever *in our presence*:

> If anyone worships the beast and his image, and receives a mark on his forehead or on his hand, he also will drink of the wine of the wrath of God, which is mixed in full strength in the cup of His anger; and he will be testing (basanizo) with fire (pur) and brimstone (theion) in the presence of the holy messengers and *in the presence of the Lamb*. And the smoke of their testing ascends into the eon of the eons (Rev. 14:9–11, MLT).

Aren't we also going to be in the presence of the Lamb in the coming ages, where these people are portrayed?

Lastly, but also very important is Revelation 20:13–14. If spiritual death (or any kind of death) is everlasting, how could the following be possible? "Then death and Hades were thrown into the lake of fire."

I still have a long way to go in understanding all the symbolism in Revelation, but here I believe the idea is conveyed that the dead are brought back to life, judged for their deeds (the way they treated others), and *death AND the grave* (Hades—place of the unknown) are both consumed once and for all because their purpose is ended. They are swallowed up in victory, just as God has declared. How then does orthodox Christianity teach that for most people, death never ends?

Does Satan Really Win?

Is God's own creation spinning out of His control? Does man's "free will" or even Satan's will trump God's will in the end? If you believe that billions of people are headed toward everlasting separation from God in fiery torment, perhaps most of them out of ignorance, or because of their bad or misinformed choices, or because Satan successfully deceived them, you essentially believe that Satan wins and God loses. In this scenario, the world is nothing more than a cosmic game of tug-of-war, and in the end, God lets go of the rope and allows most of His children to be overtaken by unstoppable, unpreventable, and everlasting evil. At this point, He must admit to defeat. He must also admit that most of His children are nothing more than throwaways not worth fighting for. Do these sound like the traits of a loving and all-powerful Father?

A friend of mine compiled a forty-something page document of verses that firmly declare God's absolute power, sovereignty, and unstoppable will over His creation. Here are just a few highlights of hundreds:

Job says: God stands alone, does whatever He pleases, no one can ultimately oppose Him, and no plan of His can be thwarted or foiled (Job 23:13; 42:2).

David says: The Lord does what pleases Him, His plans stand through all generations (Ps. 33:10–11; 135:6).

Solomon says: He works out everything for His own ends, determines the steps and destiny of man, directs the hearts of rulers, and all His purposes prevail (Pr. 16:4, 9, 33; 19:21; 21:1).

Daniel says: He does as He pleases with the powers of heaven and the peoples of the earth (Dan. 4:35).

God says...

"I am the Lord, the God of all flesh; is anything too difficult for me" (Jer. 32:27)?

"I have sworn by Myself, the word has gone forth from My mouth in righteousness and will not turn back, that to Me every knee will bow, every tongue will swear allegiance" (Is. 45:23).

"Surely, just as I have intended so it has happened, and just as I have planned so it will stand" (Is. 14:24).

"So is My Word that goes out of my mouth: It will not return to Me empty, but will accomplish what I desire, and achieve the purpose for which I sent it" (Is. 55:11, NIV).

"My purpose will be established, and I will accomplish all my good pleasure...I have planned it, surely I will do it" (Is. 46:10–11).

If all these verses are true, we can only conclude one of two things. Either God wills for most of His children to suffer eternal loss, or God wills for them to be brought back and reconciled to Himself. Either way, it is clear that He is going to have His way.

So then…what exactly is it that God wants?

> For this is good and acceptable in the sight of God our Savior; *who will have all men to be saved*, and to come unto the knowledge of the truth. For there is one God, and one mediator between God and men, the man Christ Jesus; *Who gave himself a ransom for all, to be testified in due time* (1 Tim. 2:3-6, KJV).

If it's all true, that God wills all people to be saved, Jesus actually gave Himself for everybody—not just in theory—and hell is nothing more than a myth of men. Is there evidence to support such a notion, and what might it look like on a practical level?

It's time to explore the truth about the character and heart of a Father who is the definition of LOVE. Let me introduce you to the greatest marvel of all time—truly the greatest Story ever told. It has completely transformed my heart and my life forever!

Part 2
Love Does Not Fail…

(1 Corinthians 13:8)

CHAPTER EIGHT

LOVE NEVER FAILS FOR CHILDREN

"Can a mother forget the baby at her breast
and have no compassion on the child she has borne?
Though she may forget, I will not forget you!" –Isaiah 49:15

At a writer's conference a few years back, I had the privilege of meeting Kent Whitaker, a writer who was there to present his manuscript to editors in hopes of sharing his story with the world. Kent's unforgettable experience involved the murders of his wife and youngest of two sons in 2003. When his family of four returned home from celebrating their oldest son's college graduation over dinner, they met a gunman lying in wait near their front porch. The gunman fired several shots at the family, but only Kent and the oldest son made it out alive.

The night of the murders, Kent lay seriously injured in the hospital, trying to make sense of losing two of the dearest people in his life. "On the one hand I was beginning to absorb how radically things had changed," Kent writes in his book *Murder by Family*, "while on the other I had a calm assurance that I was not alone and that God would knit whatever happened into His plans for good." [25]

Somehow Kent vowed that night to trust God, regardless of what was in store for him in the coming days. But that wasn't all. On his hospital bed, Kent sensed the unmistakable prompting of God, asking him to do the unthinkable — *to forgive the murderer*. Though a large part of him fought for revenge, another voice prodded his heart toward mercy.

"My heart told me that I wanted whoever was responsible to come to Christ and repent for this awful act," he writes. "At that moment I felt myself completely forgiving him. This forgiveness astounded me, because earlier I had experienced feelings of incredible sadness and intense anger — even the desire to kill the person responsible with my own hands. Little did I realize just how important my decision to forgive would be in the coming months." [26]

As the investigation unfolded, the shocking truth emerged: the mastermind behind the murder plot was none other than his oldest son Bart! Serious psychological issues starting in his youth led Bart down a path that culminated in hiring an assassin to shoot his own family. Little did Kent know that night in the hospital that God actually urged him to forgive his own son — before his son had even repented!

The moral of this story makes a deep impression on me. If God can quit on His own children for lesser offenses, why would He ask someone like Kent to forgive his son for one of the worst imaginable offenses? Does God expect that Kent should be more loving and merciful than Himself? Does God ask earthly parents to do what He Himself is unable or unwilling to do?

Earthly Parental Love

Most parents will never know the degree of forgiveness toward our children that Kent knows first hand. Most of us are dealing with small acts of rebellion and inconsideration, by comparison. But the question remains: Is there *anything* — as a functional, loving parent — that my children could do that would erase or cancel my love for them? Is there anything they could do that I would deem as deserving endless or even overly harsh punishment? Is not my "punishment" upon them intended to be completely corrective and restorative? I've had this conversation with certain folks, and it usually goes into something like this:

Me: "As the perfect Parent of all people,* God would never overly punish or abuse His children in ways that you and I, as loving parents, wouldn't do to our own children. If He would, you'd have to say we earthly parents love our children more than God loves His children."

Folks: "Well, God's ways are above our ways and we can't fully understand them now. His justice demands consequences — either His children believe in this lifetime or they face everlasting punishment and condemnation. Our perspective is too limited to understand this now — we're only human. But someday we will fully and willingly accept it when we see the big picture."

Me: "Huh? Let me see if I get what you're saying. God makes us in His image and 'likeness,' instilling in us His fatherly heart and tenderness toward our children. We are commanded to love our children (and all of His) selflessly and unconditionally (1 Cor. 13:4-8) and, like the prodigal son's father, not to give up on them. Yet you believe the original Father is

---

* See Gen. 1:26; Acts, 17:26-28; Col. 1:16; James 3:9.

going to give up on most of His own children, though most of them were estranged from Him since birth, by no choice of their own?"

Folks: "Yep. That pretty much sums it up."

Me: "That kind of god sounds more like a cruel, hypocritical, deadbeat dad than a loving, longing Father. Abba Father says, 'Mercy triumphs over judgment' (James 2:13)," and it is this Abba (daddy or papa) kind of Father we see in the Jewish tradition. Rabbi Stephen Wylen addresses the contrast between the Jewish and Christian views of God:

> When Jews read the Bible, the God whom we Jews meet there is in the image of a father who loves his children with an overwhelming passion. This father has very high expectations of his children, but he also indulges them. He loves to treat them well and make them happy. Some Christians believe that the God of the Old Testament is a stern God of strict judgment without mercy, but a religious Jew would not be able to discover such a deity in the Hebrew Bible.[27]

If God is truly the perfect Parent who supposedly loves and longs to be intimately connected to all of His children — His very own offspring — is it really possible that He is going to throw most of them away or lock them away in a fiery dungeon? Wouldn't that suggest that I have more love than God does? God says His love is unfailing, patient, and relentless, but if in fact it does fail and cease for most of His children, that would make Him nothing more than a liar.

Obviously God is no liar; He *is* love. All people who have lived since the dawn of time are a continued expression of that love. Our opportunity to participate in parenting is so that we can more fully understand His unfailing love for and His attachment to each and every one of us.

Characteristics of Loving Parents

One of the best ways to begin grasping the truer character of our Father God is by studying characteristics of loving parents.

Loving parents only intend good for their children. No good parent ever asks, "How can I ruin my kids' lives today?" Our kids may see our discipline that way, but ultimately everything we do is with the intent of helping them become successful, contributing members of society with the ability to nurture loving relationships throughout their lives. Could God's intent be any less for His children?

In his 1843 book, *The Plain Guide to Universalism*, Thomas Whittemore wrote:

> God is the Creator of all men. "He hath made of one blood, all nations of men, to dwell on all the face of the earth" (Acts 17:26, KJV). He would not have created intelligent beings, had He known they were to be forever miserable. To suppose that God would bring beings into existence, who He knew would be infinite losers by that existence, is to charge Him with the utmost malignity. The existence itself would not be a blessing, but a curse; the greatness of which cannot be described. As God is infinite in knowledge, and as He sees the end from the beginning, He must have known before the creation, the result of the existence He was about to confer, and whether, upon the whole, it would be a blessing; and, as He was not under any necessity to create man, being also infinitely benevolent, He could not have conferred an existence that He knew would end in the worst possible consequences to His creatures.[28]

Loving parents make sure the punishment fits the crime. Can you imagine punishing your children for the rest of their lives for an act (or season) of rebellion? I have a good friend whose eighteen-year-old son was out drinking one night and got into a fatal car accident. This son, though good-natured and very loving, had been giving her problems for a couple years through a season of rebellion against the values of the home. After he died, the thought never entered her mind, "Well, it's too late for my son, I want nothing more to do with him because of his rebellion. Sure it's sad, but he went too far and now he's getting his fair punishment."

No! The mom was heartbroken, longing for her son...aching for the days when she had a living, loving relationship with him. She will *never* stop loving or longing for her son, no matter what he did.

One little understood intent of the Levitical Law, "an eye for an eye and a tooth for a tooth," is the admonition to not over-punish the offender, while at the same time providing a way of restoration to the community. Yet many Christian teachers have turned this law on its head, making it about getting even. This is not God's way.

Loving parents understand that there are factors behind disobedience. Frequently you hear parents of toddlers defending their behavior: *Johnny is acting out because he didn't get his nap today...Susie is cutting a tooth and she's been cranky and defiant all week.* A good parent, knowing their child intimately, is able to offer patient understanding when the need arises. As this same child grows up, life often inflicts wounds and scars on his or her heart. Good parents know that there are factors that contribute to why their children do the things they do—physical pain, exhaustion, sin or dysfunction of those around them, emotional hurts and scars, injuries caused by others, disabilities, genetic disorders, chemical imbalances, and disappointments of life. How much more must God understand why His children act the way they do and plan ways to help them overcome?

It's easy to think that we all have a choice to "be good," especially if we have grown up in a loving home with little pain and suffering. But many of us have never tasted the hard life. Many of us have never been severely mistreated, abandoned, abused, or exploited. How could we not expect and believe that the heavenly Parent understands the deception of and resulting rebellion by His children who are offered little love or kindness during their mortal lives? How could we be so narrow-minded and unloving to judge that any of these people "chose this path" or "deserve what they get?"

Even God's seemingly hardened and rebellious children are treated with patience. "He will not always strive with us, nor will He keep His anger forever.* He has not dealt with us according to our sins, nor rewarded us according to our iniquities" (Psalm 103:9–10, NIV).

Loving parents demonstrate fair and consistent character. Suppose you had a set of "loving parents" who had four children. For whatever reason (rebellion, disobedience, or personality conflict) the parents locked one of the children in the basement where they isolated and punished the child for days at a time. The other children knew about their sibling in the basement and even heard the tortured screams and pleadings from time to time. Do you think the three children upstairs, loved and cared for as they were, could really trust parents who could do this to "one of them"?

In his book, *A Child Called It,* Dave Pelzer gives a most disturbing account of his childhood that was not unlike the above scenario. Growing up in a household with three siblings, Dave was singled out for some of the worst abuse imaginable. He was starved frequently—up to two weeks at a time—while having to serve dinner to the rest of the family and do their dishes. If his mom caught him putting the smallest morsel in his

---

* Literal: "into the age."

mouth, she made him throw up. He was made to sleep on a cot in the cold garage with only a thin blanket, while the rest of the family rested warm and comfortably in their beds. The horrendous list of abuses continued with probably the worst psychological abuse of all being that the mom demonstrated love and thoughtful care to the rest of the children in front of Dave, while snubbing him and requiring all of the other children to do the same. The underlying message to the children was that they were to snub Dave too, or they would receive the same treatment.

As I consider how Christianity is portrayed to the world, is this not the "loving parent" image we have unwittingly pinned on God? Is this perhaps the reason many people are not willing to trust in "a god like that" and why so many violent atrocities have been done in God's name?

Truly loving parents demonstrate trustworthiness, fairness, and consistency with all their children, creating a sense of fearlessness and security that leads to thriving in the home. And if the children are to emulate these kinds of parents, such behavior breeds peace, acceptance, and unconditional love among the whole family.

Loving parents ultimately long to be restored in relationship. Every loving parent longs to be reconciled to his or her wayward child. A large part of the Levitical Law was to teach people that reconciliation is the satisfaction (atonement) for sin and broken relationships, not destruction or casting away. The intent of the Torah was to recompense the one injured and restore the offender to society. In the case where there was no recompense in this lifetime for certain crimes against a victim (like murder), death was the allowable (not desirable) consequence so that the offender would face his or her day in the Divine Court for appropriate reconciliatory judgment. This reconciliatory emphasis of the Torah is the reminder a certain woman offered King David when he would not reconcile with his son Absalom, who was guilty of murdering his own brother out of revenge:

> The woman said, "...the king is as one who is guilty, in that the king does not bring back his banished one. For we will surely die and are like water spilled on the ground, which cannot be gathered up again. *Yet God does not take away life, but plans ways so that the banished one will not be cast out from Him*" (2 Sam. 14:13–14).

Philosopher Thomas Talbott offers similar thoughts:

So what, specifically, does perfect justice require? What sort of thing would make up for, or cancel out sin? If we accept the Christian view, according to which sin is anything that separates us from God and from each other, then the answer to our question is clear: *Perfect justice requires reconciliation and restoration.* It requires, first, that sinners repent of their sin and turn away from everything that would separate them from others; it requires, second, that God forgive repentant sinners and that they forgive each other; and it requires, third, that God overcome, perhaps with their own cooperation, any harm that sinners do either to others or to themselves.[29]

It is true that sometimes as parents we have to take a heavy hand with our children, causing pain or separation of relationship for a time. Ultimately however, our deepest desire is to weed out rebellion. Sometimes a short term separation or conflict is worth the end result — a child who learns a valuable lesson through pressure, who does not want to repeat that behavior, and who comes to us in humility, realizing the error of his or her ways and desiring a restored relationship. This is the sentiment behind the Prodigal Son we looked at earlier in Luke 15:18–20:

"...I will get up and go to my father, and will say to him, 'Father, I have sinned against heaven, and in your sight; I am no longer worthy to be called your son; make me as one of your hired men.' So he got up and came to his father." You know the rest. The father runs to meet his son and welcomes him home with open arms, no strings attached.

Loving parents never give up. We don't realize how double-minded we sound to the world when we say that God loves them unconditionally, yet if they don't pray a certain prayer before they die, this love becomes very conditional and temporary. Interview 100, 1,000, or 1,000,000 healthy, loving parents and you will not find one that would give up on their children — *ever.* How could we then ever think that the ultimate, perfect Parent would give up on any of His children? How could we truly believe His love could cease just because we go to the grave? Consider the following verses as they read in the Greek Interlinear Bible:

John 10:9: "I am the door; if EVER anyone may be entering through me he shall be being saved and shall be entering and shall be coming out and shall be finding pasture" (MLT).

Romans 10:9: "That if EVER you should be avowing with your mouth Jesus is Lord and should be believing in your heart that God rouses him out of the dead ones, you shall be being saved" (MLT).

That little word "ever" is very important because it implies that it is never too late.

According to the Scriptures, all people who have ever lived on the earth are God's very own offspring through Jesus Christ, the "first born of all creation" (Col. 1:15). That's right. You don't have to be a Christian to be one of God's children, as Paul explained to the Greek idol worshipers in Acts 17. God gave us our own offspring so we could understand how we are produced of Him—how valuable we are as His image bearers. Just as our children are physiologically the sum total of the genes we have passed onto them—no more, no less—we each possess the spiritual DNA of our heavenly Father. In order for His nature to be fully expressed and for creation to be perfectly restored and working together, all of the divinely patterned expressions of Him (us) must be gathered back to Him in perfect unity of purpose (love), yet retaining our unique individuality.

In light of the Scriptures describing God as a "consuming fire," ancient Hebrew teachings describe all people as "divine sparks" out of that Fire (God), expressing His vitality and passion in the world. This is why people everywhere are stunning, unique, and magnificent reflections of the Divine through our gifts, dreams, talents, and desires. Through each of us is revealed a different aspect of the God-nature. For Him to lose even one of those sparks would mean He loses an aspect of Himself.

Is it not the same with our own children, each their own yet fully out of us? When I think of the bond earthly parents have with our children, I know it is utterly impossible that God would ever ask us to lose a part of ourselves forever, any more than He would ever intend to give up a part of Himself. His answer is not damnation, but regeneration of all His children into *pur*ified sparks!

Jesus always esteemed children because He came to show the heart of the Father toward His children. A true father's love cannot be earned, and it cannot be done away with. Just as we would never give up on our children, God will never give up on His children; His love will not fail them.*

---

* 1 Corinthians 13:8.

CHAPTER NINE

LOVE NEVER FAILS THE HELPLESS OR THE HOPELESS

*"An act of love, a voluntary taking on oneself
of some of the pain of the world, increases the courage
and love and hope of all." –Dorothy Day*

In my inspirational parenting book, *One Million Arrows: Raising Your Children to Change the World*, I open by describing the impact 9/11 had on me. As if it wasn't surreal and haunting enough just watching it on TV, then there were the personal accounts. One man I read about, Cary Sheih, barely made it out alive. Working at his 72nd floor desk, he heard an explosion, followed by tremendous building sways and vibrations. Learning that a plane had struck the building, he joined the others on his floor in a hurried evacuation. Here's an excerpt from my book:

> With the heavy, choking stench of jet fuel, descending the tower proved difficult. But if it was difficult for Cary, he couldn't imagine how difficult it was for the rescue crews he passed, huffing their way up an endless corkscrew of stairs and then hurrying back down, carrying badly injured and burned victims. He recalls, "Sometime around the 30th or 40th floor, we passed the first firefighters coming up the stairs. They reassured people that we were safe and that we would all get out fine. By this point, they were absolutely breathless, but still pushing upward, slowly and unyieldingly, one step at a time. I could only imagine how tired they were, carrying their axes, hoses, and heavy outfits, climbing up all those stairs. Young men started offering [to help] the firemen carry up their gear for a few flights, but they all refused. Each and every one of them."[30]

While there were many, many heroes and selfless individuals working tirelessly to assist throughout this tragic period, it was the *firemen* who undoubtedly made some of the greatest sacrifices of all, and whose ultimate acts of bravery impacted lives worldwide. While most everyone else scrambled for the exit signs to save themselves (which I'm positive I would have done, too), these rescue workers fearlessly headed up into the towering infernos that day.

Cary Sheih said, "I am so grateful for the courage of the firemen and policemen who gave up their lives to help us down the burning tower. As I relive this moment over and over in my mind, I can't help but think that these courageous firemen already knew in their minds that they would not make it out of the building alive, and that they didn't want to endanger any more civilians or prevent one less person from making it to safety."[31]

I have often thought of these firemen in the years since. I'm sure that at least some of them were probably not "saved" in the traditional Christian sense of the word. Most of them were young men—singles, husbands, and fathers—with their whole lives ahead of them. Yet, they willingly and perhaps knowingly made the greatest sacrifice known to mankind, and they did it for total strangers. Surely in these situations it is the love of a heavenly Father that inspires such heroic efforts in saving the helpless.

Before my theological shift I used to wonder, *what happens to the rescue workers who did not profess faith in Jesus before they died? Did they selflessly take the hit for others, cutting short their one shot at life, only to be doomed forever?* Certain passages began to surface as I thought about these men:

"I command you to love each other in the same way that I love you. And here is how to measure it—the greatest love is shown when people lay down their lives for their friends" (John 15:12-13, NLT).

"Above all, keep fervent in your love for one another, because love covers a multitude of sins" (1 Peter 4:8).

"We are aware that we have proceeded out of death into life, because we are loving our brothers and sisters" (1 John 3:14, MLT).

When I have suggested on my blog or Facebook that people's love for others might trump the necessity of "the sinner's prayer" in future judgment, I've gotten plenty of responses like this one: "The 'good atheist' (or agnostic), no matter how benevolent and kindhearted, will be judged by God and found infinitely lacking." I can't be overly critical of this kind of ignorance because I once believed that way too. These days, I know better than to think they are "infinitely lacking." There's an awesome passage about this very topic by Paul in Romans 2:12-16:

> For all who have sinned without the Law will also die without the Law, and all who have sinned under the Law will be judged by the Law; *for it is not the hearers of the Law who are just before God, but the doers of the Law will be justified.* For when Gentiles *who do not have the Law do instinctively the things of the Law, these, not having the Law, are a law to themselves, in that they show the work of the Law written in their hearts,* their conscience bearing witness and their thoughts alternately accusing or else defending them, on the day when, according to my gospel, God will judge the secrets of men through Christ Jesus.

One of the two greatest commands, which summed up the entire law according to Jesus, is to love your neighbor as yourself. How could God ignore the sacrifices of these rescue workers in light of His own measuring stick? It would be completely contrary to His nature and His name! The 9/11 firemen (and many other selfless heroes throughout history) deliberately put themselves in harm's way so that those individuals they rescued could have a second chance at mortal life. I believe it was love — not duty — that truly made them heroes of the day. They chose to love in a way that few ever consider or demonstrate in this world. I believe that when these people are resurrected, they will stand before the Judge and He will declare that, because they learned how to love, they are justified as doers of His law and they are already sons of Love. Love truly never fails, whether in accomplishing its mission or in receiving its reward.

Widows and Orphans

There are an estimated 147,000,000 orphans in our world today, not to mention widows, lepers, and other destitute. One who believes in hell should find it strange that, though God frequently speaks of assisting orphans and widows throughout His Word, He almost exclusively exhorts His followers only to defend their rights and feed them. "Pure and undefiled religion in the sight of our God and Father is this: to visit orphans and widows in their distress..." (James 1:27). Never once does He (or anyone else) say to share the Gospel with them or snatch them from eternal flames.

If God were planning to send most of the world's poorest of the poor to hell because they don't believe in Him, why would He care about meeting their physical needs while they're alive? I don't see what difference it would make for these outcasts to have a few extra years of full stomachs while living in a "hell on earth" in every other way. We'd basically be prolonging their suffering and giving them a little pat on the back before sending them off to everlasting doom.

Many of the orphans I've met would likely welcome a quick departure from the horrible existence they face daily in this world—sickness, starvation, terror, abuse, complete rejection, sex slavery, and other forms of exploitation. Should I expect that, because nobody told them the Gospel, they will still endlessly burn in hell after a few years of hell on earth?

The simple fact is that all orphans and widows are very near and dear to the heart of the Father. He has no intention of rejecting them or sending them to hell. His intention is for us to demonstrate His Fatherly heart toward them, feeding them, defending them, and caring for their needs as an extension of "God's love with skin on." Perhaps we will come to recognize that we are also orphans who need a hand out of the gutter of life. Because of sin and separation from our true Father (and each other), we have all been orphaned and hung out to dry. Yet we will all be found— adopted back into the family as sons and daughters—every last one. "I will not leave you as orphans; I will come to you" (John 14:18).

Though their lives in this world are so difficult, orphans and widows are the very heartbeat of God. His greatest desire is to see us alleviate their suffering, recognizing those less fortunate as an extension of ourselves. In the mean time, I feel so much happier knowing that all those who we are unable to reach now will someday be given a front row ticket to provision, protection, and happiness. Every tear will be wiped away, and every want will be filled. Can you imagine the happy heart of the longing Abba when He brings all of His estranged children home from the gutters?

Blind, Deaf, Lame, And Sick

When Jesus went about doing His public ministry, He was known for healing all of the sick people who came to Him. One fine Sabbath day, He got up to do the reading in the synagogue before the people, quoting from Isaiah out of the Septuagint Greek Scriptures:

> "The Spirit of the Lord is upon me, because He anointed me to announce good news to the poor. He has sent me to heal the ones being broken in heart; to proclaim a release to captives, and recovery of sight to the blind; to call acceptable the year of the Lord, and day of recompense; to comfort all the ones mourning" (Isaiah 61:1-2, Septuagint). After Jesus quoted this, he sat down, and told the listening crowd, "Today this Scripture has been fulfilled in your hearing" (Luke 4:21).

At first read, one might think that Jesus was saying He came for those who are physically lame, blind, and deaf. It is true that Jesus healed many physical ailments of the people, but their physical ailments were not ultimately their problem. Those He healed would eventually get sick again and die, so a physical healing was not all that impressive in the grand scheme. What Jesus declared was much deeper—He came to bring permanent healing to those who are spiritually sick. This is why He first told the paralytic that his sins were forgiven before healing his physical condition (Matt. 9:2). He healed the enduring spiritual condition first, and next gave temporary relief to the mortal, physical condition, to demonstrate His legitimate power.

Notice that the text in Isaiah is not a half-hearted or timid invitation. Jesus came to declare Good News to those who are "poor in spirit." He came to proclaim a release to the captives of sin and death. He came to give recovery of sight to those who are spiritually blind and cannot see truth. He came to unstop the ears of those who cannot hear or perceive the truth (Is. 35:5). Are any left out of that equation? Though all people fit these descriptions, not all people see themselves as sick, broken, lame, blind, and deaf, particularly not many "church people." It's easy as Christians to see ourselves as somewhat healthy and whole, and above falling into life-altering sin or being taken captive by deception. I have certainly fallen prey to that blind spot in my own life and it set me up for great failure. Jesus resisted these kinds of proud people in His day.

A large part of Jesus's mission in God's plan for the ages is bringing all people to an understanding of our connectedness as a loving family in the plan and purposes of God. We are awakening to the value of humanity on a level playing field where no one is more special than the next when it comes to the need and promise of our total spiritual healing:

> The Pharisees and their scribes began grumbling at His disciples, saying, "Why do you eat and drink with the tax collectors and sinners?" And Jesus answered and said to them, "It is not those who are well who need a physician, but those who are sick. I have not come to call the righteous but sinners to repentance" (Luke 5:30–32).

If you think about it, the Pharisees, Sadducees, and scribes were the equivalent of those prominent church leaders, teachers, and theologians today who think they are more worthy than the rest of us to study and interpret Scriptures, taking pride or credit in their knowledge, spirituality, infallibility, or position. The same are convinced that they are above falling into deception, yet many of today's spiritual leaders proliferate mass injustice through lies they believe about God's character. Jesus did not come to call these kinds of people to hold positions of leadership in His Kingdom. The ultimate truth is that many of these kinds of people will at some point have their eyes opened to their spiritual poverty, and they will finally and fully realize their need as well as the fact that the Kingdom of God has no social stratification. Jesus made it clear that God actually takes away what little sight these kinds of people think they have:

> Jesus said, "For judgment I came into this world, so that those who do not see may see, and that those who see may become blind."
>
> Those of the Pharisees who were with Him heard these things and said to Him, "We are not blind too, are we?"
>
> Jesus said to them, "If you were blind, you would have no sin; but since you say, 'We see,' your sin remains" (John 9:39–41).

What God searches the horizon is the child who recognizes his impoverished state and need of a Father's Love. He will never, never turn such a person away. In Jesus's day, it was easy to find these types of people from among the physically weak and sick, because they were already humbled and broken by society. Before the end of *The Story*, I believe all people will be awakened to their deep lack and absolute need of this Love encounter, from resistant atheists to prideful religious leaders.

I see the mission of Jesus as two-fold—healing those now who are aware of their incompleteness, and later revealing to those who thought they were "well" how to recognize their lack so that He might also extend healing to them. One of my favorite accounts of Jesus's tender welcome toward weakness is found in Luke 7:

> Now one of the Pharisees was requesting Him to dine with him, and He entered the Pharisee's house and reclined at the table. And there was a woman in the city who was a sinner; and when she learned that He was reclining at the table in the Pharisee's house, she brought an alabaster vial of perfume, and standing behind Him at His feet, weeping, she began to wet His feet with her tears, and kept wiping them with the hair of her head, and kissing His feet and anointing them with the perfume. Now when the Pharisee who had invited Him saw this, he said to himself, "If this man were a prophet He would know who and what sort of person this woman is who is touching Him, that she is a sinner."

> And Jesus answered him, "Simon, I have something to say to you. …A moneylender had two debtors: one owed five hundred denarii, and the other fifty. When they were unable to repay, he graciously forgave them both. So which of them will love him more?"

> Simon answered and said, "I suppose the one whom he forgave more."

> And [Jesus] said to him, "You have judged correctly." Turning toward the woman, He said to Simon, "Do you see this woman? I entered your house; you gave Me no water for My feet, but she has wet My feet with her tears and wiped them with her hair. You gave Me no kiss; but she, since the time I came in, has not ceased to kiss My feet. You did not anoint My head with oil, but she anointed My feet with perfume. For this reason I say to you, her sins, which are many, have been forgiven, for she loved much; but he who is forgiven little, loves little" (Luke 7:37–47).

In the end, it always comes down to love, and God's love never fails for the weak or broken of heart and spirit.

CHAPTER TEN

LOVE NEVER FAILS WITH ENEMIES

"Am I not destroying my enemies when I make friends of them?"
–Abraham Lincoln

The thought never occurred to me before now that my church upbringing taught me to believe that God expects more loving, forgiving, and tolerant behaviors from me than He does from Himself. Check it out:

"Never pay back evil for evil to anyone."

"Love your enemies and pray for those who persecute you."

"Love your enemies, do good to those who hate you."

"Be merciful."

"Bless those who curse you, pray for those who mistreat you."

"Do not be overcome by evil, but overcome evil with good."

"Love your enemies, and do good, and lend, expecting nothing in return; and your reward will be great, and you will be sons of the Most High…" *

Hmmmm. God asks me to forgive my enemies, to be kind to them, to show them mercy, and to overcome their evil with good, yet He's ultimately *not* going to forgive His enemies, to be kind to them, to show them mercy, or to overcome their evil with good? How absurd and hypocritical is that? If this is what "our Father" is really like, and we are to imitate Him as "sons of the Most High," shouldn't we turn our backs on our enemies, damn them, and then build torture chambers for them? Incidentally, history bears record that many Christians throughout the centuries have actually believed this is what we should do to our enemies.

---

* Rom. 12:17; Matt. 5:44; Luke 6:27–28; Luke 6:35–36; Rom. 12:21.

Romans 5 says that God showed His love for us *while* we were still sinners and that we were reconciled to God *while* we were still His enemies. If He did this for you and me, why should He not do it for everybody? This passage says to me that God has already overcome His children's evil with good, even if we haven't had enough time to observe it yet. Luke 6:35, the one quoted above about loving your enemies in order to be sons of the Most High finishes by saying, "...for [God] Himself is kind to ungrateful and evil men."

If that's true, then why would we who have been overcome by His mercy be considered any more worthy, special, or privileged than someone who hasn't *yet* been overcome by it? Why do we believe that death magically makes God's love and mercy disappear for most of His children, especially when Scripture teaches that Jesus defeated death for all, the evidence to be seen in due season? What would compel enemies of God to be lured by some kind of "unconditional love" offered until the moment they die, only to then turn into unquenchable hate? In his book, *Love Wins,* Rob Bell tackles the rationale of this kind of god:

> Millions have been taught that if they don't believe, if they don't accept in the right way, that is, the way the person telling them the Gospel does, and they were hit by a car and died later that same day, God would have no choice but to punish them forever in conscious torment in hell. God would, in essence, become a fundamentally different being to them in that moment of death, a different being to them forever. A loving heavenly Father who will go to extraordinary lengths to have a relationship with them would, in the blink of an eye, become a cruel, mean, vicious tormenter who would ensure that they had no escape from an endless future of agony.

> Does God become somebody totally different the moment you die? That kind of God is simply devastating. Psychologically crushing. We can't bear it. No one can. And that is the secret deep in the heart of many people, especially Christians: they don't love God. They can't, because the God they've been presented with and taught about can't be loved. That God is terrifying and traumatizing and unbearable.

> And so there are conferences about how churches can be more "relevant" and "missional" and "welcoming," and there are vast resources, many, many books and films, for those who want to "reach

out" and "connect" and "build relationships" with people who aren't part of the church. And that can be helpful. But at the heart of it, we have to ask: Just what kind of God is behind all this?

> Because if something is wrong with your God, if your God is loving one second and cruel the next, if your God will punish people for all of eternity for sins committed in a few short years, no amount of clever marketing or compelling language or good music or great coffee will be able to disguise that one, true, glaring, untenable, unacceptable, awful reality.[32]

Nothing could be further from the truth than the idea that God quits on His children. It's just a matter of time (and realization) until God's truly unfailing, unconditional love works its magic on even His worst enemies.

1976 Olympic athlete, Jerome Milton, is an example of a man who experienced the glowing success rate of unfailing love. Spending most of his childhood being shuffled between orphanages and foster homes, Jerome became the helpless victim of terrible abuse at the hands of ill-intentioned adults. We can only imagine the anger and rebellion that developed inside a little boy's heart, while living in constant terrorizing fear, physical and psychological pain, and utter rejection. Finally, he landed in the foster home of Datie Florence Brown.

When Jerome came to Datie's home, hardened by his experiences, she realized he was going to be a tough case to crack. It seemed that no matter how hard she tried to love him, he despised and rejected it. But she didn't give up; she was determined to break through the fear and distrust to show this boy his first look at real, unconditional love. Eventually, Datie's love broke through. According to Jerome, "she loved the hate and rebellion right out of me."[33] Datie then raised Jerome with the motto, "Don't let your abuse be your excuse," and he went on to become a successful athlete, student, pastor, and as an adult started a home for children in need.

It's becoming obvious to me that many people who act mean, selfish, and hateful usually, if not always, operate out of a place of conditioned self-protection from deep injury, pain, rejection, or fear—all accompanied by the belief of lies—especially when those injuries occur in their childhood. Many people are so injured that they can't initially receive love or help, because they don't know how to recognize genuine love, or to trust long enough to let down the drawbridge. But, given enough time and persistence, love never fails for even the most hardened and hateful person, even if it takes a subsequent age of persistent demonstration.

Why People Reject A Loving God

This is pretty simple, really. Just like any good parent experiences at times (or continuously) from one or more of their children, people reject the heavenly Parent over half-truths, distortions, or outright lies they believe about His character or intentions. They don't see their Father for who He really is because certain truths have been hidden from view, distorted by outside influences, or not perceived correctly through jaded lenses. They do not understand His sovereign intent of good for them because they are taught that even God has His limits and conditions on love. But in time, these lies will be disarmed, one layer at a time. Ken Eckerty at Savior-of-All.com says:

> There's a story of a blind man whom Jesus touched in order to heal. After the first touch, the man could only see "men as trees, walking." It took a second touch from Jesus to complete the healing (Mk. 8:22–25). Jesus showed us that "healing" is a process where, over time, things become clearer and clearer to us concerning the things of God.
>
> The same thing happens to us as we are trying to find the Source of true happiness. As each idol of man is torn down piece by piece, he slowly comes to realize that there must be more to life than what merely meets the eye [think: prodigal son]. So until the last illusion of man is shattered, his rejection of God is *not* a rejection of God Himself, but rather of who he "thinks" God is, or as He is represented by those who call themselves Christians. He sees contradiction and division in the Church and has a tendency to judge God based on the behavior of those who are supposed to represent Him. This is why our example is so important. If Christians are not walking as if they are clearly seeing God, then how can we expect an unbeliever to see God the way He truly is? It is a sad fact that Christians are often the biggest stumbling block as to why men *cannot* see God.[34]

"Father Forgive Them..."

From start to finish, Jesus taught and demonstrated how to treat enemies, instructing His followers to forgive their enemies as many times as necessary. In fact, when Jesus told Peter to forgive his enemies in the amount of "seventy times seven," there is an underlying meaning. In Hebrew, seven is the number for God and for perfection. Jesus taught Peter (and us) that the way to forgive enemies is to do it like our Father — perfectly. We should forgive others for each and every offense. Could God then turn around and not do the same? Wouldn't that again be hypocritical if He told us to have no limits on our forgiveness, yet limited His own capacity to forgive? Would this not then make imperfect humans more forgiving than Jesus Himself? But we find, even in His last few breaths, Jesus demonstrates the way:

> When they came to the place called The Skull, there they crucified Him and the criminals, one on the right and the other on the left. But Jesus was saying, "Father, forgive them; for they do not know what they are doing" (Luke 23:33–34).

Who is Jesus asking His Father to forgive? His *enemies* — the ones who had just rejected Him, condemned Him, spit on Him, cursed Him, abused Him, and nailed Him to a tree. Why on earth would He be asking God to forgive them at a time like this unless, #1: He genuinely desired it, and #2: He intended for His request to be granted? He wouldn't possibly be asking forgiveness or showing love to people He was planning to condemn to hell forever. He wouldn't have even bothered asking His Father to forgive them if they were hopelessly damned. Besides, wasn't it these very people He hid truth from during His public ministry? How could He hold their blindness against them now?

What many people have failed to understand for centuries, as they launched hatred campaigns and persecution toward the Jews for their part in the death of Jesus, is that the Jews were divinely appointed for this task. Someone had to do the deed — someone had to play the part in *The Story* of the betrayer — the scapegoat. It just so happens that the very "chosen people" of God (also called "Judahites") were chosen to bring about His Son's demise through one of the chosen disciples, Judas, in order to bring salvation to the rest of the world. Were they then a blessing or a curse? Did this act send them to hell? What does Paul say?

For if [the rejection of the Jews] is the reconciliation of the world, what will their *acceptance* be but life from the dead? ...For I do not want you, brethren, to be uninformed of this mystery—so that you will not be wise in your own estimation—that a partial hardening has happened to Israel until the fullness of the Gentiles has come in; and so *all Israel will be saved*; just as it is written, "The deliverer will come from Zion, He will remove ungodliness from Jacob. This is my covenant with them, when I take away their sins." From the standpoint of the gospel they are enemies for your sake, but from the standpoint of God's choice they are beloved for the sake of the fathers; for the gifts and the calling of God are irrevocable. For just as you once were disobedient to God, but now have been shown mercy because of their disobedience, so these also now have been disobedient, that because of the mercy shown to you they also may now be shown mercy. *For God has shut up all in disobedience so that He may show mercy to all* (Romans 11:15, 25–32).

Recently I was talking to a friend who is attending seminary and who is convinced that God "hates" His enemies and will have no problem condemning them forever because of His "just" nature. He confidently rattled off verses like Hosea 9:15: "All [Israel's] evil is at Gilgal; Indeed, I came to hate them there! Because of the wickedness of their deeds I will drive them out of My house! I will love them no more..." My friend is also big about accusing people like me of "proof texting," or pulling verses out of context to try to prove my point—even verses that clearly stand on their own and need no context (like "love never fails"). In this case, I suggested we keep reading a little further in Hosea so we could keep the proper context.

If you read far enough in Hosea—and other prophets—you see that God refines and restores all people. Even the worst-case, hopeless apostates are eventually reformed through (inner) judgment, heart change, and being realigned to the ways of justice. The message of the prophets always becomes a complete, full-circle story—one that ends with something like Hosea's final thoughts on the matter:

"I will heal [Israel's] apostasy, I will love them freely, for My anger has turned away from them" (Hosea 14:4).

A hateful person is still someone's child, and ultimately God's child. Any truly loving parent could never give up on hoping to see their child overcome resistance, insecurities, and fear. As devoted and unfailing is the love of a typical earthly parent for their children, it's only a minuscule, infinitely inferior representation of the heavenly Parent's love.

What about Hitler?

Whenever I tell someone I no longer believe in hell and that I now believe in the ultimate reconciliation of all people, one of the first things they undoubtedly ask me is, *"What about Hitler?"* For some reason, Hitler appears to be the "poster child" for the necessity of the doctrine of hell.

Before I address the question about Hitler, let me emphasize that I do not believe anyone who causes intentional injury to others is off the hook. There is definitely going to be some future day of accountability for people like Hitler (and you...and me), and at that time he will receive a fair hearing from The Judge who knows all. As we move through this book, we will explore what future accountability and judgment might look like for people like Hitler, from what we glean in the Scriptures.

So what about Hitler? Well first of all, how can we be the ones to decide that he is too evil or too corrupt to save and reform? I am convinced that until you live in someone else's shoes — which is never — you cannot make a true judgment about them. Who knows the kind of household Hitler grew up in? Perhaps they were all Jew-haters. Perhaps he was abused himself and carried with him a lot of bitterness and insecurities. There are reports that his father was quite driven and may have beaten his children for underachieving, but it is also suggested that he was particularly close to his mother, who died when he was only eighteen.

In addition, we have not personally experienced the cultural, religious, and social pressures that Hitler was affected by in his day. For example, in my "History of Modern Germany" class in college, I learned how popular religious and scientific views during Hitler Germany revolved around the powerful legend of a special, ancient race of people (Aryans) who were superior to all other "races" in intelligence and physical strength. The Germans wholeheartedly believed they were descendants of this race and that it was necessary and good to the future success of their country (and the world) to eradicate the weak among them, lest they contaminate the

gene pool. In addition, Hitler took power in Germany at a most opportune
time, on the heels of the Black Plague and following several decades of
political, social, and economic instability and division. The people of
Germany were desperate for a strong leader who would alleviate the dire
state of their impoverished nation (and empty stomachs). All these
perspectives shaped his society and his own young life.

It's no secret that European Jews have been hated, uprooted, and
sequestered into slums throughout the centuries, often under the blessing
and direction of the Church, both Catholic and Protestant. The sentiment
many held at the time was that you were doing God a favor to mistreat
and even to eradicate Jews. Perhaps that is the real reason Hitler had so
much support and cooperation in his quest — it was a popular opinion of
the day. Apparently Hitler and his army truly believed, most likely
influenced by religion, that they were being noble by "cleansing the gene
pool" of those they deemed evil. For every Jew he destroyed, perhaps
Hitler felt he purged the world of one more "Christ-killer" and political
dissident.

History has proven that it is human nature, whether in governments or
religions, to justify the means to an end (killing) in the name of ridding the
world of evil. Yet eradicating evil is merely a point of perspective,
depending on which side of a border or belief system you're on. What we
must consider is, what did Jesus teach? He told Peter to put his sword
away; evil is overcome with good, not violence.

In the course of the conversation about my belief in the savability and
eventual restoration of Hitler, I usually ask the skeptic, "Let's put the shoe
on the other foot and talk about the Jews Hitler killed. Were they believers
in Christ?"

"No," they reply.

"So do you think it's fair that the Jews who were led into the gas
chambers, perhaps under the influence of Christianity, left hell on earth for
hell in eternity? Whether we're speaking of Hitler or the Jews he put to
death (many of whom were probably nice, loving people), is it really fair
to endlessly punish both parties the same? And would we really expect the
Jews — fairly innocent victims who were put to death centuries after Christ,
perhaps in His name — to want to put their faith in such a "loving savior"?

Even in light of his colossal offenses, I can't imagine that anyone who
has had an authentic grace-encounter themselves would truly want Hitler

to burn in a torture chamber for millions of years for crimes he committed over a few years of his earthly life – especially if you can possibly entertain the idea that every one of His victims are ultimately to be restored with healing and happiness. And if they are to be restored, would the knowledge of Hitler's endless punishment ultimately satisfy any of his victims? Or do you think they might be more satisfied if he were to be transformed into a remorseful, loving, serving person, and reintroduced to them as a caring friend and brother?

I once heard the saying, "Absolute power corrupts absolutely." Hitler undoubtedly had a lot more power than you or I will ever have. Certainly, in our limited sphere of influence, you and I have caused significant pain or damage to others at some point. Let's be thankful that God did not allow us to have the kind of influence and power where our bad decisions and unloving behavior could affect millions of people and several generations to come. If we were in Hitler's shoes, we can't decisively say what we would have done with that power, or that we would not have become a person just like him.

I think it's pretty arrogant when fellow Christians are quick to condemn people like Hitler to hell when it's only possible to think that way because they aren't headed to a place like that themselves. Though they may claim it is "by grace alone" that they have been saved, their sentiments show that they don't truly understand the depth of their own sin and what the free gift of grace really means. If these people truly got grace and realized they would fare no better without the work of Christ in their lives, they'd be flat on their faces, acknowledging God's boundless love and forgiveness, rather than tweeting modern sentiments like, "Welcome to hell, Bin Laden."

If we're going to point the finger at Hitler for his part in the Holocaust, we'd better include Martin Luther, one of the revered fathers of the Protestant Reformation and hence, the modern Church. Though he lived a few hundred years before Hitler, Luther had a significant influence on Hitler's thinking and persecution of the Jews:

> In 1523, Luther advised kindness toward the Jews in that Jesus Christ was born a Jew, but only with the aim of converting them to Christianity. When his efforts at conversion failed, he grew increasingly bitter toward them. Luther's other major works on the Jews was his 60,000-word treatise *Von den Juden und Ihren Lügen* (On

the Jews and Their Lies)...published in 1543, three years before his death. Luther argued that the Jews were no longer the chosen people but "the devil's people." He referred to them with violent, vile language. Luther advocated setting synagogues on fire, destroying Jewish prayer books, forbidding rabbis from preaching, seizing Jews' property and money, and smashing up their homes, so that these "poisonous envenomed worms" would be forced into labor or expelled "for all time." ...Luther's words, "We are at fault in not slaying them," amounted to a sanction for murder.[35]

In the Church of England Newspaper on August 4, 1944, William Ralph Inge, a retired Dean of London's St. Paul's, wrote:

"If we wish to find a scapegoat on whose shoulders we may lay the miseries which Germany has brought upon the world...I am more and more convinced that the worst evil genius of that country is not Hitler or Bismarck or Frederick the Great, but Martin Luther..."[36]

In addition to Martin Luther, the Catholic Church had its share of influence. "[Hitler's] family moved to Lambach in 1897. There, Hitler [age 8] attended a Catholic school located in an 11th-century Benedictine cloister whose walls were engraved in a number of places with crests containing the symbol of the swastika (a symbol that came to be associated with white supremacy)."[37]

Some say that when Hitler committed suicide in 1945, he was holding a photograph of his mother. Everything about this act clearly reveals the heart of a troubled man. Though his mother never lived to see her son's brutality against the Jews, there's little doubt she loved him deeply and probably would not have given up on him.

It's difficult not to bring the parental love application into any and all of our scenarios because, at the heart of love for the blind, weak, lame, helpless, hopeless, enemies, and children, is the love of a devoted Father. No decent parent ever gives up longing to be restored in relationship with his or her child, and in turn to help that child succeed in life as a decent, loving human being. Anything less would reveal a serious character flaw in that parent, yet that is the kind of horrible character we have unwittingly pinned on the Father who first loved us.

Let us not be deceived. God's perfect love will NOT fail, even for Hitler.

Ultimate Atonement

In light of our worst-case scenarios – people like Hitler, Ted Bundy, Saddam Hussein, and Osama Bin Laden – is it possible that these types of people have been appointed roles in *The Story* for the very purpose of demonstrating to us the limitlessness of God's patience and love, when He one day overcomes their heinous acts and deranged character with good?

I never quite understood Romans 9 until I was able to put on these new lenses, but now I see the whole chapter addressing this very idea:

> For He says to Moses, "I will have mercy on whom I have mercy, and I will have compassion on whom I have compassion." So then it does not depend on the man who wills (thelema)* or the man who runs, but on God who has mercy. For the Scripture says to Pharaoh, "For this very purpose I raised you up, to demonstrate my power in you, and that my name† might be proclaimed throughout the whole earth." So then He has mercy on whom He desires (thelema), and He hardens whom He desires (thelema) (vs. 15–18).

Consider also Ephesians 2:7–9:

> ...so that *in the ages to come* He might show the surpassing riches of His grace in kindness toward us in Christ Jesus. For by grace you have been saved through faith; and that not of yourselves, it is the gift of God; not as a result of works, so that no one may boast.

A while back we looked at Acts 17:31, which states that belief or faith will be furnished to all people at some point in the plan of ages. This is why Paul said it is a *gift* in which no one may boast – it is not a respecter of persons, positions, locations, or circumstances. It is not for a few. Faith is a gift for all, to be manifested (made visible) in due season (1 Timothy 2:6)!

Romans 6:10: "For the death that He died, He died to sin *once for all*..."

Hebrews 7:27: "...because this [sacrifice] He did *once for all* when He offered up Himself."

---

* I point out the three occurrences of the Greek word "thelema" (wills) in this passage because I wanted you to see how translators render "wills" when speaking of man, but use "desires," when speaking of God, lest they make it sound like God wills people to go to hell with the way they translate this passage.

† In Jewish thought, your name represented your character, not only what people called you. God desires that people understand His true character.

Hebrews 9:12: "…through His own blood, He entered the holy place *once for all*, having obtained eonian (age-enduring) redemption…" (MLT).

1 Peter 3:18: "Christ also died for sins *once for all*, the just for the unjust, so that He might bring us to God…"

Jesus provided the ultimate atonement (at-one-ment), once for all. The modern definition of atonement is:

> A repair done for the sake of a damaged relationship; compensation for a wrong; reparation for an offense or injury.

We haven't seen it with our limited vision yet, but we will. Christ's atonement for sin will be fully manifested and experienced at a future time when offenders will "put on Christ," (Rom. 13:14), wholeheartedly desiring to repair damages they've caused, restoring relationships with God and people. This is the meaning of being "crucified with Christ," (Gal. 2:20) laying down our lives for others. It's not "works-based salvation," because a person is only saved from death through the grace offered in the name of Jesus Christ. However beyond that, Scriptures are clear that nobody is getting away with injurious treatment of others. This is why Paul referred to a "judgment age." There are many passages that speak of this age, such as Luke 12:43–48 (please note that these "punishments" are metaphorical, not literal — this is a parable):

> "Blessed is that [faithful, sensible] servant whom his master finds when he comes. Truly I say to you that he will put him in charge of all his possessions. But if that servant says in his heart, 'My master will be a long time in coming,' and begins to beat the servants, and to eat and drink and get drunk; the master of that servant will come on a day when he does not expect him and at an hour he does not know, and will cut him in pieces (think: "sword of the Spirit" — he's not dead), and assign him a place with the unfaithful. And that servant who knew his master's will and did not get ready or act in accord with his will, will receive many lashes, but the one who did not know it, and committed deeds worthy of a flogging, will receive but few. From everyone who has been given much, much will be required; and to whom they entrusted much, of him they will ask all the more."

I used to think this was some kind of heavy-handed external judgment, but I have come to realize that nobody ever had a change of heart or felt remorse over coercion or punishment. I believe this "sword" pierces from the inside, our own hearts convicting us with life-changing realizations about how we have treated others. This is exactly what happened to the Prodigal before he came home (and what happened to me). He realized what he had done, and his own heart led him home. In his article, "Fifteen Bombs that Sank my Theological Ship," V.E. Jacobson says:

> Of course we do not wish to insinuate for a moment that the son of stubbornness will escape judgment. All the dead, great and small…will have to stand before the Great White Throne to be judged. They will be judged according to the truth (Luke 8:17; Rom. 3:4); according to deeds (Rom. 2:6; Rev. 20:12–13); and, according to the light they have (Rom. 2:12).[38]

The biblical "Great White Throne" could very well be symbolic for the seat of your own cleansed heart, with the proper King now reigning in his rightful place. As you contemplate those who have significantly hurt you in your lifetime, ask yourself which would be more satisfying to you — knowing these offenders were put away for endless, torturous punishment, or knowing that they will become remorseful for their actions — to the point that they genuinely desire to do whatever it takes to amend all their wrongs?

Corrie Ten Boom, a German woman whose family assisted in hiding Jews during the Holocaust, suffered some of the worst injustices under the hand of Hitler. She lost her whole family in concentration camps, yet she did not covet hell for their offenders. Rather, she completely forgave her persecutors their debt. In her elderly years, she even described the joyful opportunity she encountered to reconcile with one of her prison camp guards. I believe she would be elated to see all the rest of her earthly enemies again — standing alongside her family — watching them become enlightened, loving, serving, and redeemed sons and daughters of God. If you or I want any less, then God's love has not been perfected in us and we cannot yet be called genuine children of God.

> "Beloved, let us love one another, for love is from God; and everyone who loves is generated from God and knows God. The one who does not love does not know God, for God is love. …By this, love is perfected with us, so that we may have boldness in the day of judgment; because as He is, so also are we in this world. We love,

because He first loved us. If someone says, 'I love God,' and hates his brother, he is a liar; for the one who does not love his brother whom he has seen, cannot love God whom he has not seen." (1 John 4:7–20, MLT, selected).

Remember, we don't know the whole story. The prison camp guards in Nazi Germany were under unimaginable pressure (and brainwashing) to fulfill their duty to their country, which at the time was basically eat or be eaten. We see time and again in Scriptures that our enemy is also our brother, and we are to love both without judgment. In one of my favorite e-books by Stephen Jones, *Creation's Jubilee*, we read:

> We have a punishment mentality, rather than having the mind of Christ, which would lead us to know the precise measure of restitution to be paid that would correct the injustice and restore the lawful order. ...In cases where restitution is impossible, due to the nature of the crime, the penalty is death...what is done cannot be undone except by the direct power of God. And so in such cases, God instructed earthly courts to set aside the case and await the final judgment at the end of the age.[39]

After reading that, a friend wrote, "Man, now it makes sense! It wasn't that the OT God was callous or didn't care or give much value to human lives. It was that He knew the big picture and this life is just a small part of it. Death resulting from sin didn't automatically mean eternal torture, it just meant you had to await His judgment. Suddenly I can see God's love where before I just saw...well, un-love or unforgiveness. It's a principle of God's Law that, once full restitution has been paid to the victims of injustice, the sinner is forgiven by the Law, and their sins are *not* to be remembered. Such is the power of forgiveness. Now that's Good News!"

In his book, *The Inescapable Love of God*, Thomas Talbott adds:

> Contrary to popular belief, the OT principle of retaliatory justice — "an eye for an eye and a tooth for a tooth" — was never instituted for the purpose of justifying harsh punishment for serious crimes, something that no one at the time would have questioned; instead, it was instituted for the purpose of eliminating excessive punishment, such as capital punishment in exchange for a tooth.

The idea was very simple. We must measure the seriousness of a crime according to the degree of harm done, and we must proportion the punishment to the seriousness of the crime. ...This may seem harsh and unforgiving (eye for eye, tooth for tooth, life for life, Lev. 24:17-20), as indeed it is, but it also has the effect of placing strict limits upon allowable punishment. And it raises an intriguing question: *Given the [scriptural] principle of equal retaliation (lex talionis), for what sort of crime might everlasting torment be a just retaliation?* ...Why should anyone think that everlasting torment is a just punishment for any act of rebellion, whether it be yours, or mine, or Adam's, or even of Satan himself? How could any finite being, limited in power and knowledge and wisdom, subject to deception and blindness, ever do anything that would deserve such punishment by way of a just recompense?[40]

I have read Jewish commentaries that confirm Talbott's assessment in that the purpose of Lex Talionis (the "eye for an eye" law) was to limit excessive punishment for a crime so that offenders were not over-punished. If you study the Levitical Law, there is a whole teaching on the restoration requirements for the offended party. Sure the intent of the Law was to satisfy the demands of justice for the offended, but also included was a responsibility to restore the offender to society, not to cast them out. Doesn't this sound more in line with a just and loving God?

It is important to consider the implications here—not only for our own personal offenders, but also to consider whom we have offended. If you and I have wrongs we have done against others intentionally in this lifetime that we have not attempted to reconcile, we are merely putting off our own day in "court." I believe that restitution attempted here and now will be far easier than if we wait until later. This is why we are admonished to forgive and to make sure we keep clear accounts as much as possible with all men whom we have wronged. Hopefully you can spot the spiritual meaning in Jesus's words:

Matthew 5:23-26: "Therefore if you are presenting your offering at the altar, and there remember that your brother has something against you, leave your offering there before the altar and go; first be reconciled to your brother, and then come and present your offering. Make friends quickly with your opponent at law while you are with him on the way, so that your opponent may not hand you over to the judge, and the judge to the officer, and you be thrown into prison. Truly I say to you, you will not come out of there until you have paid up the last cent."

Matthew 21:44: "And he who falls on this stone will be broken to pieces; but on whomever it falls, it will scatter him like dust." Either fall on The Rock in self-imposed repentance and reconciliation toward those we've wronged, or The Rock will fall on us and we will be shattered.

What's Good for Neb and Paul is also Good for Hitler

In considering whether God will redeem (buy back) all people from the consequence of Adam, I think it's difficult for most people to get past two obstacles. First, that everyone is redeemable and second, that it's possible for someone to have the opportunity to believe in Christ after rejecting Him (knowingly or unknowingly) during this lifetime. Let's explore both of these obstacles.

Is there something redeemable in every person? Is the worst offender or criminal worth saving? Could any good come out of the Hitlers, the Kim Jong-Ils, the Saddam Husseins, the Bundys or, closer to home, the heartless boss, abusive family member, or total jerk living next door?

We need look no further for the answers than to our own apostle Paul. Paul was chosen precisely to show us God's intent for *all people*, no matter how hopeless, mean-spirited, prideful, sinful, blind, hypocritical, or lost they may be. He said:

> "I'm grateful to Him Who strengthens me, Christ Jesus, our Lord, for He deems me faithful, assigning me a service, I, who formerly was a blasphemer and a persecutor and a violent aggressor. But I was shown mercy, because I acted in ignorance and unbelief. Yet the grace of our Lord overwhelms with faith and love in Christ Jesus. Faithful is the saying, and worthy of all welcome, that Christ Jesus came into the world to save sinners, of whom I am foremost. But therefore was I shown mercy, that in me, the foremost, Jesus Christ should be displaying all His patience, for a pattern of those who are about to be believing on Him for age-abiding life" (1 Tim. 1:12–16, MLT).

Paul was not looking for a coming to Jesus experience. His "conversion" was not because he was seeking, worthy, good, or even a good bet. It was because God picked the seemingly most hopeless case—

the Hitler of his day — to reveal that within everyone lays an ungerminated good seed, ready to be quickened by a life-giving encounter with Love. If Paul, the self-righteous, ignorant, unbelieving, blasphemous, murderous, self-acclaimed "chief of sinners," should qualify to be overpowered by an illuminating grace that led him to repentance, why should Hitler not qualify? Who would fail to qualify? Paul, stricken with a genuinely repentant heart, declared that he was a "pattern" of God's mercy and patience for others like himself who would eventually come to belief.

Now back up a few centuries. In Daniel, Nebuchadnezzar (Neb, for short) is another stellar example of the sole work of God in bringing a hopeless, dormant seed to life. Neb was king of Babylon, the greatest empire on earth, comprising a large portion of the inhabited world. He was full of pride in his accomplishments, and did not give God the glory for his power or position — nor did he desire to. Regardless of Neb's will or opinion in the matter, God humbled him for seven years, turning him into a "wild beast." Whether this story is literal or metaphorical doesn't really matter. Neb was cursed to live in the wild, crawling around on his hands and knees, eating a steady diet of grass. After seven years, he was restored to sanity by the hand of God, and given proper understanding of his absolute need for God and subjection to a greater authority. At this time, God actually restored Neb to greater power and glory than before, and for the rest of his days, Neb gave credit where credit was due.

> "At that time my reason returned to me. And my majesty and splendor were restored to me for the glory of my kingdom, and my counselors and my nobles began seeking me out; so I was reestablished in my sovereignty, and surpassing greatness was added to me. Now I, Nebuchadnezzar, praise, exalt and honor the King of heaven, for all His works are true and His ways just, and He is able to humble those who walk in pride" (Daniel 4:36–37).

This was not just a nice little story with an inconsequential happy ending. This is the story of our enemies. This is *our story*. What is good for Nebuchadnezzar, and Paul, and Hitler, is also good for you, and me, and everyone we know that ever wandered in darkness, searching for anything and everything but God. Everyone is infinitely valuable and ultimately redeemable to God, no matter how seemingly hopeless.

So far we've addressed the first major obstacle people raise in contemplating whether God's plan of redemption could really be that all-inclusive. This brings us to the second major obstacle people encounter. Can people really get another chance to believe after rejecting God in this lifetime?

CHAPTER ELEVEN

LOVE NEVER FAILS FOR ANY...OR ALL

"The only victory love can enjoy is the day when
its offer of love is answered by the return of love.
The only possible final triumph
is a universe loved by God and in love with God."
–William Barclay

I'm positively stumped whenever I share the good, wonderful, awesome news of God's plan to save everybody with my Christian friends and some of them, without even stopping to consider a few of my valid points, or to question the process that led me to this belief, or to take any time whatsoever to look into the possibilities, respond with, "I'm sad for you, Julie."

Maybe they are genuinely sad because they believe I have gone astray and am now leading others astray. Some have suggested I'm going to be guilty of sending people to hell and others have said I will also end up there. It's really hard to get upset about going to a place you're 200% sure doesn't exist. There are many others who respond with, "That's depressing news." Huh? God saving everyone is *depressing*? Sort of makes you wonder why these people make any attempt at evangelism.

After sharing my beliefs about God's fool-proof salvation plan on my blog, I once had a reader respond with, "That kind of teaching is unpalatable and at odds with the image of a loving God."

I've had to think long and hard about why anyone could possibly feel this way and the only thing I can come up with is this: If hell is not true and God is going to save everybody, then these people feel that they are no longer "special."

Perhaps that kind of God would seem unfair and "unloving" to them because He does not ultimately reject total, undeserving sinners, regardless of the many factors involved. Perhaps these people also feel that their "decision" to follow Jesus would be cheapened. They have been raised in church under the impression that they are more deserving of a place in "heaven" than all those sinners and unbelievers, especially since they believe they "chose Jesus now," which resulted in many sacrifices, good works, and proper behavior throughout their lives to go along with that decision. Should they stop long enough to consider the possibility of everyone being included as equally special, they might feel depressed that their "free will decision" was seemingly all for naught. The grace or undeserved favor that they have professed all their lives is not really all that free or favorable when it comes to certain others. In essence, their sadness for me must really be sadness for themselves.

If they are sad, I am even more sad that these people are not willing to consider the possibility that their God is more unconditionally loving and more victorious over His creation than they have ever heard about or given Him credit for. They do not want to entertain the thought that God might one day awaken every person to the full beauty, clarity, and purity of God's love for them in such a way that is irresistible. They do not want to allow for the possibility that each person is on a different timetable in being drawn into a relationship with God, perhaps most not seeing this reality come to fruition during this lifetime.

On her blog, *Written Not With Ink,* my friend Barb Riley encapsulates beautifully the individual process of awakening to Love and Light:

> Whenever I need to wake up my daughter in the morning, all I have to do is crack open her blinds, allowing the tiniest ray of sunshine to peek into her bedroom, and voila`...she's awake. And not just barely awake, but wide awake. And I'll be darned if she doesn't look like she's about to declare, "Carpe diem!" before proceeding to do ten push-ups. Her reaction is almost always immediate.
>
> Then there's my son. I can fully raise his blinds, pull back his curtains, and turn on his bedroom light, but even after all that, he can, and often will, continue to catch his precious Z's, totally unaffected by his brightened surroundings. He doesn't respond to the light in the same urgent way my daughter does. And I don't believe he has much of a choice in the matter either, considering he's in an unconscious state, "dead to the world" as the expression goes.
>
> How is it that he is so opposite from my daughter, yet created by the same set of parents? Could it be that God, the ultimate Creator, made him that way? If so, do you suppose there's any merit in

comparing his physical limitation (unresponsiveness to light) to what the Bible teaches about understanding one's spiritual limitations? Since Jesus refers to Himself as "the light of the world," I thought I'd take a look at this possibility.

In John 6:44, Jesus says this to His disciples, "No one can come to Me unless the Father who sent Me draws them." The first time I read that, I remember thinking, *well, that's not fair; what if the Father doesn't draw someone? Does that mean there's nothing anyone can do?*

As I continued to read through the Bible, I noticed several more verses where it's quite clear Who, exactly, is in control when it comes to responding to the light of Christ:

"Yet to this day the Lord has not given you a heart to know, nor eyes to see, nor ears to hear" (Deut. 29:4).

"The hearing ear and the seeing eye, the Lord has made both of them" (Prov. 20:12).

"For this reason they could not believe, because, as Isaiah says elsewhere: He has blinded their eyes and deadened their hearts, so they can neither see with their eyes, nor understand with their hearts, nor turn—and I [Jesus] would heal them" (John 12:39–40, NIV).

"While they were talking and discussing, Jesus Himself approached them and began traveling with them. But their eyes were prevented from recognizing Him" (Luke 24:15–16).

Yikes, what do you do if you are one of the many people written about above, who won't be able to turn to Jesus to heal you because God has prevented you from doing so? It hardly seems fair.

The good news is—and this is truly Good News—just a few chapters after Jesus tells His disciples that no one can come to Him unless the Father draws them, He then says, "But I, when I am lifted up from the earth, will draw all men to Myself" (John 12:32, NIV). How beautiful is this three-letter word: *ALL!* Someday this verse will be true of all people:

"Then He opened their minds to understand the Scriptures" (Luke 24:45).[41]

Only One Chance?

I have asked people the question, "Where in the Bible does it say that this mortal lifetime is the only opportunity we get to be saved?" To which they usually respond with Hebrews 9:27, "And inasmuch as it is appointed for men to die once and after this comes judgment." This is certainly the verse I was also taught to use in such cases in my years of evangelism training, but if you examine the verse more closely, does it really say anything about having only one chance to be saved? All men are appointed to die, fact established. Yes, there will be some kind of Judgment — the Bible teaches that it will last for a whole age. But where in this verse is the one-chance-or-you're-damned-forever teaching? I'm pretty sure people make the mental leap because they assume the Judgment is a "you're in or you're out" situation, based on their church teachings. This is not the case, which we will examine more in depth shortly.

I also believe this notion of "only one chance" is most often conveyed by certain verses with an erroneous translation of the word "eternal," where passages suggest we only get one chance before facing the threat of "eternal judgment" or "eternal punishment." Chapter 14 is devoted to revealing just why these verses are critical mistranslations. What many Christians don't realize is that our mortal lives are just a small part of a bigger, more complete story where God is locating and developing a few people ahead of the rest to help Him finish His plan of growing and harvesting the seedlings of all mankind into His ever-growing Kingdom:

> In all wisdom and insight He made known to us the mystery of His will, according to His delight which He purposed in Him with a view to an administration suitable to the filling of the seasons (with people), that is, heading up all in Christ, both in the heavens and on the earth. In Him also we were chosen by lot,* having been designated beforehand according to His purpose who works all after the counsel of His will, for us to be in high praise of His glory, of the ones hoping earlier in Christ (Ephesians 1:8–12, MLT).

Another verse often quoted in support of "only one chance" is John

---

* Being chosen by sacred lot is frequently used in the Scriptures. This suggests that God was truly fair in deciding who would play which roles in *The Story*, choosing roles by lot or random drawing, similar to throwing dice.

3:16: "For God so loved the world, that He gave His only begotten Son, that whoever believes in Him shall not perish, but have eternal life." This verse surely seems like it could be saying that belief must take place in this lifetime — or else — but this is another example of a mistranslation as well as a misunderstanding of what life really is. Understood properly, this verse is talking about having the abundant life of Christ *now*, beginning in this age, not exclusively later. Here is a more literal translation:

> For thus God loves the world, so that He gives His only-begotten Son, that everyone who is believing in Him should not be perishing, but may be having age-abiding life (CLT).

Notice the present, progressive tense of the Greek. This is significant because there are plenty of places where the Greek uses past or future tenses, but present progressive tense was used intentionally to convey specific meaning about the onset and continuation of life in the ages. As we will thoroughly explore later, this verse declares an often-repeated theme of the NT — at any point in time that you put your faith in Christ, you immediately begin to experience "eonian life," or life beginning in the current age and continuing throughout the coming ages. And for anyone who has not put their faith in Christ, they are in the process of "perishing" — right now, in this age (John 15:1–11). Think of it like a green plant thriving by a water source, or withering away for lack of water.

Growing up in church I was always taught that life and death are eternal conditions, and that the only way I would be exempt from eternal, spiritual death is if I put my faith in Jesus. But does that really make sense? If Jesus paid my debt, and that debt was *eternal* punishment, wouldn't that mean that Jesus had to go to hell eternally in my place? If that's my due punishment, and if He took it, how come the only thing that happened to Him is that *He died*? Without a doubt, He overcame death at the cross, but the fact is, He didn't exactly remove the consequence of sin. I still have to die. What He did do is take on death with me and declare victory over it, making a way of deliverance so that I could be brought to life again.

Paul referred to Jesus as the "second Adam." The second Adam* came, not to take away the consequence of first Adam's sin (death), but to reverse the effects of sin and death by conquering their permanence.

---

* Rom. 5:14 and 1 Cor. 15:45.

Through Jesus, our perfect sacrifice, all the offspring of Adam (all people) will be raised again to imperishable life. Now that I understand that people are not limited to believing in Christ in this mortal lifetime, and that Jesus came to conquer death, not hell, other once-confusing or irrelevant verses now come under new light:

Rom. 5:18: "So then as through one transgression there resulted judgment toward all men, even so through one act of justice there resulted the just pronouncement of life to all men" (MLT).

1 Cor. 15:22-23: "For as in Adam all die, so also in Christ all will be made alive. But each in his own order..."

1 Tim. 2:5-6: "For there is one God, and one mediator also between God and men, the man Christ Jesus, who gave Himself as a ransom for all, the testimony given in its own due season" (MLT).*

The key concept in the last two verses is that all people will be reconciled (or harvested)—like crops—in their own season of ripening. The part about "each in his own order" in 1 Cor. 15:22-23 never used to make sense to me, but now I understand that there are actually three "seasons" of crops representing mankind spoken of repeatedly throughout Scripture, and they do not all ripen in this age. I am introducing several new topics here, but this too will be covered more in depth in chapter 17, dealing with the Harvests. In that chapter, we'll learn more about the Jewish view of God's beautiful, purposeful plan for the coming ages.

A few times we have brought up the Calvinist idea of being chosen for salvation while everyone else is damned. The Bible does indeed teach about a chosen people, but they are not the elite few while others are doomed. The "chosen people," have always been about a few being chosen ahead of the rest to assist in bringing God's plan of salvation to all.

Who are those chosen ahead of time to assist in this marvelous plan? Some might still say, "Israel," since they were first called the "chosen people," but that is not exactly correct. Physical Israel (the nation) was a chosen people in the flesh who would be a "type" or picture of a chosen spiritual people (by lot) who would help God work His plan for mankind upon the earth because of their loving service, sacrificial lifestyle, and unwavering trust in the power of God during this lifetime. These people

---

* The NASB reads, "the testimony to be given at the proper time," but the Greek reads, "idios kairos" and translates, "due season." The notion of seasons is in keeping with the larger theme in Scripture of a harvest of people (chapter 17).

are not merely "chosen for salvation" as taught in the tenets of Christianity, but chosen for a great purpose of future leadership:

> These will wage war against the Lamb, and the Lamb will overcome them, because He is Lord of lords and King of kings; those who are with Him are the called and chosen and faithful (Rev. 17:14).

Consider Paul's words in Romans 9:6-7: "For they are not all Israel who are descended from Israel; nor are they all [Abraham's] children because they are Abraham's descendants..." Paul's point is that it is a spiritual lineage of Abraham who is chosen to help win the harvest, not a physical lineage, whether Jews or non-Jews. He makes the same point in Romans 2:29: "But he is a Jew who is one inwardly; and circumcision is that which is of the heart, by the Spirit, not by the letter; and his praise is not from men, but from God." Other passages teach what the job description will look like for this spiritual people:

2 Timothy 2:11-12: "It is a trustworthy statement: For if we died with Him, we will also live with Him; If we endure, we will also reign with Him."

Rev. 5:9-10: "You were slain and purchased for God...men from every tribe and tongue and people and nation. You have made them to be a kingdom and priests to our God; and they will reign upon the earth."

Rev. 20:6: "Blessed and holy is the one who has a part in the *first resurrection;* over these the second death has no power, but they will be priests of God and of Christ and will reign with Him..."

Reigning with Christ is actively participating in the redeeming of creation, according to God's planned design. This was the idea behind the dominion given to Adam in the Garden. Just as Adam was assigned physical dominion, those who are chosen to reign with Christ will be given spiritual dominion. Understand that "reigning" with Christ will not be a Lord-it-over, heavy-handed position, but that of a servant. It should be apparent that not every Christian (or Israelite) is living a life worthy of leading the world with Christ as humble servants. *The chosen and faithful* are the few "priests" who will be establishing true mercy and justice on earth with Christ, restoring love and relationships in the ages to come.

Do you remember the job of priests in the OT? They entered the Holy of Holies in order to make atonement (at-one-ment) between the people and God. Jesus, the Great High Priest, will be joined by a company of "priests," to administer this atonement for all people for all time. I believe Revelation offers a symbolic picture of this:

> On either side of the river was the tree of life, bearing twelve kinds of fruit, yielding its fruit every month; and the leaves of the tree were for the healing of the nations (22:2).

Jesus, the tree of life, offers healing leaves (priests) to the nations as an extension of Himself. The result? Fruit is being yielded every month as people flock to Jesus and His priests for this healing and wholeness.

And just what does it mean to "reign" with Christ? According to Strong's #936 (Greek: basileuo):

1) to be king, to exercise kingly power, to reign

    a) of the governor of a province

    b) of the rule of the Messiah

    c) of the reign of Christians in the millennium *

2) metaph. to exercise the highest influence

It should be getting clearer that some kind of judicial process is going on in the coming ages. What need would there be for Jesus and His chosen to be ruling and reigning over people if the "unsaved" were sent to hell and the rest were a faithful, unified body of believers? Paul addressed this when he said, "Or do you not know that the saints will judge the world? If the world will be judged by you, are you not competent to constitute the smallest law courts? Do you not know that we will judge angels? How much more matters of this life" (1 Cor. 6:2–3)?

Because of the exemplary demonstration of self-sacrificing love, forgiveness, and service in this lifetime, these "called, chosen, and faithful"† people will be the very ones "conquering" the enemies of God through *invitation* — invitation to life, love, and kindness by example. These will pattern themselves after Jesus' example, not by the old (current) order

---

* According to some Hebrew interpretations of Scripture, the Millennial Kingdom is the next temporary phase or age after this. Its purpose is for God to fulfill promises He made to Israel (not the country but the true followers of God, under the Mosaic Covenant. True Israel, according to Paul, is not a nationality, but a heart condition. Quite possibly there will be both mortals and immortals living during this time on earth, a concept we will cover later in the Covenants, chapter 16.

† Revelation 17:14.

of coercion, fear, and bloodshed. It is possible that these future priests will no longer be mortals, but will be powerful people who have been resurrected into imperishable life.

Does Everyone Really Get A Fair Chance *Now*?

If you are like me, and you don't have a Calvinist bent, perhaps you have wondered how everyone on earth could possibly have had the same fair opportunity to hear about and believe in Jesus before they die. If you haven't asked that question, perhaps it's because you've had a pretty fair chance to hear and have disregarded the fact that most of the rest of the world hasn't. When you really think about it, mainstream Christianity endorses that one's opportunity to be saved is most directly related to the geographic location of where they were born.

For example, the majority of people reading this book were probably born in a country where the teachings of Christianity were interwoven throughout society. You may have even grown up in a town where there were as many churches as restaurants. You were likely raised in a Bible-teaching, church-attending home, and heard the Scriptures often. Even if none of that is exactly true of your circumstances, you probably watched Billy Graham or some other evangelist on TV, or you were invited to church, or you had a friend who shared the get-saved-from-hell version of the gospel with you: "pray the sinner's prayer and accept Jesus into your heart before it's too late." In short, your opportunity to believe in Jesus is really most strongly correlated to the family you had the good fortune of being born into, which determined the city and country in which you were raised. If this was a country in the Western hemisphere where you had freedom of religion and plenty of Christian influence, then you are likely to have had ample opportunities to hear about and "accept" Jesus.

If you ascribe to Calvinism, it's miraculously coincidental that most of the "elect" are born into the same general geographic location. Wouldn't it have made more sense for God's elect to have been scattered evenly in every culture? Even if you believe in Arminianism, wouldn't God have been a lot more fair had He scattered salvation evenly among the nations, so that people would actually be "without excuse" for rejecting Him?

Once again, we see special club mentality in action. It's sure great if you're born into *The Club*, but "it sucks to be you" if you are one of the billions who were not. It should make us all a little uncomfortable that, not unlike Hitler's era, Christianity is rather a "white man's religion." A large majority of the world who has historically not heard about Christ are Asian, African, and Indian. We've tried to soften the blow by saying that God has been fair because He somehow revealed Himself to these people, but if that's truly the case, why have we been sending missionaries? And what about people living in all the centuries without missionaries?

Most Christians would probably object to comparing Christianity to a club membership, stating that anyone can join. But can anyone really join if they don't know the club exists, or would most people even want to join if they haven't been conditioned from birth to play by the rules, such as "join this club or burn forever in hell?"

If you're still not convinced that there are some big problems with our traditional salvation theology, contrast your life and upbringing to that of an orphan girl living on the streets of India, far, far away from the West. This child, one of 80 million like her on the streets, was abandoned on a city sidewalk before she had a chance to learn much of anything about survival, let alone matters of any deity. Every day is a battle to survive by stealing food, figuring out which adults want to help her and which ones want to use her body or sell her for money, and figuring out where she is going to safely sleep next.

Add to that, since she was born into the lowest caste (social strata), most of the people she sees every day think she is under a curse from the gods for the way she lived a previous life, so they feel justified and even honored for abusing her. Even if she did somehow, by a stroke of good luck, get the chance to be taken in by an unusually caring family, she would likely be taught the religion of Hinduism, and that she must spend the rest of her life trying to appease the anger of 330 million gods. The chance of meeting anyone who has ever heard about Jesus would be nearly impossible, as there are still many hundreds of thousand of communities in India today that know nothing about Jesus or even the "hell version of the gospel." Even if she did happen to encounter the message, what are the chances, with all that baggage, that she would care enough (or be able) to *hear*? What good is "Jesus saving her from her sins," when all she cares about is where she's going to get her next meal?

We could also apply this contrast to many other down and out people in life—the mentally, physically, or psychologically handicapped, severe addicts who are powerless to break out of their cycles of addiction, other poverty-stricken people scrounging to survive the day, children who are physically abused or abandoned by parents, or anyone who is spiritually abused by "Christian" parents or churches. And what do we do with all those millions of people who lived before Jesus? Are they going to be faulted for "rejecting" Him? How about the billions who have been raised devout followers of their religions and that's all they've ever known?

As soon as I suggest that most people have not had a fair chance to hear and believe the Gospel, I often get verses like Romans 1:20 quoted by people who have not read or understood this passage in context: "For since the creation of the world His invisible attributes, His eternal power and divine nature, have been clearly seen, being understood through what has been made, so that men are without excuse." Sure sounds like a straightforward declaration that everyone for all time has had a fair chance to believe, right?

But wait a minute. If you read this passage *in context* and especially in a more literal rendering *(vs. 18–25)*, you find quite a different message:

> For God's anger is being revealed from heaven on all the irreverence and injustice of *people who are unjustly suppressing the truth,* because that which is known of God *is apparent among them,* for God makes it apparent it to them. For since the creation of the world His invisible attributes, His enduring power and divine nature, have been clearly seen, being understood through what has been made, so that [these] people are without excuse. *The ones knowing God* did not glorify or thank Him but were made vain in their reasonings and darkened is their unintelligent heart. Alleging themselves to be wise, they are made stupid, and *they change the glory of the incorruptible God into the likeness of an image of a corruptible human...* (Rom. 1:18–25, MLT)!

The people being talked about in this passage were those who already knew God, stopped acknowledging the truth about His character, suppressed the truth that had been revealed to them, and then taught lies. This is not saying that all people everywhere have had the truth of God revealed to them, but rather that those who did were not faithful with it, becoming darkened in their understanding. It is *these people* who are without excuse.

Set Up for Failure

Too many people try to divorce God's love from His justice. Sure, He demands and requires justice. But tell me, how could torturing someone endlessly, even for the most grievous behaviors over the course of eighty years, be considered fair? Paul plainly states in Romans 11:32: "For God has shut up *all* in disobedience so that He may show mercy to *all*." Apparently, the same "all" who have been locked up in disobedience will be shown mercy. Perfect justice demands a loving, restorative remedy for all sin because, even though much of Christianity doesn't teach it this way, we were all created inherently flawed and "shut up in disobedience." Mankind was basically "set up" for utter failure, perhaps in order to learn what can be learned no other way.

Many churches today teach that the fall of Adam and Eve was basically "Plan B." Adam and Eve, they say, were created perfect, were intended to stay perfect, and God was merely doing "damage control" by setting in motion a solution for their unexpected sin. But if Plan B is even possible, and God did not fully plan out and expect what went down in the Garden ahead of time, and if God threw His hands up helplessly because of man's "free will," what's to keep His creation from necessitating a Plan C, or a Plan D? If God really must work around the "free will" of humans, what's to keep man from messing up the plan continuously?*

Nothing could be more off base than saying that Adam and Eve "messed up Plan A." The fall of Adam was Plan A all along. Adam and Eve were created to fall, and it appears they were created mortals, not immortals, because Adam was formed out of dust. Dust is not the stuff of immortality; it is the composition of temporal clay. Even the name "Adam," secondarily means "earth" (as in soil or dirt) in Hebrew.

There's a God-made law in the Torah that sums up Plan A, whereby God takes responsibility for the fallen state of His own creation: "If a man digs a pit and does not cover it over, and an ox or a donkey falls into it, the owner of the pit shall make restitution" (Ex. 21:33–34). In his book, *Free Will*, Bible teacher Stephen Jones explains this law of liability:

---

* Chapter 19 is devoted to the impossible, unscriptural fallacy of man's unlimited free will.

The liability here is based upon ownership. If a man digs a pit and does not take the necessary steps to cover it and an ox comes along and falls in by his own free will or by his own stupidity, guess who is liable according to God's law? This is the law that sets the standard of liability. It is the owner of the pit who is liable, and he must then buy the dead ox for himself.

In applying the spirit of this law to Adam's situation in the garden, God is both the owner of the pit and the owner of the ox (Adam). First, God dug a pit, because He created an opportunity for Adam to sin. God did not cover this pit in that He created Adam with the potential to sin and created a tree of knowledge, putting it within Adam's reach. He did not build a ten-foot fence around that tree of the knowledge of good and evil. God created an opportunity for Adam (the ox) to fall into the pit (sin and death). That made God legally liable by His own law and created a 'tension' that demanded a resolution.

Could God have prevented man from sinning? Of course He could have. He did not have to plant the tree in the first place, or if He did, He did not have to omit the fence. Even then, He did not have to create a tempter and allow him entrance into the garden. The fact is that God knew the end from the beginning. He was not taken by surprise. He dug that pit and left it uncovered because He had a plan, and the plan called for man to fall. And so he did. *By God's own liability laws, then, He is responsible.* So what did God do about it? He sent His only begotten Son who was lifted up on the cross in order to drag all men to Himself (John 12:32). He paid for the sin of the whole world because all of creation became subject to death through Adam's fall. He bought the dead ox. The ox is now His.[42]

I love looking for common themes or threads because, at closer inspection, the Bible is really one big interwoven Masterpiece. I looked up the Hebrew word for the "pit" that the ox fell into (Ex. 21:33–34) and, true to Mr. Jones' interpretation about the pit representing death, I found that the word is "bowr," the same word used by the Psalmist in the following:

Psalm: 30:3: "O LORD, You have brought up my soul from Sheol (grave); You have kept me alive, that I would not go down to the *pit.*"

Psalm 88:3–5: "And my life has drawn near to Sheol. I am reckoned among those who go down to the *pit*; I have become like a man without strength, forsaken among the dead, like the slain who lie in the grave..."

Does All Really Mean ALL?

I know from experience that as soon as a person suggests that all people are going to be saved, the accomplished theologian types swoop in and say, "Well, you know, 'all' doesn't really mean *ALL*." Then they will mention verses in the Bible where all didn't mean everybody on earth, but perhaps all people of a certain group or kind. That is great, and I agree that there are times that all can mean a limited amount of people in context. There are, however, several verses that are, by design, constructed in such a way that even the skeptics cannot credibly deny that *all means ALL*. As soon as you mention these verses, they either ignore the question or try to bridge to another subject because they don't have a way to combat the simple truth of the deliberately paralleled "alls" in front of them. Here are a few of the verses proving that all really does mean ALL when it comes to God providing for the ultimate salvation and reconciliation of everybody:

Romans 5:18: "So then as through one transgression there resulted *condemnation to all men*, even so through one act of righteousness there resulted *justification of life to all men.*" If we are going to say that the "all" who will be justified into life through Jesus are not really *all*, then we are going to have to admit that the condemnation brought about by Adam's sin does not affect everybody either. It's the same number and group of people being referred to on both sides of the equation.

Rom. 11:32: "For God has *shut up all in disobedience* so that He may *show mercy to all.*"

1 Corinthians 15:22: "For as in Adam *all die*, so also in Christ *all will be made alive.*" Same deal. Do all die in Adam? Yes. So it is the same all who will be made alive in Christ.

What about Jesus, did He ever declare that He would save ALL?

John 12:32: "And I, if I [Jesus] am lifted up from the earth, [I] will draw [literally "drag"] all men to Myself." Was Jesus lifted up from the earth? Did He really mean all, and if not, why did He say it?

Phil. 2:10–11: "at the name of Jesus every knee will bow, of those who are in heaven and on earth and under the earth, and that every tongue will confess that Jesus Christ is Lord, to the glory of God the Father."

Romans 14:11: "For it is written, 'As I live' says the Lord, 'every knee shall bow to me, and every tongue shall give praise to God.'"

It's crazy to think that anyone would bow in submission to God and give Him acceptable, legitimate praise under coercion on his or her way to everlasting torment. The Scriptures are clear that...

- God hates false confessions, pretenses, and praise (Matt. 15:8).

- No one can say, "Jesus is Lord," unless they are under the influence and inhabitation of the Holy Spirit (1 Cor. 12:3).

- Everyone who confesses "Jesus as Lord," will be saved (Rom. 10:9).

In his heartwarming book, *The Secret Life of God*, Jewish rabbi David Aaron states that the redemption of Israel in God's plan for mankind is not the end of the story:

> Ultimate redemption must be universal—reaching the entire world. Therefore, the finale of this great "love story" is the coming of the Messiah, who will negotiate world peace and inspire universal love. Then the awareness of the mysterious divine oneness and the ecstasy of love will embrace and fill all. "Then the knowledge of God will fill the earth as the waters fill the seas" (Isaiah 11:9). Love and peace will reign supreme.[43]

Even the Jews have embraced inclusivity all along. But without these and other invaluable historic perspectives on Scripture, the true meaning of Christ's Gospel became changed, ignored, squelched, distorted, persecuted, and eventually all but lost. Those who stood in agreement with the truth and scope of God's unlimited mercy were silenced.

But today, mainly via the Internet, the true implication of the Gospel is being revived and liberated to bring the magic and beauty of God's plan back into circulation worldwide. In his book, *Velvet Elvis*, Rob Bell says:

> For Jesus, salvation is now. ...The Bible paints a much larger picture of salvation. It describes all of creation being restored. The author of Ephesians writes that all things will be brought together under Jesus. Salvation is the entire universe being brought back into

harmony with its maker. We can join a movement that is as wide and deep and big as the universe itself. Rocks and trees and birds and swamps and ecosystems. God's desire is to restore all of it.[44]

Why Evangelize?

Some people have suggested that if my understanding of the Gospel is true, and everyone is going to be saved anyhow, then what's the point of sharing it?* On his blog, *Blogismos*, Jacob Beaver offers his perspective:

> There have been claims that if there is a possibility that God is indeed the Savior of everyone (1 Tim. 4:10), then there is no need for missionaries or sharing the Gospel with others.

> Tell that to people who are starving to death and do not have clean drinking water and are sleeping on the streets. Tell that to the people of Japan, New Orleans, or Haiti. Tell that to those living in poverty and whose countries are infested with the AIDS virus. Tell that to the abused, the oppressed, the weak, and the least of these who are all experiencing hell as we speak.

> There is always a need to give food and drink, to clothe the naked, to visit those in prison, and to take care of the sick. There is a need for missionaries, and a need for people who have experienced the unconditional love, grace, and mercy of God and who want to offer it to others.

> There is always a need for good news.

> Also, I will gladly share with anyone the Good News of Jesus Christ—that God loves them just as they are, and that there is nothing they can do to change that. I will gladly tell someone living in hell that they don't have to live that way anymore and that there is hope.

> I share my faith now more than I ever have in my life. The Gospel honestly excites me and I want others to know the Good News of Jesus. It's liberating and the best thing I have ever heard.[45]

---

* There is a section toward the end of the book that deals with questions like these.

Can We Really Love Without Love Supreme?

Awhile back, a friend expressed frustrations about her local church. She admitted that, in the many years she's been attending, she has not seen the membership grow in unity one bit. She feels as if there is a huge barrier keeping people from moving forward in their relationship with God and with each other. Her next words said it all:

"For some reason, it seems we don't know how to love."

All I could think about was the monster god image we have built a whole religion and mega-church industry around. For centuries we've been sending out missionaries and indoctrinating the entire world with our distortions and misrepresentations—however ignorant we have been of them—about the character of our heavenly Father. Thankfully God wasn't sleeping when this happened—the deception was part of Plan A— and eventually He will set the record straight. "And the great dragon was thrown down, the serpent of old who is called the devil and Satan, who deceives the whole world; he was thrown down to the earth, and his angels were thrown down with him" (Rev. 12:9).

Until we understand that love really will conquer all, that love could not possibly fail (1 Cor. 13:8), that mercy will triumph over judgment (James 2:13), and that every single person who has ever lived is a unique, infinitely valued expression of the true Father (and will someday act like it), we will never truly know what it is to love as our Father loves. But when we do finally get it, we will realize that all of His children are worth keeping. Every single person we meet will become deeply valued to us, and we will realize the great accountability we have in the way we treat them, knowing that they will be a part of our future.

One of my favorite passages in Scripture (now that I understand it) captures the essence of the plot of *The Story*. In Revelation 22 we read:

Blessed are those who are washing their robes, so that they may have the right to the tree of life, and may be entering by the gates into the city. Outside are the spiritual predators who feed off of others for corrupt gain, religious magicians who weave powerful illusions to manipulate the vulnerable or naïve, idolaters who prostitute themselves with other gods (and teach others to do the same), murderers who harbor hate towards their brothers and sisters, and everyone who loves and practices lying (vs. 14–15, MLT).

Pictured in this metaphorical story are those who wash their robes so they may enter into the spiritual city of God—the New Jerusalem. But just outside the city gates, what do we have? We have sinners! This is not hell; this is just outside the "gates" of our dwelling place with God! So what is the point of this information? The point is what Jesus says next:

> The Spirit and the bride say, "Come!" And let the one who hears say, "Come!" And let the one who is thirsty come; let the one who wishes take the water of life without cost (vs. 17).

Do you see? The Spirit and the bride of Christ (those who are eligible to reign with Him), are inviting the rebellious and unloving people outside the city gates to come in to partake of citizenship in the Kingdom, and to wash their robes in the blood—to put on the right treatment of others through Christ—and come in to drink of the water of life.

Can anyone ever be left out of the free gift awaiting them inside the city gates? Rob Bell offers his clear opinion in *Velvet Elvis*:

> While we were still sinners, Christ died for us. While we were unable to do anything about our condition, while we were helpless, while we were unaware of just how bad the situation was, Jesus died. And when Jesus died on the cross, He died for everybody. Everybody. Everywhere. Every tribe, every nation, every tongue, every people group. Jesus said that when he was lifted up, he would draw all people to himself. All people. Everywhere. Everybody's sins on the cross with Jesus. So this reality, this forgiveness, this reconciliation, is true for everybody. Paul insisted that when Jesus died on the cross, he was reconciling "all things in heaven and on earth, to God." All things, everywhere.[46]

Perhaps the thought has crossed your mind, as it did mine when I began to discover these things, "Is this a new teaching? And if not, why have I never heard any of this before now?" You would expect any credible, true teaching of the Scriptures to have a long and deep history, right? Now it's time to take a look and see what we can dig up in the musty old archives of our Christian heritage.

CHAPTER TWELVE

TRACING GOSPEL HISTORY

The Internet, with its unlimited access to information old and new, is quite possibly the most stunning, magnificent, brilliant plan of God for our world today. It used to be suggested that human knowledge doubled every century; today it is suggested that it doubles every few months and is still picking up steam. In short, knowledge is increasing exponentially.

Fortunately, the availability of information is no longer restricted to a powerful few, while the rest of us sit in idle dependence. Nearly anyone can access enough information to learn as much as the next guy about anything, if the desire is present. In this case, you and I now have the ability to research ancient writings, books, and language aids that not very long ago were only available in a few obscure libraries and even rare collections. As this information has become available to the masses of inquisitive, open-minded people, many are discovering the wonderful truth that the Gospel actually meant "good news" in every sense of the word to the majority of earliest Christians. Quoting from an 1899 book you've probably never heard your pastor read from in church, *Universalism: The Prevailing Doctrine of the Christian Church During its First Five Hundred Years*:

> An examination of the earliest Christian creeds and declarations of Christian opinion discloses the fact that no formulary of Christian belief for several centuries after Christ contained anything incompatible with the broad faith of the Gospel—the universal redemption of mankind from sin. The earliest of all the documents pertaining to this subject is the "Teaching of the Twelve Apostles,"* ...recognized as early as A.D. 200.[47]

Author J.W. Hanson continues:

> The four great General Church Councils held in the first four centuries—those at Nicaea, Constantinople, Ephesus, and

---

* In Greek, this document is known as "Didache" (variant of "didasko"), meaning to give instruction with the goal of the highest possible development of the pupil.

Chalcedon—gave no expression of condemnation of Universal Restoration even though that doctrine had been prevalent all along. The Niceo-Constantinopolitan Creed, adopted in A.D. 325 by 320 bishops, says only one thing about the future world: "Christ will come again to judge the living and the dead," and has no mention of hell or eternal torment. [48]

Are there any actual quotes by the early Church leaders (sometimes called *apostolic fathers*) that have been preserved that we might see some proof that they believed in the restoration of all? Following is a lengthy but enlightening excerpt from *Creation's Jubilee*, by Dr. Stephen Jones:[*]

1. Clement of Alexandria (150–213 A.D.)

Clement, related in some way to the Roman Emperors, was born in Athens and later moved to Alexandria, the hub of Greek culture and religion. Being very well educated, he started a Christian school of thought there from 190–203 A.D., with the aim of explaining Christ to the Greek world. He also wrote a book called *Miscellanies*, in which "the task Clement had set for himself was to make a summary of Christian knowledge up to his time" (Donald Attwater, *Saints of the East*, p. 37).

In his own words, he said plainly: "For all things are ordered both universally and in particular by the Lord of the universe, with a view to the salvation of the universe. But needful corrections, by the goodness of the great, overseeing judge, through the attendant angels, through various prior judgments, through the final judgment, compel even those who have become more callous to repent.

"So he saves all; but some he converts by penalties, others who follow him of their own will, and in accordance with the worthiness of his honor, that every knee may be bent to him of celestial, terrestrial and infernal things (Phil. 2:10), that is angels, men, and souls who before his advent migrated from this mortal life.

"For there are partial corrections (padeiai) which are called chastisements (kolasis), which many of us who have been in transgression incur by falling away from the Lord's people. But as

---

[*] Used by permission.

children are chastised by their teacher, or their father, so are we by Providence. But God does not punish (timoria), for punishment is retaliation for evil. He chastises, however, for good to those who are chastised collectively and individually" (*Stromata*, VI, ii, Pedag. 1, 8; on 1 John ii, 2).

2. Origen of Alexandria (180–253 A.D.)

Origen was by far the most influential Christian for the next century [after Clement]. He was the first to write a systematic theological commentary on the whole Bible. He took great pains to learn Hebrew, not only that he might better argue the case for Christianity among the Judeans, but also that he might correct some of the mistranslations of the Septuagint Greek version.

His writings were the most influential in the whole Greek world, though he was relatively unknown in the Latin West (Rome). In his book, *Against Celsus IV, 13*, Origen continues the teaching of Clement by writing:

"The Sacred Scripture does, indeed, call our God 'a consuming fire' (Heb. 12:29), and says that 'rivers of fire go before His face' (Dan. 7:10), and that 'He shall come as a refiner's fire and purify the people' (Mal. 3:2–3). As therefore, God is a consuming fire, what is it that is to be consumed by Him? We say it is wickedness, and whatever proceeds from it, such as is figuratively called 'wood, hay, and stubble' (1 Cor. 3:12–15) which denote the evil works of man. Our God is a consuming fire in this sense; and He shall come as a refiner's fire to purify rational nature from the alloy of wickedness and other impure matter which has adulterated the intellectual gold and silver; consuming whatever evil is admixed in all the soul."

The teachings of Clement and Origen were *not* unusual. The basic view of the Divine Fire restoring sinners was the majority opinion for many centuries in the Greek-speaking Christian Church. Unfortunately, many in the Latin Church of the West did not read the Scriptures in their Greek original, but only had a very inferior Old Latin version, which Jerome eventually re-translated as the Latin Vulgate. And so the Latin West did not set the theological tone for the Church until Augustine in 400 A.D.

3. Gregory of Nazianzus (329–389 A.D.)

One of the four Eastern Doctors of the Church, St. Gregory, was well educated in Alexandria and Athens. In addition to that, according to Robert Payne:* "Of all the Fathers of the Church, he was the only one to be granted after his death the title, 'Theologian,' which until this time was reserved for an apostle—John of Patmos" (*The Fathers of the Eastern Church*, p. 179).

Gregory was one of the most prominent Christian leaders of his day and well loved for the fruit of the Spirit, which he manifested daily and consistently.† Gregory wrote this about the lake of fire:

"These (apostates), if they will, may go our way, which indeed is Christ's; but if not, let them go their own way. In another place perhaps they shall be baptized with fire, that last baptism, which is not only very painful, but enduring also; which eats up, as if it were hay, all defiled matter, and consumes all vanity and vice" (*Orat. XXXIX*, 19). [Gregory's point, as made by many of the early Church Fathers, was that the fire was a purifying process—not for utter destruction—and would rid people of the dead works in their lives, which ultimately is anything not done in love].

4. Gregory of Nyssa (335–394 A.D.)

St. Basil, the dear friend of Gregory of Nazianzus, had a younger brother also named Gregory. He was a bishop of Nyssa in Cappadocia. Robert Payne writes of him:

"The Emperor Theodosius had recognized him as the supreme authority in all matters of theological orthodoxy, and…he was treated with extraordinary respect. Of the three Cappadocian Fathers, Gregory of Nyssa is the one closest to us, the least proud, the most subtle, the one most committed to the magnificence of man" (Robert Payne, *The Fathers of the Eastern Church*, p. 164).

---

* Robert Payne was a famous 20th Century novelist, historian, and biographer who published more than 110 books. His historical works include: *The Holy Fire: The Story of the Fathers of the Eastern Church*, St. Vladimir's Seminary, 1957.

† Gregory Nazianzus, an avowed believer in Universal Reconciliation, was appointed as the president of the second council of the Church in Constantinople in the fourth century, 325–381 A.D.

In the book, *Orat. Catech.*, based on 1 Cor. 15:28, Gregory wrote: "When all the alloy of evil that has been mixed up in the things that are, having been separated by the refining action of the cleansing fire, everything that was created by God shall have become such as it was at the beginning, when as yet it had not admitted evil...this is the end of our hope, that nothing shall be left contrary to the good, but that the Divine Life, penetrating all things shall absolutely destroy Death from among the things that are; sin having been destroyed before him, by means of which, as has been said death held his dominion over men."

Four hundred years after his death, at the Seventh General Council held in A.D. 787, the assembled princes of the Church granted him a title which exceeded in their eyes all the other titles granted to men: he was called "Father of Fathers" (Robert Payne, *The Fathers of the Eastern Church*, p. 168 – 169). This was an ironic twist of history, for that same council also pronounced a curse upon all who taught that the fire of God would cleanse, rather than torture men for eternity! One might think that perhaps Gregory was out of step with mainstream Christian thought for believing and teaching the restoration of all mankind, but *Funk & Wagnall's New Encyclopedia* says of him: "Gregory's religious position was strictly orthodox" (his views were considered mainstream Christianity in his day). In fact, he was called "the bulwark of the church against heresy," taking part in the Council of Nicea and other later Church Councils.

It is well known by those who have studied early Church writings, that [Universal Reconciliation] was the majority view. In fact, it was practically the *only view* for the first few centuries after Christ and the apostles. The early Church had quite a number of doctrinal disputes, but the universality of salvation was *not even disputed*. In fact, it was taught by all the major theologians of the day in the churches that the Apostle Paul founded.

Six Schools of Christian Learning

There were six Christian theological schools of thought known to have existed in the first few centuries. The first and earliest was in Alexandria, where Clement, and others taught that sinners are purged [purified] by the lake of fire. The theological school at Caesarea in

Palestine was next. The writings of both Origen and Clement were highly esteemed there, and Origen actually lived there during his most productive years.

The school of Antioch, which had its feet more firmly planted on the ground, disputed with Origen over his allegorical method of interpretation, but they agreed wholeheartedly with his purging and reconciliatory view on the "lake of fire."* The same with the school founded at Edessa in the fifth century.

It was only the Latin school (based in Carthage, Africa, but which included Rome) that taught the doctrine of endless punishment. Augustine, the "champion" of endless torments, wrote that there were "...indeed *very many* (who)...do not believe that such things [eternal torment] will be. *Not that they would go counter to divine Scripture*" (*Enchiridion*, 112).

Titus, bishop of Bostra, also wrote a book around 364 A.D. entitled, *Against Manicheans*, where he said, "The punishments of God are Holy, as they are remedial and salutary in their effect upon transgressors; for they are inflicted, not to preserve them in their wickedness, but to make them cease from their sins. The abyss...is indeed the place of punishment, but it is not endless. The anguish of their sufferings compels them to break off from their sins."

One other very influential theologian was Theodore of Mopsuestia (d. 428). He asked, "Who is so great a fool as to believe that God would resurrect men merely to destroy them forever with torments?" (*Fragment IV*).

During the Dark Ages, when the doctrine of eternal torment had become "orthodox" in Europe, its judicial shadow came with it— burning people at the stake. It was argued that God was going to throw them into an endless torment of fire anyway, so the Church was only initiating it a few insignificant years early. Besides, such "justice"

---

* Origen was labeled a heretic in 553 A.D., 300 years after his death, by the Fifth General Council, attended by 148 church bishops. They spelled out fifteen "anathemas" (false teachings) against Origen, including his allegorical interpretation of Scripture, but not one of them condemned his teaching that all men would be saved.

served to instill fear into the hearts of people going against the Church in any way—not only to avoid the stake, but to avoid the burning hell.

This tactic was certainly effective; no one can argue that point. But if one has opportunity to study the divine justice of Bible Law, it soon becomes apparent that such punishment is of heathen origin, rather that of the Bible. In every nation, the popular belief about divine justice has always served as a model for the justice of man. In the Dark Ages, they thought they were imitating God; in reality, however, they were imitating the heathen who burned their children to Molech in the valley of Ben-hinnom.[49]

Other Well Known Advocates in History

One thing I found quite surprising is the substantial list of well-known people in history who believed and proclaimed Universal Reconciliation through their writings and recorded public speeches. Recently I have located and read some of their quotes or books, but before the recent days of the Internet, most publishers, pastors, and theologians had largely suppressed their beliefs from public view.

Here are a few that you might recognize: Pantaenus, Didymus, Basil the Great, Eusibius, the Anabaptists, William Law, Sir Isaac Newton, Victor Hugo, Anne Bronte, Lord and Lady Byron, Robert and Elizabeth Browning, George Washington, Florence Nightingale, Abraham Lincoln, Hans Christian Anderson, Harriet Beecher Stowe, George MacDonald, Hannah Hurnard (*Hinds' Feet on High Places*), William Barclay, and Andrew Murray. You should be able to Google any of these people as I did, and find sites that offer some of their universal quotes, writings, or other teachings.

One of my favorite writers of the early 20th century is Hannah Whitall Smith. Though I'd read her biography and some of her works, I had no idea she believed in Universal Reconciliation until a couple years ago. In fact, she penned a book about her journey to belief in God's plan to save all called, *The Unselfishness of God*. I've sat in sermons where pastors unsuspectingly quote from this "heretical" book, because unconscionable editors who republished her works in recent decades took out three entire chapters chronicling her main point: the dawn of her inclusive beliefs.

Here are some stirring thoughts randomly selected out of the climactic, final (deleted) chapter entitled, "The Unselfishness of God" (duh!):

> I have always felt that this time my real discovery of the unselfishness of God began. Up to then, while I had rejoiced in the salvation for myself that I had discovered, I had been secretly beset from time to time with a torturing feeling that, after all, it was rather a selfish salvation, both for Him and for me. How could a good God enjoy Himself in heaven, knowing all the while that a large proportion of the beings He had Himself created were doomed to eternal misery, unless He were a selfish God?

> I had known that the Bible said that He was a God of love, and I had supposed that it must be true, but always there had been at the bottom of my mind this secret feeling that His love could not stand the test of comparison with the ideal of love in my own heart. I knew that, poor and imperfect as my love must be, I could never have enjoyed myself in heaven while one of my children, no matter how naughty, was shut out. That [God] could and did enjoy Himself, while countless thousands of His children were shut out, seemed to me a failure in the most essential element of love. So that, grateful as I had felt for the blessings of forgiveness and of a sure and certain hope of heaven for myself, I still had often felt as if, after all, the God I worshiped was a selfish God, who cared more for His own comfort and His own glory than He did for the poor suffering beings He had made.

> But now I began to see that the wideness of God's love was far beyond any wideness that I could even conceive of; and that if I took all the unselfish love of every mother's heart the whole world over, and piled it all together, and multiplied it by millions, I would still only get a faint idea of the unselfishness of God.

> Every doubting question was answered, and I was filled with an illimitable delight in the thought of having been created by such an unselfish God. Our Creator, by the laws of common morality, is compelled to take proper care of the creatures He has created, and must be held responsible for their well being. I saw that God was good — not religiously good only — but really and actually good in the

truest sense of the word, and that a good Creator was of course bound to make everything go right with the creatures He had created.

My own feelings as a mother, which had heretofore seemed to war with what I had believed of God, now came into perfect harmony. ...Most of my ideas of the love and goodness of God have come from my own experience as a mother, because I could not conceive that God would create me with a greater capacity for unselfishness and self-sacrifice than He possessed Himself...

Since I had this insight of the mother-heart of God, I have never been able to feel the slightest anxiety for any of His children; and by His children I do not mean only the good ones, but I mean the bad ones just as much. I had, in short, such an overwhelming revelation of the intrinsic and inherent goodness and unselfishness of God that nothing since has been able to shake it.

Still to this day, the one thing which I find it very hard to tolerate, is any thing which libels the character of God. Nothing else matters like this, for all our salvation depends wholly and entirely upon what God is; and unless He can be proved to be absolutely good, and absolutely unselfish, and absolutely just, our case is absolutely hopeless. God is our salvation, and, if He fails us, in even the slightest degree, we have nowhere else to turn.[*]

My Own Story

When I read those words, everything in my mother's heart, mind, and spirit resonated with Hannah's. Believing in the vile superstition of hell has jaded my life and my perception of God for too many years. How many millions in this world have also been injured beyond repair in this lifetime because of the false view of God thrust upon them?

In my trips to developing countries like Haiti and India, I was once critical about the seeming ridiculousness of many of their religious superstitions, thinking I was above that kind of deception and ignorance. These days, I realize that I was perhaps worse off (and in some ways even

---

[*] To read the three awesomely inspiring chapters edited out of Hannah's original book, go to: tentmaker.org/books/unselfishness-of-god.htm.

more deceived) than they, for I believed and declared lies about the character of God while believing and professing that I was somehow above error. I have lived in the same bondage to fear as any other world religion, the same superstitions, the same blind traditions of men, and I called it *truth*.

So how did we get so far off, ending up on such a major "calf path"? Perhaps as the result of Roman persecution against anything "Jewish," Christianity veered off course from the teachings of those who were first entrusted with meaningful, yet obscure symbolism interwoven throughout their own history and Scriptures. But it's not too late to get back on track. It's time to put on some new glasses and take a look at the Scriptures like you've never seen them before.

Part 3
Hebrew Perspectives on Scripture

CHAPTER THIRTEEN

HEBREW ABCS

There's a well-known East Indian fable about seven blind mice who come to a large object in their path. It's so immense that they decide to split up, explore it, and come back to report their observations in hopes that they can determine together what it is. Each mouse sets off with high hopes of solving the mystery.

When they all return, there's a cacophony of excitement, each believing he has been able to determine the nature of the object. One mouse declares that it's a great cliff. The next is sure it's a sharp spear. The third believes it's a dangling rope. The fourth makes a case for a magnificent pillar. The fifth announces it's a powerful fan. And the sixth is positive he has encountered a giant snake. The seventh mouse, lagging behind and somewhat baffled since none of those things are remotely close to the same thing, ventures out with plans to explore more methodically. After a thorough examination, he comes back to report that all the others are mistaken; the object is actually *an elephant*. Each of the other mice only explored a small portion and, being blind, they incorrectly interpreted only a swath of evidence.

The moral of this story for us is that, over time, Christian theologians and their prodigy—pastors and churchgoers—have become like those six blind mice in approaching Scripture. This explains the often times vast chasm between Bible versions and the teachings of theologians, denominations, and churches. They have resembled the mice, exploring only part of the evidence as the result of centuries of inherited debilitating blindness. What is the nature of the blindness in modern orthodoxy?

When approaching the Scriptures, the only way we will begin to see more clearly is by pursuing a view of Scripture through the lenses of early Hebrew culture, thought, and intent. Without it, we cannot possibly make sense of the scriptural foundation, concepts, themes, and prophetic significance. The suppression and rejection of this crucial information in the early centuries after Christ began failing the Church in trying to interpret and understand the Bible. Certainly there is a modern effort being made by many at understanding and unlocking the mysteries of the OT, but for most of Church history, several key concepts have been seriously neglected, three of which are central in understanding God's plan to redeem and restore all of His creation—namely *the Jewish Covenants, Feasts, and Harvests*. We'll take a look at all three in this section but first, let's look at a few "rules" of Hebrew Scripture interpretation.

History Unfolds in Repetitive Cycles

Contemporary western thinking, borrowed from the Greeks, sees history and prophecy unfolding chronologically, on a linear timeline. This view basically limits scriptural prophecy to one occurrence of fulfillment (in time) and breeds a lot of confusion, limitation, and misunderstanding of Scripture. One particular linear-based theology that originated in the 1800s is called *dispensationalism*. Dispensationalism essentially chops up the Scriptures with claims that God works differently with His creation at different times in history (a partial truth), teaches that the Law and most of the OT no longer apply to us today, and suggests that God deals differently (even today) with Jewish and non-Jewish believers.

When you understand God's intent for mankind—an intent that is veiled within the symbolism of the Law and the OT—you find that these beliefs veer substantially off course. God's plan has always been all about restoring *unity* among His creation and his observable method about fulfilling His word in many repeated cycles or layers throughout history (like fractals, for you science geeks).

According to Hebrew thought, the Scriptures are multi-layered in that, one symbolic picture or passage is typically fulfilled or made evident repeatedly, perhaps throughout all ages and on different levels of understanding. Earlier I mentioned that even one verse of the Torah could have as many as seventy layers of meaning and fulfillment.

Let me give you one simple example. The tabernacle,* or dwelling place of God, was first established in the mystical Garden of Eden—a place also

---

* The word "temple" as a special dwelling place of God is a bit of a misnomer—finite locations cannot confine the Infinite (Acts 7:48; 17:24). God dwells in and through all creation at all times (Rom. 11:36, 1 Cor. 8:6, Eph. 4:10, Col. 1:16). Perhaps the shifting, expanding "temple" locations are more of a reflection of the developing human understanding. Each subsequent layer is "true," but the full truth or deepest layer is finally found in, "God's dwelling place is in us all."

containing many layers of meaning. Next, it moved into the wilderness as a temporary shelter in the days of Moses, following the people around before they settled in the Promised Land. After their entrance into the Promised Land, it became a somewhat permanent structure with the construction of the first and second temples (Solomon's Temple, and Ezra's Temple, respectively). Jesus became the fifth fulfillment of the anointed tabernacle or temple of God. The sixth anointed dwelling place of God, incidentally the "number of man" in Jewish teachings, is within all of those who have put their faith in Jesus in this lifetime. And finally, the seventh (number for Divine *completion**) dwelling place of God will be permanently established *and completed* in all people, after the plan of the ages has been consummated with restoration of all.

> Behold, the tabernacle of God is among men, and He will dwell among them, and they shall be His people, and God Himself will be among them... (Rev. 21:3).

The layers God's dwelling places started many millennia ago, is but one example of the many symbols and teachings in Scriptures that continue to be expanded and repeated throughout the plan of ages.

Transitioning Patterns of Fulfillment

The way I understand it, biblical prophecy follows a progressive pattern of shifting from the natural world (flesh and blood—OT) to the spiritual relationship (metaphorical—NT), and perhaps moves to encompass both levels together in the coming ages. Here's what I mean. The entire OT tells a prophetic story through natural world elements (Garden of Eden, Egypt, Promised Land, Jordan River, manna, sacrifices, feasts, etc.), and types (Joseph, Moses, Elijah, etc.).

Hundreds of years later, many of these prophetic pictures were fulfilled spiritually in the life, death, and resurrection of Jesus, who conquered the ultimate enemy—the grave. To many Jews, this is why Jesus was insignificant. They had waited for a king to come and physically conquer their external enemies, not understanding or accepting the far superior, lasting victory over a much greater enemy in the inner, spiritual sense. Paul elaborates on the spiritual fulfillment through Jesus:

---

* See "Ask Rabbi Simmons," Judaism.about.com.

For He rescued us from the dominion of darkness, and transferred us to the kingdom of His beloved Son, in whom we have redemption, the forgiveness of sins. He is the image of the invisible God, the firstborn of all creation. For He created all things, both in the heavens and on earth, visible and invisible, whether thrones or dominions or rulers or authorities — all things have been created through Him and for Him. He is before all things, and in Him all things hold together. He is also head of the body, those called out (for faith now); and He is the beginning, the firstborn from the dead, so that He Himself will come to have first place in all things. For it was the Father's good pleasure for all the fullness to dwell in Him, and through Him to reconcile all things to Himself, having made peace through the blood of His cross; through Him, I say, whether on earth or in heaven (Col. 1:13-20, MLT).

Paul also points out the gravitation of natural to spiritual fulfillment in 1 Cor. 15:45–46:

The first man, Adam, became a living soul. The last Adam became a life-giving spirit. However, *the spiritual is not first, but the natural; then the spiritual.*

As you consider the perspectives in next few chapters, keep this and the last point in mind (repeated cycles). Whether these Jewish symbols are fulfilled in the natural world at a later time or not, they have been repeatedly fulfilled in different ways and times in history.

Again, the next phase of the Kingdom could possibly unite these two levels together as a spiritual-natural Kingdom on earth. If this happens, those who are alive will see, feel, touch, and experience the two realms meeting in an exciting, powerful way that has not happened since the beginning of *The Story*. Jesus's dominion would be administered in both the natural realm on earth and in the heavens, and there would be ever-expanding peace and harmony, in both the seen and the unseen.

Earlier we used the example of the tabernacle as a repeated prophetic cycle, but notice how it also follows a pattern of fulfillment from tangible (in a external building) to spiritual (within people). Another tangible example can be seen using the "Kingdom" theme. In the OT, there was the imperfect, fallible kingdom of Israel with a physical king, land, and subjects. This natural world kingdom was merely a type of an *infallible* spiritual Kingdom to come. There are many verses about this future Kingdom rising above all other kingdoms and filling the earth, but one of my favorites is Daniel 2:35. Feel free to read this in context so you can see how the different composite parts of the statue represent kingdoms:

> Then the iron, the clay, the bronze, the silver and the gold (earthly kingdoms) were crushed all at the same time and became like chaff from the summer threshing floors; and the wind carried them away so that not a trace of them was found. But the stone (Jesus) that struck the statue became a great mountain* filling the whole earth.†

When He conquered the grave, Jesus established the beginning of an infallible, all-powerful Kingdom that will not be stopped until it fills the earth. However, we will not see the fulfillment of this prophecy until the next age. John recorded the onset of this event in Revelation 11:15: "The kingdom of the world has become the Kingdom of our Lord and of His Christ (Anointed); and He will reign into the ages of the ages" (MLT).

No Reference to Eternity in Scripture

Eternity‡ had no place in the mind of the early Hebrews, probably because neither their Scriptures nor their dealings with God included any such concept. In fact, the Scriptures in Hebrew and Greek were solely written with the perspective of generations or long periods of time (eons or ages), unfolding like a chapter book. About the closest you get in the Scriptures to the concept of never-ending is the word for "immortality," (athanasia) which literally means "un-death." The word athanasia is only used three times in the entire Greek Scriptures, once to describe the state of God (1 Tim. 6:16), and twice to describe the future state of man (1 Cor.

---

* A "mountain" in Bible prophecy symbolizes a kingdom.
† See also Isaiah 11:9 and Habakkuk 2:14.
‡ The concept (not the word) of eternity originated with the Greeks and was introduced into the Church teachings by Tertullian (160–220 AD). It was made popular in Church and Scripture in the 5th Century by Jerome and St. Augustine. Because of his enormous (and mostly erroneous) contributions to the doctrines of the Church, Augustine is considered to be one of the most important figures in the development of Western Christianity. Read a thorough history of the introduction of this concept into Church Theology, "Whence Eternity? How Eternity Slipped In" (http://thetencommandmentsministry.us/ministry/free_bible/whence_eternity).

15:53-54). There is also a Greek word that is often mistranslated as immortal/immortality but it actually means incorruptible (aphthartos).

According to the Ancient Hebrew Research Center:

> First rule in Hebrew study—Hebrews think in concrete and Greeks think in abstracts. Concrete thinkers think in relation to things that can be seen, touched, smelled, heard, or tasted. Some examples of this are trees, singing, smell of baking, etc. Abstract thoughts are such things as belief, faith, grace, etc. These cannot be sensed by the five senses. The word *everlasting* (the modern translation of the Hebrew word "olam") is an abstract word. The Hebrew meaning of olam is something like 'behind the horizon.' It is something that is beyond what you can see (or understand) at the moment but may be revealed as you travel closer. The abstract idea of "everlasting" would have been a foreign concept to the ancient Hebrews.[50]

It's Different Than We Thought

The following chapters piece together my thoughts and understanding so far on the Hebrew view of *God's Plan of the Ages*. The biblical account of the ages—not eternity—reveals this plan for a set period of time, perhaps unfolding in 1,000-year increments called "millennia." Modern Hebrew perspectives teach these millennia correspond to the seven days of creation, with each "day" representing certain features of the millennium it represents. Perhaps this is why in Hebrew understanding, "a day" can also signify a thousand years and can be used interchangeably.

From Jewish view, there have been approximately six millennia (or six "days") since the account of Adam, but we have yet to experience the seventh millennium or "seventh day," of which many people believe we are on the cusp. Paul actually refers to this age metaphorically in Hebrews chapter 4, when he refers to it as "the Sabbath Rest" (seventh day). Jewish people understand this as the *Millennial Kingdom*, but what is it and who is it for? Perhaps we can learn more about God's plan for mankind revealed in the ancient Hebrew teachings and culture!

CHAPTER FOURTEEN

ETERNITY VS. AGES

Throughout previous chapters I have mentioned the non-existence of eternity in Scripture. This chapter is crucial to our understanding of the false teaching of a place of eternal torment or even everlasting separation from God, without reducing the implications of our future life with God.

Why then did translators go awry and begin inserting the concept of eternity into the Scriptures? Earlier we learned that the Hebrew word, *olam* (Strong's #5956), actually means something like, "behind the horizon" or "concealed from view," pertaining to times ahead, and simply does not mean or imply eternal. It has been frequently mistranslated as *everlasting* and *eternal* throughout the OT, though most literal translations and the Interlinear render *olam* as "age."*

So now let's turn to the Greek word frequently translated *eternal, forever,* or *everlasting* in the NT. *Aion* is a noun that actually translates as "eon," or the more common modern English equivalent, "age" (Strong's #165), and is one of the most mistranslated and also inconsistently translated words in the Bible.

Like its English counterpart, "age," the word *aion* is defined as "a period of time with a beginning and an end." Yet, consider the myriad of ways this simple word has been translated in two of our more popular NT versions today:

- *Age* or ages: NAS–26, KJV–2
- Ancient time: NAS–1
- Beginning of time: NAS–1
- *World* or worlds: NAS–7, KJV–78
- World without end: KJV–1
- *Course*: NAS–1
- *Eternal*: NAS–2, KJV–2

---

* The scribes of the OT Greek Septuagint translated the Hebrew word olam as the noun, *aion* (age) or the adjective, *aionios* (pertaining to an age), depending on usage.

- Eternity: NAS–1
- *Ever*: NAS–2, KJV–71
- *Forever*: NAS–27, KJV–30
- *Forever and ever*: NAS–20, KJV–21
- Forevermore: NAS–2
- Long ago: NAS–1
- *Never*: NAS–1, KJV–6
- *Old*: NAS–1
- *Time*: NAS–1
- "Miscellaneous": KJV–5

For your further entertainment, I have taken some screen captures of the noun, *aion*, and its adjective form, *aionios*, from an online Lexicon at http://biblestudytools.com. I have also boxed in the particular contradictory definitions to which I wish to draw your attention:

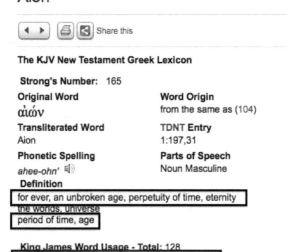

Aionios

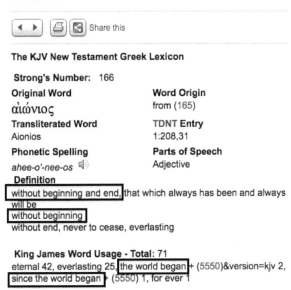

The KJV New Testament Greek Lexicon

Strong's Number: 166

Original Word	**Word Origin**
αἰώνιος	from (165)
Transliterated Word	**TDNT Entry**
Aionios	1:208,31
Phonetic Spelling	**Parts of Speech**
ahee-o'-nee-os 🔊	Adjective

Definition
without beginning and end, that which always has been and always will be
without beginning
without end, never to cease, everlasting

King James Word Usage - Total: 71
eternal 42, everlasting 25, the world began + (5550)&version=kjv 2, since the world began + (5550) 1, for ever 1

As you can see, Strong's lists the definition of *aion* as both a "period of time" and "forever." Also, for the adjective form, *aionios*, the definition says, "without *beginning* and end" (twice), yet KJV also translates it as, "since the world *began*."

Aion is decisively a noun, yet it has frequently (and erroneously) been replaced with adjectives or adverbs (such as forever and ever, everlasting, eternal). Though Strong's Concordance makes no mention of it, some of the various words it's translated into already have their own Greek word, such as *world* (kosmos), *time* (chronos), *beginning* (arche), and *end* (telos*). The adjective form, *aionios*, most literally means, "pertaining to an age."

The use of the word *aion* for such a variety of words, phrases, and concepts in and of itself should raise a major red flag. The ancient Koine Greek language of the NT was much more methodical and consistent than later languages. Greek words also typically have more precise meanings. For instance, Greek has at least three words for *love*: brotherly love (phileo), romantic love (eros), and unconditional parental love (agape). Regardless, the words *aion* and *aionios* each have one primary meaning

---

* Though *telos* is usually translated *end*, it's the word from which we get telescope and more accurately means arriving at or completing upon a distant target.

and should always be translated *age* or *pertaining to an age*, respectively. While many Bible students or theologians will defend the gamut of translation liberties taken of these two words, there are many prominent, respected Bible scholars today who argue for a more consistent and literal translation.*

While I understand the need for translating the Bible so that it is more relevant to modern readers, the fact of the matter is that *aion* and *aionios* are not words that change with time or context. This can be verified by reading an Interlinear Bible or literal translation where both words are always translated accurately and consistently. Just compare any passage in the NT to one of these two resources where everlasting, eternal, or forever and ever are used in your common Bible versions, and you will see it for yourself.

When you view the plan of the ages through the Hebrew lenses, using the correct translations of *aion* and *aionios* make sense in every single passage, whereas the many faulty translation occurrences of these words result frequently in critical distortions. Here's one less critical but obvious example from Ephesians 3:21:

YLT (*Young's Literal*): "…to Him [is] the glory in the assembly in Christ Jesus, *to all the generations of the age of the ages.*"

KJV: "Unto him [be] glory in the church by Christ Jesus *throughout all ages, world without end.*"

NKJV: "…to Him be glory in the church by Christ Jesus *to all generations, forever and ever.*"

NLT: "May he be given glory in the church and in Christ Jesus *forever and ever through endless ages.*"

As you might have guessed, *Young's Literal* is the most accurate and true to the Greek. Notice that KJV and NKJV differ in that KJV leaves the ages idea intact, whereas NKJV completely drops the ages and renders "forever and ever." Which brings up a valid point. Why even include "and ever"? Can you have more than one forever? Also, while KJV does get "ages" correct in this instance, they also insert the phrase, "world without end," which is just another example of translators inserting something that is rather nonsense (and not there).

---

* To see a lengthy list of quotes from recognized, respected modern day scholars who have openly admitted that *aion* and *aionios* pertain only to time and ages (not eternity), check out the Resources section.

Suddenly, verses that once conveyed absolute, eternal destruction now can be viewed in a new light. Compare Mark 3:29 in *Young's Literal Translation*, a more accurate translation for both Hebrew and Greek:

NASB: "...but whoever blasphemes against the Holy Spirit *never has forgiveness*, but is guilty of an *eternal sin.*"

YLT: "...but whoever may speak evil in regard to the Holy Spirit *hath not forgiveness – to the age*, but is in danger of *age-during judgment*."

Can *Aion* Ever Mean Eternity?

We've already answered this, but let's look at it from a logical point of view. If *aion* could possibly mean eternity, what does its plural form, "aions" mean? Can eternity be plural? In some passages *aion* is used in the singular form, while in other passages it is used in the plural form:

Ephesians 1:21: "not only in this age (aion) but also in the one to come..."

Ephesians 2:7: "...the ages (aions) to come..."

Colossians 1:26 "...hidden from the past ages (aions)..."

Try substituting "eternity" for the age-related words above and it's easy to see why it shouldn't be done. Though *aion* simply means age, translators pick and choose how to translate it, depending on the theological bias they are trying to preserve in any given passage. Think about it. Can one word possibly mean both a finite period of time *and* outside of time or infinite? And even if we have words in English that have double, contradictory meanings (bad, dust, root, trim), and we use phrases like, "I've been waiting forever," Koine Greek is fairly precise and perhaps that's a primary reason why God chose it as the language of the Gospel, since it would be passed down through many generations and translated into many languages. Let's continue to look at more examples.

Before Eternity?

Referring to the Strong's screen capture a couple pages back, you can see that *aionios* is the word most often mistranslated as "forever" or "eternal." In 2 Timothy 1:9 and Titus 1:2, the Greek phrase, "pro chronon

aionion" occurs and, translated exactly, means "before times eonian."* If
aionios should be translated eternal, what is meant by "before times
eternal"? Isn't that contradictory and impossible? Every translator must
surely have recognized this dilemma and, instead of translating it
accurately, attempted to solve this conundrum by making up something
that sounded plausible. Let's compare Titus 1:2 in a few translations and
you can see how each one tries to make *aionios,* occurring *twice* within the
verse (italicized), somehow fit in with their doctrinal slant:

KJV: "In hope of *eternal* (aionios) life, which God, that cannot lie,
promised *before the world began (aionios)...*"

NASB: "in the hope of *eternal* life, which God, who cannot lie, promised
long ages ago..."

NIV: "...on the hope of *eternal* life, which God, who does not lie,
promised *before the beginning of time...*"

BBE (Bible in Basic English): "In the hope of *eternal* life, which was
made certain *before eternal time...*"

When you see all the different and inconsistent ways that this one
word is translated within and between all of our modern Bible versions, it
becomes apparent that some mighty painful contortions are happening to
try to get everything to fit with the "eternal torment" agenda. The more
literal translation of this verse reads, "...upon hope of life *age-during,*
which God, who doth not lie, did promise before times of ages" (YLT).

If *Aion* Means Forever...

NASB translates the noun *aion* as "forever" or "forever and ever" forty-
seven out of about 100 occurrences in the NT. KJV translates it that way
seventy-one times out of 100. If they had consistently translated this one
word 100/100 times (which they should have done if they were being
honest), the following verses would have read as such:

Matt. 13:39: "...the harvest is the end of the forever (aion)"

1 Cor. 2:7: "...before the forevers (aions)..."

1 Cor. 10:11: "...upon whom the ends of the forevers (aions) have
come..."

---

* See the Greek Interlinear for confirmation of exact translation. "Before times
eonian," means before the times of the ages. In context, this verse means that God
promised age-enduring life to us before the times of the ages began.

Gal. 1:4: "...so that He might rescue us from the present evil forever (aion)."

Eph. 2:7: "...so that in the forevers (aions) to come..."

Heb. 9:26: "...at the consummation of the forevers (aions)..." *

BUT...if *aion* means simply "age," and if you understand that the current Story we're living in unfolds in time and ages, then you can translate *aion* consistently 100% of the time, be true to the text, and find that the Bible makes a lot more sense the way it was actually written — without all the necessary "damage control" of translators. Just for fun, you should try looking up these aforementioned verses in a parallel Bible, which can be easily located online, comparing how each popular version translates *aion*. It's quite entertaining.

How Many Ages?

A case can be made for specific ages throughout time and based in early Jewish thought, as referenced in Scriptures, but that can be a rather complex topic and is outside the scope of this book. Rather, let's simply consider some specific references to the ages in the NT.

- Before the ages (2 Timothy 1:9–10; Titus 1:1–3; 1 Cor. 2:6–8)

- The current age — at the time of the writing (Matt. 12:32; 13:22; Mark 4:19; Luke 16:8; 20:34; Romans 12:2; 1 Cor. 1:20; 2:6–8; 3:18; 2 Cor. 4:4; Gal. 1:3–5; 1 Tim. 6:17; 2 Tim. 4:9–10; Titus 2:11–13)

- The age to come (Luke 18:30, Eph. 2:2)

- Other ages to come (Eph. 2:7)

---

* See 1 Cor. 15:20–28 for the description of what is meant by "consummation of the ages," when all enemies of Jesus are defeated (having been made "friends"), death is abolished for all time, Jesus turns over the Kingdom to His Father, and God becomes "all in all." This is what I believe to be the "happily ever after" description in the storybook of the ages, as described in Isaiah 25:6-8 and Revelation 21:1-7.

Eonian Theme in Scripture:

Eonian, the English counterpart for *aionios* or, "pertaining to an age," is used in a variety of ways in the Scriptures.

- eonian times
- eonian life
- eonian salvation
- eonian redemption
- eonian covenant
- eonian allotment

- eonian kingdom
- eonian gospel
- eonian consolation
- eonian glory
- eonian God
- eonian fire/refining

These phrases, depending on context and intent, could mean things that last for one age, multiple ages, or all of the ages in *The Story*, but none of them mean eternal or never-ending. Each passage must be studied to find out what is the duration and for what purpose.

Eonian God

One of the first questions people usually ask at this point is, "How can eonian not mean eternal since it's the adjective used to describe God?"

Does the fact that God is described as "eonian" negate His everlasting (or outside of time) quality? Absolutely not! This use of words by the original writers is merely describing one of God's many attributes as being the "God of the ages," reigning supreme over His time-bound plan.

Consider 1 Tim. 1:17, the *only* verse that uses this phrase. Most modern versions render something like this: "Now to *the King eternal*, immortal, invisible, the only God, be honor and glory *forever and ever*." But check out *Young's Literal*[*]:

> ...and to *the King of the ages*, the incorruptible, invisible, only wise God, [is] honour and glory — *to the ages of the ages*! Amen (YLT).

This verse says nothing about God's enduring quality, but it is speaking directly about His reign as the King of the ages (not unlike Jesus being referred to as the "rock of the ages"). Hence, God will receive glory

---

[*] Also check the Greek Interlinear and Concordant Literal, both available online — see resources section for more info.

throughout them and especially at their consummation! The ages definitely come to an end (see Heb. 9:26 and 1 Cor. 10:11). As to what the early Hebrews understood about the duration of God, I don't think He ever had to explain to anyone that He was enduring (even though they didn't grasp a word like "eternal" yet). That would have been like referring to "cold ice" or a "wet shower."

There is actually a Greek word used only once in the NT to reveal more of God's enduring, incomprehensible nature. "For since the creation of the world His invisible attributes, His eternal (*aidios*) power and divine nature, have been clearly seen, being understood through what has been made, so that they are without excuse" (Romans 1:20). *Aidios* offers a greater sense of His unperceived and *perpetual* nature, unlimited by space and time, but still does not mean eternal in the sense we regard it today.

What's interesting about the word *eternal* is that it wasn't even derived from Greek (the original language of the NT), but was derived from Latin. In other words, the word eternity did not have roots in the Greek (or Hebrew) Scriptures. I looked up the etymology for the word eternal in an etymological dictionary. The English word is *a late 14th century word*, derived from the Latin word *aeternus*, which is defined as,

> Of an age, lasting, enduring, permanent, endless, contraction of aeviternus "of great age," from aevum "age" (see eon).[51]

As you consider the somewhat contradictory definitions of this Latin (Roman) word, keep in mind how many centuries, church leaders, and church doctrines influenced the definition along the way.

Eonian Life

The next question people raise is Matt. 25:46: "These will go away into eternal punishment, but the righteous into eternal life." When I offer the more literal translation, "These will go away into eonian correction*, but the just into eonian life," people question how this passage could possibly mean anything less or different than what they have always been taught—

---

* Of note in this verse is that the word for "punishment" in Greek is kolasis, which actually means "correction." All the difference. See kolasis definition at: (http://www.studylight.org/isb/view.cgi?number=2851).

that Jesus is speaking of "eternal life," and therefore He must also be referring to "eternal punishment."

Here is what they are missing; *"eonian life" is not eternal life*. It means coming into life (relationship with Jesus) in the age that the Bible writer is referring to and continuing through the remaining ages. In any age you live that you are connected to Jesus – the life source or "Vine" – you are enjoying life in that age. For instance, as a believer in Christ, I am currently enjoying life pertaining to this age. When the next age arrives, perhaps the seventh age of the "Wedding Feast" or "Sabbath Rest," I will no longer be enjoying life in this age, but then it will be life pertaining to that age. Eonian life, then, is not so much about a time that begins after we die, but more about a quality and vitality of life *right now*, lived in fellowship with God through His Son. Consider the following, paying close attention to the Greek Scripture writer's specific use of the present progressive verbs:

John 3:15 – 16 "Everyone believing in Him should not be perishing but may be having eonian life" (MLT).

John 5:24: "Verily, verily I say to you that the one hearing my word and believing the One who sent me is having eonian life and is not coming into judging but has stepped out of death into life" (MLT).

John 6:47: "I am saying to you, the one believing in me is having eonian life" (MLT).

John 17:3: *"This is eonian life – that they may be knowing you, the only true God, and Jesus Christ whom you commission"* (MLT). You can't get any clearer on a definition of eonian life than that!

Rom. 6:22-23: "But *now* having been freed from sin and enslaved to God, you are having...the outcome, eonian life. For the wages of sin is death, but the grace gift of God is eonian life in Christ Jesus our Lord" (MLT).

Gal. 6:8-10: "For the one sowing in his flesh will be reaping corruption out of the flesh. Yet the one sowing in the Spirit, out of the Spirit shall be reaping eonian life." (MLT).

1 John 3:14: "We have perceived that we have stepped out of death and into life because we are loving the brothers. The one not loving the brother is remaining in death." (MLT).

1 John 5:11-12: "This is the testimony, that God gives us eonian life. And this life is in His Son. The one having the Son is having life; the one not having the Son of God is not having life" MLT).

There are many more such verses you can look up, correcting them with *eonian life* and the proper verb tense to experience the greater truth that *Jesus came to give us life right now*—not just later—and that people's lives are markedly improved when they believe, understand, and live the true Gospel message.

Because the understanding of eonian life is so crucial, let's consider two more parallel passages—Mark 10:29-30 and Luke 18:29-30:

"Now He said to them, 'Verily, I am saying to you that there is no one who leaves house, or wife, or brothers, or parents, or children on account of the kingdom of God, who will not by all means be getting back many fold in this season, *and in the coming age, eonian life.*'" Looking at the Greek words, it is obvious that this is not speaking of both an age and eternity, like the modern versions lead you to believe,* but about a coming age, and life pertaining to that age.

There are many, many verses that teach, even without the words "eonian life," that when we believe in Christ, we enjoy life immediately, regardless of which age we live in. As Paul said in Rom. 8:6, "For the mind set on the flesh is death, but the mind set on the Spirit is *life* and peace..."

We are living in a plan of ages, but the purpose of these ages—at least the ages we know about—is going to come to an end, as will all of the eonian (temporary) elements in them. The Scriptures do not provide detail as to what happens after the Story of the ages is complete, when all prodigals have been reconciled to their true Father, but we do know that all forms of death will have been destroyed and God will be "all in all" (1 Cor. 15:28). Perhaps at that point, a brand new story will commence.

As for now, what about *this* story? What is the purpose of the ages— does the Bible give us any clues?

---

* The NASB says, "...and in the age to come, eternal life."

CHAPTER FIFTEEN

THE PURPOSE OF THE AGES

What is the purpose of these ages referred to in the Bible? Though nobody knows for sure what comes after this lifetime, I favor the Jewish take on the plan of ages. The way they piece together themes out of the rich symbolism of their culture and history opens our minds to the possibilities of a much bigger story than most of us ever hear in church. Though the Jewish traditions have been largely dismissed or forgotten in recent centuries, I now present an overview here.

The obvious confusion of most Bible translators (and their diverse translations), theologians, pastors, and all the resulting denominational doctrines has resulted in disjointed views of the Bible and ill-understood passages. For one such example, I didn't know of a more confusing, enigmatic Biblical author than Paul—until I was finally offered a more authentic translation and interpretation of his message. Despite apparent evidence to the contrary, Paul offers what seems to be a consistently clear view of God's ultimate plan and purpose for all of His creation:

Eph. 1:9–10: "...He made known to us the mystery of His will, according to His kind intention which He purposed...the fullness of the seasons·, that is, the summing up of all in Christ—in the heavens and on the earth..." (MLT).

Phil. 2:9–11: "...at the name of Jesus every knee will bow, of those who are in heaven and on earth and under the earth, and that every tongue will confess that Jesus Christ is Lord, to the glory of God the Father."

Col. 1:20: "...and through [Jesus] to reconcile all to Himself" (MLT).

At the heart of it, I believe the purpose of the ages is for a loving Father to reveal Himself to His estranged, prodigal children through story. In order to do so, He brought forth a firstborn Son out of Himself, and out of that Son He is bringing forth the rest of His family—all people—who will become coheirs of His inheritance (Rom. 8:17), partaking in His divine

---

* In chapter 17 (The Harvests) you will find out why the "fullness of the seasons" is such an important concept in Scripture. The Greek word used, "kairos" (seasons), reveals a message about the harvest of all people who "ripen" in different seasons.

nature (2 Peter 1:4), and living in perfect fellowship with Him in the coming ages and beyond (Eph. 2:7). Paul and the prophets declare that this plan is accomplished through a firstborn Son, the pattern or type of what we are all to become, and then continues on through each person as they are awakened in their "season of ripening," until God's Kingdom fills the earth (Is. 11:9, Hab. 2:14).

Many people question why there is so much evil and suffering in the world if God has such "kind intentions" toward us. But how could we truly discover who our Father is unless we have a portion of *The Story* that includes what He is not? And how can we make an accurate judgment of whether it is a good story until we have "read" it through to the finish? I suggest that by the time we have read the last chapter, we will over-whelmingly agree that all the hardships of this mortal lifetime made for a necessary contrast, leading to the ultimate glorious climax and conclusion of a Good Story. And as we make our journey to knowing our Father through this Story, perhaps we find that this is the only way we can individually and collectively learn how to love, how to recognize and reject unlove for all its hurtful emptiness, and how to live like true sons and daughters of the Most High.

Is the purpose of ages revealed in the OT? Yes, it can be extracted from many different symbolic rituals and types, some of which we will discuss in greater detail in the next couple chapters. But for starters, consider how the "seven days of creation" in Genesis correlate to the ages. Earlier I mentioned that the Hebrew perspective on these seven days in Genesis 1 foreshadow seven ages* or perhaps millennia. Six ages correspond to the "ages of man" (toil upon the earth), while the seventh† corresponds to the "age of God" or "age of perfect completion," during what some people refer to as the *Millennial Kingdom*. Paul called this future age, "The Sabbath Rest" in Hebrews 4. Deuteronomy and the prophets seem to foretell inspiring details about this age, especially Isaiah and Zechariah.

But early Hebrews also celebrated the "8th day" of creation. They included an additional day of celebration at the end of their seven-day

---

* The seven days-to-ages theory offers a purposeful view of a particular finite period of time, certainly within an otherwise larger period of time (plan of ages and beyond), and does not make a case regarding the age of the earth.

† In Hebrew, seven is the number for God, or the number for Divine completion.

Feasts, marked by repentance, new beginnings, and circumcision (cutting away flesh, signifying death of fleshly nature and renewal). Many of the symbolic rituals performed during the Feast celebrations were actually what the Hebrews called "dress rehearsals," reminding them of much greater realities to come in the distant future.

In the online book, *Hebrew Roots*, we find a lengthy but awe-inspiring discussion of the symbolic meaning of the Eighth Day:

> Shemini Atzeret is an eighth day extension of the seven-day Sukkot season (Feast of Tabernacles[t] or Ingathering, celebrated in early fall) and concludes it, and yet it is a separate festival with its own significance. Yahweh gave His instructions regarding this day: "...on the eighth day you shall have a holy convocation; and you shall offer an offering made by fire unto Yahweh[:] it is a sacred assembly; and you shall do no customary work on it" (Lev. 23:36).

> "Shemini" means *eighth*, while "Atzeret" means *conclusion* or *gathering*. It comes from the Hebrew root "atzar" meaning "to hold back" or to "tarry." In that connotation it is seen as an added day to spend with Yahweh, which brings the feast to a conclusion, but also it also prepares for the beginning of a new cycle.

Historical Observation of the Feast

> In Hebraic tradition Shemini Atzeret was a closure on the festivities of Sukkot [Tabernacles] and a new beginning. ...The people had gone from the days of awe and repentance in *Feast of Trumpets* and *Day of Atonement*, into a festival of joy in *Tabernacles*, and the

---

[*] There are seven Hebrew "Feasts" (celebrations of remembrance or "spiritual feasting on God") as detailed in the OT, each carrying an agricultural theme. In some Jewish thought, the seven Biblical Feasts correspond to seven ages or possibly millennia, which ultimately reveals the seasons and harvests of all people. They are, in order: Passover, Unleavened Bread, Firstfruits, Pentecost, Trumpets, Day of Atonement, and Tabernacles (or Ingathering). It is outside the scope of this book to cover the significance of each, but an informative DVD series can be ordered on the Messianic Jewish website: http://ElShaddaiMinistries.us.

[t] The word "tabernacle" means tent or dwelling, signifying the age when God makes His dwelling place with people (Rev. 21:1-3).

[‡] I find it fascinating that the 8th Day, with *an offering made by fire*, corresponds to the "age of judgment" (following the Sabbath Rest age). During this age, Revelation's symbolic "lake of fire" burns away the impurities in people's lives, but not people!

eighth day was decreed as a memento of all that had been gained throughout the period, so that its collective benefits could be savored and enjoyed in one more day of intimacy with Yahweh. *The rabbis understood that in a special sense, this day was to consolidate all the knowledge, spiritual food, and instruction that had been gained in the preceding holy days for spiritual growth and maturity.*

On this eighth and final Day there was a gathering of all the women of Israel in the Court of the Women. They sang songs of rejoicing and praise, they danced before Yahweh waving banners and flags and torches. Then, they proceeded from the Temple Mount into the streets of Jerusalem. As they danced through the streets, the city came alive with rejoicing and with the light of the flames as the procession passed by.

When they returned to the Temple Mount, in the Court of the Women, a Menorah was erected there. This menorah was 80 feet tall and had at each of the seven places, a bath of 30 gallons of fine oil. The torches were given to the husbands of the dancers to light the Menorah. When the Menorah was lit, the entire city of Jerusalem was awash in its glow. Because the city sits within the bowl of the hills that surround it, and because this Menorah was so high and so bright, *every corner of every home in the city was alight with its radiance.*

The rabbis say that to see Jerusalem in those days was to experience the Radiant Glory of God that had been lost since the Shekinah [glory] left the first Temple. They called this the "Light of Jerusalem." So it was in this glorious setting that Y'shua (Jesus) proclaimed Himself as "the Light of the World" (John 8:12). He was the prophetic fulfillment of light and glory, which is to fill the earth with its radiance (Numbers 14:21).

Spiritual Significance of the Feast

The picture of Shemini Atzeret is that of a very intimate union and fellowship, *which follows after the broad-based and universal Feast of Sukkot whose focus is on the harvest and ingathering of the nations.*

There is great significance in the number "eight" in the name of the Feast. Numerically the number eight, as the Eighth Day, *is symbolic of perfect completion, and yet the first of a new series.* Its very name identifies it as a "new beginning."

"He that sat upon the throne said, 'Behold, I make all things new'" (Rev. 21: 5).

"For, behold, I create new heavens and a new earth: and the former shall not be remembered, nor come into mind. But be glad and rejoice continually in that which I create: for, behold, I create Jerusalem a rejoicing, and her people a joy" (Isaiah 65:17-18).

The harvest has been reaped. All sin, iniquity and transgression are finished, having been dealt with at the final resurrection and judgment. Everlasting righteousness is ushered in and the former things are not to even be remembered again. There has been a completion of one cycle, and the beginning of another *new* cycle, according to the Father's Plan.

As the prayers for rain in Shemini Atzeret indicate, there is another season of planting and harvest, but this time it is in righteousness, producing..."after our own kind."

What new vistas or horizons lay beyond in the ages to come? Paul said, "For I reckon that the sufferings of this present time are not worthy to be compared with the Glory that shall be revealed in us" (Romans 8:18).

This is a level of glory that is beyond our perception — to actually be included as one and in perfect union with Yahweh... That is the prayer that Y'shua prayed, and it will be fulfilled (John 17:22-24)!

Summing Up All In Christ

The plan and purpose of the ages is summed up in 1 Cor. 15:22-28. Here's a snapshot from the more literal Greek:

For as in Adam all are dying, so also in Christ all shall be made to live. But each in his own order: the anointed Firstfruit, after that the ones anointed in His presence, thereafter the consummation when He will

---

* Want to follow along? scripture4all.org/OnlineInterlinear/Greek_Index.htm.

be giving up the Kingdom to His God and Father, when He shall be abolishing all sovereignty and every authority and power. For He must be reigning until He places all His enemies under His feet. The last enemy being abolished is death. ...When all are subjected to Him, then the Son Himself also will be subjected to the One who subjected all to Him, *that God may be all in all* (MLT).

The 8th and concluding "Day" in *The Story* of ages—described as the "age of judgment"—is when people, having been given "hearts of flesh for their hearts of stone" (Ez. 36:26), will make use of the final opportunity for making amends. After all that has been broken and lost has been recovered and restored, the Judge will finally pronounce a final *Jubilee,* where all "debts" are cancelled and all "slaves (to the Law) and criminals" set free, followed by the last great *Feast of Tabernacles*, when God finally makes His permanent, tangible home (tabernacles) with all people.

> Then I saw a new heaven and a new earth; for the first heaven and the first earth passed away, and there is no longer any sea. And I saw the holy city, New Jerusalem, coming down out of heaven from God, made ready as a bride adorned for her husband. And I heard a loud voice from the throne, saying, "Behold, the tabernacle of God is among men, and He will dwell among them, and they shall be His people, and God Himself will be among them..." (Rev. 21:1-3).

As you can see, "going to heaven" isn't really about leaving earth, but about bringing heaven here. According to the Jews, we were made for earth where the future Kingdom becomes a unified citizenship here, with God living perceivably, intimately among all people. But if we're not going off into the "heavenly cosmos" on some permanent vacation, what might the coming ages look like? What are they really about and what might we expect? Let's start by taking a look at The Covenants.

---

* The *Year of Jubilee* falls every 49th or 50th year on the *Day of Atonement* (*Yom Kippur*), just five days before *Feast of Tabernacles* in early autumn. I say 49th or 50th because there is debate among Hebrew scholars.

† In Bible prophecy, *seas* are symbolic for the masses of people who are not called out to faith during their mortal lifetime. The reason there are "no longer any seas" is because all these masses of people have now been fully awakened to their Father.

CHAPTER SIXTEEN

TWO MAJOR COVENANTS

A *covenant* is a formal, solemn, and binding agreement between two or more parties for the performance or completion of some action. Although there are many different covenants in the OT, there are two that are foundational to understanding the Jewish interpretation of the plan of ages — the *Abrahamic Covenant* and the *Mosaic Covenant*. These could each be studied much more extensively, but it will suffice for us to look at a simplified overview of what they mean and how they apply to us.

Abrahamic Covenant

When God made this Covenant with Abraham, He signed it for both parties (Genesis 15) because it was a *unilateral, unconditional Covenant,* meaning that its fulfillment was not contingent upon the actions or agreement of both parties. In this case, the Covenant fulfillment was only conditional upon God keeping His promise, requiring no response from Abraham or his descendants. In Genesis 12:1-3, we find the terms of this Covenant repeated to Abraham's son Isaac and grandson Jacob:

> Now the LORD said to Abram, "Go forth from your country, and from your relatives and from your father's house, to the land which I will show you; and I will make you a great nation, and I will bless you, and make your name great; and so you shall be a blessing; and I will bless those who bless you, and the one who curses you I will curse.* *And in you all the families of the earth will be blessed."*

Through Abraham's physical seed or lineage would come the long-awaited Anointed One. Jesus, a physical descendant of Abraham of whom Isaac was a type,† is both the genealogical and spiritual fulfillment of this

---

* Despite the seeming severity of being under a curse, curses are temporary. God revoked the curse on the earth after the flood (Gen. 8:21), He turned Israel from a curse into a blessing (Zech. 8:13), and Jesus redeemed us from the curse and even "became a curse for us" (Gal. 3:13). Jesus is not still under a curse.

† Abraham's son, Isaac, put on the altar and "brought back to life" was a symbol or "dress rehearsal" of this plot.

promise. How could *all the families of the earth* possibly be blessed through the fulfillment of this promise unless Jesus (The "Second Adam") reversed the effects of any kind of curse for all physical offspring of the First Adam? It would be otherwise impossible to take God at His word that all families for all time could benefit from this covenant blessing.

It is to this particular all-inclusive Covenant that Paul referred throughout his letters when he wrote of all people being saved:

> ...*all Israel will be saved*; just as it is written, "The deliverer will come from Zion, He will remove ungodliness from Jacob. *This is my Covenant with them*, when I take away their sins." (Rom. 11:26–27).

> So then as through one transgression there resulted condemnation to all men, even so through one act of righteousness there resulted justification of life to all men... For as in Adam all die, so also in Christ all will be made alive... The first man, Adam, became a living soul. The last Adam became a life-giving spirit (Rom. 5:18; 1 Cor. 15:22, 45, respectively).

But there is another layer to this promise. There would also come a line of spiritual descendants from Abraham who would help the Messiah deliver this blessing upon the whole earth. As we saw earlier, these spiritual descendants are called "the elect" or "the chosen" by Paul. This is not the "elect of Calvinism" — some special by-invitation-only club pass into heaven — because it was never about just a few being saved and the rest damned. Paul said,

"...it is not the offspring of the flesh who are offspring of God, but the offspring of the promise are regarded as seed" (Rom. 9:6–8, MLT).

Once again, this offspring and seed are a line of people who are not the *only people saved*, but are the people saved* ahead of others. What is the job of seed? It is to be planted in order to bring forth fruit. This spiritual "seed of Abraham" will be planted among the rest to bring a fruit-bearing harvest of all peoples, blessing all families of the earth.

In summary, the *Abrahamic Covenant* is an unconditional covenant that results in salvation (healing from all forms of death) and restoration of all

---

* The Greek word for *saved* (sozo) actually means delivered, healed, and made whole. People are being delivered and healed from the curse of death and made whole from their separation from God and each other. Find more on sozo in the Resources section under "Simple Tools for Identifying Mistranslations."

people through Christ's victory over death.* This salvation will be proliferated through Abraham's spiritual seed to bring all people into a willingly restored, desired relationship with the Father. Remember, these "chosen" are obtained by lot for their role in the first act of *The Story*—not by their own intelligence, merit, or ability. They are then matured and trained to bless and teach the rest of the nations, now and in the ages to come, how to love and joyfully serve others.

Mosaic Covenant

This *conditional* Covenant, summed up in Exodus 19:1–8 and 24:1–8, promises rewards for obedience and faithfulness to those "called out" of spiritual darkness in this first lifetime (ahead of the rest). In other words, this Covenant is completely different from the Abrahamic Covenant in that the outcome is contingent upon actions from both parties. Its rewards are for whom Jesus referred to as "the good and faithful servant," the "overcomer" who made good returns of the "talents" given to him or her (Matt. 25:14–30). These are whom Paul referred to as "chosen."

Here is the gist of this Covenant:

> "Now then, *if* you will indeed obey My voice and keep My covenant, *then* you shall be My own possession among all the peoples, for all the earth is Mine; and *you shall be to Me a kingdom of priests* and a holy nation" (Ex. 19:5–6).

These future promises of the Mosaic Covenant are not only to Jews and Israelites; they are promises to all Covenant keepers, Jew and non-Jew alike. We see a couple parallel promises to Covenant keepers in the NT:

1 Pet. 2:9: "But you are *a chosen generation, a royal priesthood*, a holy nation, a people for God's own possession, *so that you may proclaim the excellencies of Him who has called you out of darkness* into His marvelous light."†

---

* Is. 25:8, 1 Cor. 15:54–55, Rev. 20:13–14.

† NASB cross-references these verses with Isaiah 9:2; 42:16; Acts 26:18; 2 Cor. 4:6. Some people argue that Peter wrote this book to Jews only, but Paul declares, "there is no Jew or Greek...for all are one in Christ Jesus" (Gal. 3:28). Therefore, Peter's writings applied to both Jew and non-Jew who were *spiritually* "chosen according to the foreknowledge of God the Father" (1 Peter 1:2).

Rev. 20:6: "*Blessed and holy is the one who has a part in the first resurrection; over these the second death has no power, but they will be priests of God and of Christ and will reign with Him for a thousand years.*"

In Jewish thought, there are indeed wonderful promises declared in Scripture for those who keep the Mosaic Covenant. Deuteronomy, Psalms, and Isaiah contain visions of and references to these promised rewards, foreshadowed through natural world pictures and prophecies.

Consider the iconic *Promised Land*. I used to think the Promised Land — and other prophecies throughout the OT describing some kind of future blissful state — was about "eternity in heaven" for believers only. Today I lean toward the Hebrew interpretation whereby the Scripture writers (including Paul) foresaw some kind of heavenly Kingdom *on earth*, an age of peace and possible rewards for Covenant-keepers, which again has been referred to as the "Millennial Kingdom," "Wedding Feast," or "Sabbath Rest." Here's one such (possible) prophetic description:

> Therefore, *you shall keep the commandments of the LORD your God, to walk in His ways and to fear Him.* For the LORD your God is bringing you into a good land, a land of brooks of water, of fountains and springs, flowing forth in valleys and hills; a land of wheat and barley, of vines and fig trees and pomegranates, a land of olive oil and honey; a land where you will eat food without scarcity... (Deut. 8:6–9)*

The promises of rewards in passages like these are contingent upon belief and obedience. This is why Moses did not get to go into the Promised Land — he was made into an example when he defied a command of the Lord during his leadership! The greater the authority and understanding a person is given, the greater the accountability and corrective process. Come to think of it, do you know how many people actually got into the Promised Land out of the first generation of Israelites who had been called out of Egypt to possess it as their reward? That number would be *two*.

If the OT Promised Land was meant to be a prophetic picture of Christianity's idea of "heaven," or "eternal life," do you really think that only *two* out of a few million (and excluding Moses!) would make it in? No, I believe this was a prophecy of the type of faith it would take to

---

* See also passages like Isaiah 65:17–25.

qualify to reign with Christ on earth in the next age! How did these two men qualify? After being called out and delivered from Egypt by God, they willingly responded with uncharacteristic belief (compared to the rest of the nation) in the power and might of their God, and they were ready to act on it. After scouting the land, Joshua and Caleb gave a "good report." In essence, "Our God *saves*! He is all-powerful and will surely deliver us ALL safely into the Kingdom. The odds don't appear in our favor, but we will trust in our God." Everyone else gave a bad report—"Our god isn't big enough to save us all. He's going to let most of us perish."

It's worth mentioning that those who are not "called out of Egypt" in this mortal lifetime apparently don't have the option of taking part in the rewards of the Mosaic Covenant (although I could be wrong about that). While this might not seem fair, I truly believe that by the end of the ages everyone will be enjoying exactly the same level playing field and privileges. Also, because of their inability during this lifetime to participate, who knows how God might especially reward them or give them opportunities during the next ages? Many of them may even be included in the leadership, so we can't rule anything out. Either way, the point is that the only thing lost is *time* (which is not all that tragic in the scope of eternity), not privilege or being included in all the best a Father has to offer equally to all His children.

Citizenship in the Kingdom

Jesus spoke frequently to the Jews about what it takes to enter into or be cast out of the Kingdom, but this had nothing to do with "going to heaven or hell." In case you hadn't noticed, the contingency for getting into His Kingdom frequently, if not always, rested on *obedience* and *fair treatment of others* (a.k.a. "works"), *not belief.* Some pastors and Bible teachers I have talked to, who believe and teach that Jesus was talking about going to heaven and hell (the way the Church teaches today), try to explain away Jesus's emphasis on good works by saying that God deals differently with Jews than Gentiles, in that Jews are saved by works but Gentiles are saved by faith. However, I think they miss the whole point. I believe that when Jesus referred to *the Kingdom*, He taught people what citizenship in His Kingdom looks like—both now and later—so those he exhorted could take part in the age of rewards—something they already envisioned. Being cast out of the Kingdom was not about going to hell, but about not being in right relationship with God and people, and reportedly not being included in the first resurrection to enjoy the next age of rest and rewards.

The "Kingdom" or "Kingdom of heaven"* *is not a place,* but a citizenship, a judicial position of authority, and a political system of heavenly justice, set up on earth. Strong's definition (#932) of the Greek word used for "kingdom" throughout the NT is:

1. Royal power, kingship, dominion, rule.

> a. Not to be confused with an actual kingdom but rather the right or authority to rule over a kingdom.

> b. Of the royal power of Jesus as the triumphant Messiah.

> c. Of the royal power and dignity conferred on Christians in the Messiah's kingdom.

2. A kingdom, the territory subject to the rule of a king.

3. Used in the New Testament to refer to the reign of the Messiah.

Jesus warned that many of the original, natural "sons of the Kingdom" would be cast out of the Kingdom for their disobedience. He also made it clear that nobody will get (or retain) citizenship or position in His Kingdom until they've learned obedience to the greatest commandment. Anyone who misses out on in the School of Love here will experience full transformation during the age of judgment, or the "8th Day."

Part of Jesus's warning to the Jews of His day was also in reference to their missing out on what is described as the greatest joy of the next age — the Wedding Feast. Jesus spoke on occasion about being shut out of the Wedding, cast into "outer darkness" where there is "weeping and gnashing of teeth."

Contrary to popular teaching, if you study carefully the place of "weeping and gnashing of teeth" from a Hebrew perspective, it is not hell or eternal torment, but a place "on the outside looking in," for a time of the necessary inner reflection that leads to longing and transformation. *Outer darkness* is a figurative description of living outside the light of the city —

---

* "Kingdom of heaven" and "Kingdom of God" can be used interchangeably — see next footnote.

the New Jerusalem—away from the felt or experiential presence of the Lamb. Consider Matt. 8:11–12:

> "I say to you that many [spiritual children] will come from east and west (non-Jews), and recline at the table with Abraham, Isaac and Jacob in the kingdom (citizenship and reign) of heaven; but the [flesh, unbelieving] sons of the kingdom will be cast out into the outer darkness; in that place there will be weeping and gnashing of teeth."

Bible teacher Chuck Missler says:

> The controversy seems to revolve around the passages in Matthew (which speak about the coming "kingdom of heaven"*) that use the term "outer darkness." Briefly, the "outer darkness" is defined by several prominent scholars, including Kenneth Wuest, Dr. Spiros Zodhiates, Erwin Lutzer, and Charles Stanley, not as "hell," but as "the darkness outside." As Stanley puts it, "The outer darkness refers to being thrown outside a building into the dark." He goes on to say that the point of the three parables in Matthew that use the term "outer darkness," is that "in God's future kingdom, those who were faithful in this life (those who produced fruit for the kingdom) will be given more privileges than those who were not."
>
> Consequently, the "outer darkness" is not a description of hell or a place of punishment, like the Catholics use of the term "purgatory," but a place of restoration, renewal and re-instruction in the ways of the Lord. …His desire is that all His children be reestablished in holiness. The Bible does not say how long an individual might be in this "outer darkness" to be restored, but the concept certainly does encourage us to be wise and heed our accountability here and now. 'Fruit' does matter to the Lord.[53]

---

* Matthew is the only NT book that uses the expression "Kingdom of heaven." The rest of the NT writers use "Kingdom of God." This is because the book of Matthew ministered to the Jewish believers who regarded the name of God (original Greek NT manuscripts probably used "Yahweh" rather than "God") too holy to speak.

Millennial Kingdom Belief in Early Church History

It's rare to hear teachings today on the Millennial Kingdom—the period of restoration of an Eden-like earth—even though it's frequently depicted throughout the OT. Most churches and denominations teach that we die and go to "heaven," and that's it. And if they do talk about the Kingdom, they usually do so in a way that is synonymous with their false impressions of heaven as a destination in the cosmos somewhere.

In his article, "Millennial Views," Dr. Renald Showers, author of *What on Earth is God Doing*, shares his findings on the teaching of the Millennial Kingdom in the early Church:

> Numerous historians declare that Premillennialism* (initially called chiliasm) was the first major millennial view of the Church, and that it was the predominant view of orthodox believers from the first to the third centuries. A sampling of historians will be quoted as evidence for this declaration.
>
> Edward Gibbon (1737-1794), the noted English historian who wrote the classic work, *The History of the Decline and Fall of the Roman Empire*, stated the following:
>
> "The ancient and popular doctrine of the Millennium was intimately connected with the second coming of Christ. As the works of the creation had been finished in six days, their duration in their present state, according to a tradition which was attributed to the prophet Elijah, was fixed to six thousand years. By the same analogy it was inferred, that this long period of labor and contention, which was now almost elapsed, would be succeeded by a joyful Sabbath of a thousand years; and that Christ, with the triumphant band of the saints and the elect who had escaped death, or who had been miraculously revived, would reign upon earth till the time appointed for the last and general resurrection...."

---

* *Premillennialism* is the view we've been exploring of a literal 1,000-year reign of Christ on earth, a political kingdom of peace and prosperity. A plausible case is made that in Scripture, mortals, immortals (resurrected), sinners, and saints will all be living together in this Kingdom (see Isaiah 65–66). *Immortals* would be those from all centuries who were included in the *first resurrection* – those who qualify under the Mosaic Covenant. *Mortals* would be those living on earth during the first resurrection who are not part of that particular resurrection (see Revelation 20:1–7).

"The assurance of such a Millennium was carefully inculcated by a succession of [Church] fathers from Justin Martyr (103–165) and Irenaeus, who conversed with the immediate disciples of the apostle [Paul], down to Lactantius (240–320), who was preceptor to the son of Constantine. Though it might not be universally received, it appears to have been the reigning sentiment of the orthodox believers" (Edward Gibbon, *History of Christianity*. New York: Peter Eckler Publishing Company, 1916, pp. 141–4).[54]

This view potentially sheds much light on the NT, especially when considering the teachings of the Calvinists and the Arminians, who don't have logical answers to the seeming contradictions of both Paul's and Jesus's teachings. At times, both Jesus and Paul appear to teach salvation by works *and* grace.

Jesus

Matt. 7:21–23: "Not everyone who says to Me, 'Lord, Lord,' shall be entering into the kingdom of the heavens, *but he who does the will of My Father who is in heaven.* [...] depart from me, *you who practice lawlessness'*" ((MLT) works).

Matt. 19:23–24: "Truly I say to you, it is hard for a rich man to enter the kingdom of heaven. Again I say to you, *it is easier for a camel to go through the eye of a needle, than for a rich man to enter the kingdom of God*" (works).

John 6:47: "Truly, truly, I say to you, *he who believes has eonian life*" ((MLT) faith).

Paul

1 Cor. 9:27: "...but I discipline my body and make it my slave, so that, after I have preached to others, *I myself will not be disqualified*" (works).

Gal. 5:19–21, (selected): "Now the deeds of the flesh are evident, which are: immorality, impurity, sensuality, idolatry...enmities, strife, jealousy, outbursts of anger, disputes, dissensions, factions, envying...and things like these, *of which I forewarn you...that those who practice such things will not inherit the kingdom of God*" (works).

Heb. 4:1, 11: "Therefore, let us fear if, while a promise remains of entering His rest, *any one of you may seem to have come short of it. ...Therefore let us be diligent to enter that rest, so that no one will fall, through following the same example of disobedience*" (works).

Eph. 2:8–9: "For *by grace you have been saved through faith*; and that not of yourselves, *it is the gift of God; not as a result of works*, so that no one may boast" (faith).

Gal. 2:21: "I do not nullify the grace of God, *for if righteousness comes through the Law, then Christ died needlessly*" (faith).

It's easy to see why these passages and the teachings about grace and works have been debated and caused more confusion than probably any others. Denominational doctrines (and schisms) have been formed over trying to make sense out of them, especially without the right lenses.

If you don your Hebrew glasses, these seeming contradictions vanish and the text makes perfect sense. Once again, Jesus warned the Jews about being excluded from the citizenship of his Kingdom and therefore missing out on the next phase—the age of rewards for *obedience* – not about missing out on "eternity." It was this special, temporary age of the Kingdom of which they had heard, expected, and longed for since the days of Moses. And Paul made it clear that ALL Israel—even those Jesus warned—would eventually be included in the ultimate Kingdom that grows until it covers the earth (Is. 11:9; Hab. 2:14; Rom. 11:26–29).

The Jewish teachers of the Law totally understood Jesus's warnings, which is why they were so angry. Had Jesus warned them of impending eternal torment, perhaps they would have had a different response than anger (like begging and pleading). They were incensed when He suggested that they were not worthy of reigning in His Kingdom, and that they were in danger of missing out on the greatest reward of all time at the first resurrection—the crowning age of the ages. I'm sure they all felt entitlement for all their outward observance and perfect knowledge of the Law, not to mention being natural offspring of Abraham.

Did Paul Offer to Go to Hell?

I used to think Paul actually offered to go to hell on behalf of his fellow Jews.

> For I could wish that I myself were accursed, separated from Christ for the sake of my brethren, my kinsmen according to the flesh, who are Israelites, to whom belongs the adoption as sons, and the glory and *the covenants* and the giving of the Law and the temple service and the promises… (Rom. 9:3–4).

But this never made sense to me. Who in their right mind would ever wish they could miss out on being with God and Jesus in exchange for an eternity in hell, regardless of their love and loyalty? I wouldn't want to do that for anyone. Now that I better understand the purpose of the next age, I know that Paul was merely saying he wished he could give up his place of rewards of serving under the leadership of Christ, if it meant that his brothers could experience the coming reign with Christ and the fulfillment of promises that they had looked forward to for several millennia.

Missing out on the first resurrection especially for a Jew, is really nothing to take lightly. As we covered, it is referred to in Scripture as the *Wedding Feast*, the *age of the ages*, and the *Sabbath Rest*. Those who take part are referred to in Scripture as the bride (of Christ), priests, kings, sons, barley, first fruits, gold, and overcomers. If this teaching has been interpreted correctly by many people since the days of Jesus, every "called out" person — Jew or Gentile — who falls short of fulfilling their part of the Mosaic Covenant terms, loses out on this most amazing, promised celebration! Beyond that, they miss out on a part of the joy of reaping and gathering in the harvest of humankind alongside Jesus:

> He who overcomes, and he who keeps My deeds until the end, to him I will give authority over the nations; and he shall rule them with a rod of iron, as the vessels of the potter are broken to pieces,* as I also have received authority from My Father; and I will give him the morning star (Rev. 2:26–28).

People are saved from Adam's curse of death by *grace* — a free gift — but they can't get citizenship or position in the Kingdom of God at any time without learning to overcome through trust and love. "Not everyone who says to Me, 'Lord, Lord,' shall be entering the kingdom of heaven, but he who does the will of My Father who is in heaven" (Matt. 7:21, MLT).

What is His will? Below are the requirements in becoming "chosen," true sons of God, as taught by Jesus, Paul, James, and John:

Matt. 7:12: "In everything, therefore, treat people the same way you want them to treat you, for this is the Law and the Prophets."

John 13:34: "A new commandment I give to you, that you love one another, even as I have loved you, that you also love one another."

---

* Reference Psalms 2:8–9. I believe this speaks of ruling unto "brokenness" of fleshly willfulness (pottery is made of clay) and bringing all into submission to Christ.

Rom. 13:8–10: "Owe nothing to anyone except to love one another; for he who loves his neighbor has fulfilled the law. ...And if there is any other commandment, it is summed up in this saying, 'You shall love your neighbor as yourself.' Love does no wrong to a neighbor; therefore love is the fulfillment of the law."

Gal. 5:14: "For the whole Law is fulfilled in one word, in the statement, 'You shall love your neighbor as yourself.'"

Ultimately, the "new commandment" leads to all people learning to die to themselves – the second death – that they might become conformed to Christ (Gal. 2:20), the goal and will of God for all His children.

Thankfully, all of those Israelites who did not make it into the Promised Land the first time around will be resurrected later and will go through a process of being transformed into citizens of the growing, all-encompassing Kingdom of God, with full rights as sons and daughters of the Most High:

> All the ends of the earth will remember and turn to the Lord, and all the families of the nations will worship before You. For the kingdom is the Lord's and He rules over the nations. All the prosperous of the earth will eat and worship, all those who go down to the dust will bow before Him, even he who cannot keep his soul (self) alive (Psalm 22:27–29).

I've referred many times to the harvest of people that is such an important concept throughout the Bible. Let's find out more about the three harvests—what exactly are they, and how do they fit within the scope of the coming ages?

CHAPTER SEVENTEEN

THE GREAT HARVESTS

Have you ever noticed that the Bible is blooming full of agricultural terms? There's a significant reason for this that goes far beyond a nice little farming theme. Consider the frequency of some of these words as they occur in the original languages (Hebrew and Greek):

Farmer=26

Planting (verb)=66	Season=334
Seed=300	Barley=36
Soil=76	Wheat=45
Field=332	Grapes=22
Crop/Produce=124	Vineyard=115
Harvest=78	Winepress=21

Contrary to the evidence, the Bible is not a farmers' almanac. Sure, most Bible teachers and pastors pick up on the fact that, in all His talk on growing, pruning (sometimes mistranslated as "punishing"), and harvesting, Jesus actually talked about *people*, but most fail to dig deep enough to understand these references properly. The following anecdote illustrates what happens when the Christian-doctrine-forming-committee meets Bible agricultural references without the correct lenses. See if you recognize any particular doctrinal positions developing in this analogy:

There were two farmers, each who owned sizable cherry orchards. When the time came for the harvest, they each went into their own orchards to gather the fruit of their labors.

The first farmer took a few small baskets, placed them under some of the trees, and waited while all the cherries that freely wished to do so fell or jumped into the baskets. It was an unprecedented miracle indeed, and such a small percentage was actually able to do that. But it surely was impressive! So he took his few cherries and went home and made one nice little cherry pie. The rest of the cherries fell to the ground and rotted or got eaten by worms and birds.

The second farmer took his baskets to his cherry orchard and looked for all the best cherries—the reddest, plumpest, ripest, sweetest, and free of blemishes or bug holes—only the very best of the crop would do. He took all that he deemed select-worthy and filled his basket up enough so that when he got home, his wife also was able to make a nice cherry pie for him and was also able to put up several gallons in the freezer for the winter. The rest of this farmer's cherries that didn't get picked fell to the ground and rotted or got eaten by worms and birds.

I'm sure you were able to identify the two predominant views of modern Christianity (Arminianism and Calvinism) in how God utilizes His own crops. In fact, the greatest percentage of Christians believe like the first farmer—man is saved by his own free will—yet as you can see by the near-impossible odds, it should produce the smallest crop. Whether referring to cherries or people, the Bible makes it clear that a crop is completely unable to make the smallest step toward its own harvest.

Psalm 14:2-3: "The LORD has looked down from heaven upon the sons of men to see if there are any who understand, who seek after God. They have all turned aside, together they have become corrupt; there is no one who does good, not even one."

Isaiah 65:1: "I revealed myself to those who did not ask for me; I was found by those who did not seek me. To a nation that did not call on my name, I said, 'Here am I, here am I'" (NIV).

John 6:44: "No one can come to Me unless the Father who sent Me draws him..."

From all we've explored in Scriptures and in regard to the heart and character of God, there's yet another alternative that certainly makes the most sense.

A third farmer went out to his orchard and saw that the first cherries were just ripening. So he went out and picked all that were ready. He continued picking daily, as long as there were still cherries to pick, putting them up for winter when he got them home. He canned them, dried them, froze them, gave them to friends and relatives, and he even ate lots of them immediately.

Finally, when he had picked every last cherry and safely stored them, he went back and saw many more lying on the ground underneath the trees. Some of them were too ripe, too soft, or too bug-eaten to be any good for conventional uses. But as any good farmer would do, he thought about what might be done to salvage the rest. It was such a short growing season, after all. So he gathered them up—every last one—and put them into a winepress where he made the sweetest, tastiest wine in the land. Not one cherry was wasted.

We've thoroughly covered the evidence for this hope-filled scenario of every part of the crop being utilized for a good purpose, but it's worth mentioning this verse again:

[God] *wills all men to be saved*, and to come unto the knowledge of the truth. For there is one God, and one mediator between God and men, the man Christ Jesus; *Who gave himself a ransom for all, to be witnessed (or testified) in due season* (1 Tim. 2:3-6, MLT).

What is noteworthy about this word "wills" is that some versions translate it as *wills* and some translate it as *desires*. But if you go to Strong's* (#2309), here is the primary definition of the Greek word *thelo*: "to will, have in mind, intend, to be resolved or determined, to purpose." There are many places in Scripture where God says that His "thelo" cannot be stopped or thwarted by men. It is a very strong word indicating what He intends to *make* happen.

Matt. 6:10: "Your kingdom come. Your *will* be done, on earth as it is in heaven."

Dan. 4:35: "…according to His *will* he does among the force of the heaven, and among the ones dwelling on the earth. And there is not one who shall act against His hand…" (Septuagint).

The Barley Harvest (Firstfruits)

Here's what I have gathered about the symbolic Hebrew meaning of the harvest theme in the Scriptures. There were three primary crops†

---

* http://studylight.org/isb/view.cgi?number=2309

† Corn is a fourth type of grain mentioned in some Bible translations but corn wasn't even grown in the ancient Middle East. This is a mistranslation of other grains (barley or wheat).

grown, harvested, and celebrated by Israel throughout their history. Barley was harvested in early spring, wheat harvest began late spring and continued into summer, and the grape harvest came in at the end of summer into early fall, when the crop was harvested and put through the winepress. All three of these crops reportedly correspond to types of people in their varying stages of belief (ripening) in God's plan of ages.

The barley harvest was celebrated by Israel during the Feast of Firstfruits. It is during this early spring Feast that Jesus arose from the dead as the "firstfruit" to God. Paul says, "But the fact is that Christ has been raised from the dead, and He became the firstfruit of those who have fallen asleep [in death]" (1 Cor. 15:20).

As I understand it, the barley also represents the "overcomers" who have been designated to be harvested in the first resurrection. These overcomers are also called *firstfruits*, *chosen*, and *elect*. According to Revelation 14:4, "These are the ones who follow the Lamb wherever He goes. *These have been purchased from among men as first fruits to God* and to the Lamb."

In the OT, Gideon was a "barley type." Although he was the "weakest" of his clan, and his clan was the "weakest" of Israel (which is often how barley appear in this mortal lifetime), God called Gideon out to strike down a valley full of bloodthirsty, Midianite warriors.

Gideon, though knock-kneed with fear, asked God for a reassuring sign that this mission was doable, which God graciously granted. When Gideon snuck up on the Midianite camp in the night, looking for reassurance to his request, here's the conversation he heard between two men in the camp (Jud. 7:12–14):

> Now the Midianites and the Amalekites and all the sons of the east were lying in the valley as numerous as locusts; and their camels were without number, as numerous as the sand on the seashore. When Gideon came, behold, a [Midianite] was relating a dream to his friend. And he said, "Behold, I had a dream; *a loaf of barley bread was tumbling into the camp of Midian*, and it came to the tent and struck it so that it fell, and turned it upside down so that the tent lay flat."

> His friend replied, "This is nothing less than the sword of Gideon the son of Joash, a man of Israel; God has given Midian and all the camp into his hand."

God's sign through this Midianite affirmed to Gideon that indeed, he and his men could take the whole army if only they believed. Well, the rest is history. Gideon believed, and all he had to do is stand back and watch; God did the job for him. This is the faith of barley, the overcomers of God's first harvest.

To the untrained eye, a loaf of barley seems an odd weapon for battle and would probably not make the top ten in a superhero's arsenal. On the other hand, once you understand the deeper, spiritual significance of barley and many other details in *The Story*, then a whole new perspective comes to light.

I believe this whole account of Gideon's overtake of the Midianites could be a prophetic picture of the *spiritual* (not violent or literal) takeover by the overcomers—God's special forces—at the start of the next age. I believe Gideon and his small army, whittled down to 300 men, represent the overcomers; the Midianites may represent the corrupt power systems of this world; and Gideon's sword represents the "sword of the Spirit," or the Word of God. It is the powerful Word of God that will enact justice on the world, the "spiritual weapon" of takeover. If you read the account in its entirety, you see some really cool gems, such as Gideon's men hiding their fire torches in clay jars and breaking them just before descending on the Midianite camp. I believe this is a picture of the glory being revealed in the overcomers as their mortal bodies of "clay" are broken away in the first resurrection, in exchange for new, powerful bodies empowered by the impassioned fire of God!

The Wheat Harvest (Pentecost)

Wheat is the second crop to be harvested. In the spring Feasts lineup, the start of the wheat harvest was celebrated on the Feast of Pentecost, fifty days after Jesus rose from the grave. It has been suggested that the wheat represents those who have been called out to belief in this mortal lifetime, but who were not considered *overcomers* of exemplary faith.

The wheat, as symbolically corresponding to a called out people in the OT, begins with the calling of Israel out of Egypt. By no effort, ability, or smarts of their own, God called out a nation of people to special knowledge of Him, relationship, and the resulting deliverance. And really, in order for there to be a called out people ahead of others (to pave the way for others later), there had to be people who were not called out.

Israel was no more able to deliver itself from the crushing slavery of Egypt (corresponding to law, sin, and resulting death) than anyone else, but God sent a Moses as a savior type to rescue them singlehandedly with mighty acts and miracles to defy all man-made gods* — gods that could do nothing to deliver them from death. So all Israel — every last one, regardless of personal "worthiness" or even belief — was led out of Egypt by the power of God through a savior.

Contrasting Barley and Wheat

To obtain a greater understanding of the characteristics of *barley believers* (as opposed to believers who are not considered overcomers), read Hebrews 11. First note the reference in verse 35 about the "better resurrection"† and then back up to read what kind of people qualify for it. Revelation 17:14 spells out three prerequisites:

> ...He is Lord of lords and King of kings, and those who are with Him (to rule and reign) are the *called and chosen and believing*‡ (MLT).

The barley are *chosen* to rule and reign with Christ in the coming two ages simply because they demonstrate fully matured *belief* and trust in the living God. They fulfill the Mosaic Covenant by living in obedience to the New Commandment, basing their motives in love and true justice, understanding that adherence to the Law *without love* is nothing more than clanging-gong Phariseeism and hypocrisy.

Joshua and Caleb were examples of called, chosen, and believing individuals who received the reward of the Promised Land based on their excelled belief in God's good character and power. They were willing to sacrifice and trust despite incredible odds (*giants!*). On the contrary, because of their lacking belief, the rest of Israel were disqualified from the Promised Land, but only for a season in time. What does this mean

---

* The plagues that fell upon Egypt through Moses were each an affront to a specific Egyptian god.

† Read Rev. 20:1–7 about the "first resurrection," which I believe is the same thing.

‡ Though translated in most versions as "faithful," the Greek word used here (pistos, #4103) has a greater implication of both *trustworthy (obedient) and believing*.

exactly? The wheat will have their part in the second resurrection, which is still an equally magnificent "resurrection to eonian life" (Matt. 25:46). Again, the only difference seems to be time — more time for overcomers, feasting on and enjoying the presence of God.

Something I suspect is the possibility that certain people who did not get a chance to hear and believe in this age, such as orphans, widows, lepers, oppressed people, those who laid their lives down for others, and "loving, caring people of other religions," might possibly be included in the wheat or, who knows, maybe even the barley harvest. *If this is true,* these people might be resurrected and offered immediate belief in Jesus at a time when "blind faith" is no longer required. In other words, part of their reward for either suffering or sacrificing during their mortal lifetimes could be that they are given the gift of belief immediately at their resurrection, foregoing any kind of restorative process. I'm not certain or dogmatic about this; however, it certainly fits in more with the just nature of God to me. I base this possible scenario on certain verses I read in the NT such as:

Matt. 20:16: "The last shall be first."

Luke 12:47–48: "The slave *who knew his master's will and did not get ready or act in accord with his will,* will receive many lashes, *but the one who did not know it,* and committed deeds worthy of a flogging, will receive but few."

Matt. 22:8–10: "'The wedding is ready, but *those who were invited were not worthy.* Go therefore to the main highways, and as many as you find there, invite to the wedding feast.' Those servants went out into the streets and gathered together all they found, *both evil and good*; and the wedding hall was filled with dinner guests.'"

Luke 14:22–24: "And the servant said, 'Master, what you commanded has been done, and still there is room.' And the master said to the servant, 'Go out into the highways and along the hedges, and *compel them to come in,* so that my house may be filled...'"

Rom. 2:12–15: "For all who have sinned without the Law will also perish (die) without the Law, and all who have sinned under the Law will be judged by the Law; for it is not the hearers of the Law who are just before God, *but the doers of the Law will be justified.* For when Gentiles who do not have the Law do instinctively the things of the Law, these, not having the Law, are a law to themselves, in that *they show the work of the*

Law written in their hearts, their conscience bearing witness and their thoughts alternately accusing or else defending them…"

Bible teacher Stephen Jones comments,

> We are judged according to our level of revelation and not merely by the pure standard of righteousness set forth in the Law. Everyone is raised in one culture or another, each having variations on its standards of right and wrong. God takes all of this into consideration in His wisdom. But when He calls someone, such as Abraham, out of a worldly culture and begins to train him in the revelation of the character of God, He expects more out of that person than of others.[55]

An interesting factoid about wheat versus barley is that when it comes to removing the chaff, barley is winnowed (a light blowing), while wheat is threshed (a much more rigorous process).

Grape Harvest (Ingathering & Tabernacles)

The last harvest of Israel at the end of the growing season was the grape harvest. After the grapes were brought in and pressed, the Israelites celebrated the last Feast of the season, the *Feast of Ingathering or Tabernacles (also called "Sukkot" or "Booths")*. According to Wikipedia:

> Sukkot was agricultural in origin. This is evident from the biblical name, *The Feast of Ingathering…* "At the end of the year when you gather in your labors out of the field…" (Ex. 23:16); "…after you have gathered in from your threshing-floor (wheat) and from your winepress…" (Deut. 16:13). It was a thanksgiving for the fruit harvest. Coming as it did at the completion of the harvest, Sukkot was regarded as a general thanksgiving for the bounty of nature in the year that had passed.[56]

Is it sinking in yet? Here we have the final Feast of the year, celebrating the ingathering of all types of people — even the tough, fleshy grapes!

I think Scriptures suggest that the grape harvest and process is reserved primarily for *Pharisee-types,* not "the world" or those who did not know any better. Pharisees are knowledgeable religious people (even today) who are "called out" to belief in the true God, yet who are prideful, loveless, judgmental, unjust, ignoring the needs of the poor, and full of hypocrisy. If you study out the NT, especially Jesus's interaction with them, these people's fate appears to be "eonian" judgment ("the 8th Day") in a purifying and symbolic process called, "lake of fire." In John 9:40–41:

> Those of the Pharisees who were with Him heard these things and said to Him, "We are not blind too, are we?" Jesus said to them, "If you were blind, you would have no sin; but since you say, 'We see,' your sin remains."

We could certainly make an argument that those people of the world (unbelievers) who have intentionally harmed others — the Pharaohs, Hitlers, and Bin Ladens — would also find themselves in need of the "fires of purification," but only God knows how heavy their sentence will be since it appears that He created certain people as "vessels of destruction and dishonor" (Rom. 9:22; 2 Tim. 2:20), partly as "overcomer training" and also to provide a contrast to what is good and what is the ultimate intention of God. In other words, it appears that these kinds of people did not have a choice about the evil they committed in their role in *The Story*, unlike those who were offered the truth and inwardly knew better.

In Lev. 27:28 we read, "*Anything devoted to destruction is most holy to the Lord.*" I've never heard a pastor teach from that verse before — what could it mean? Perhaps it refers to the winepress producing the most desired results of the crop; the contrast of a hateful, bitter person turned into a delightful, "sweet" person. Who wouldn't want to celebrate that?

I recently learned that the biblical word frequently translated "tribulation" to convey fearsome apocalyptic events, actually comes from the Greek word, "thlipsis" (Strong's #2347), which simply means, "to press." This word is associated with pressing of "grapes" in a winepress and is used as such in these more literally translated verses:

Rom. 2:9: "There will be *pressing* and small space for every soul of man who does evil, of the Jew first and also of the Greek" (MLT).

Rev. 7:14: "These are the ones who come out of the great *pressing*, and they have washed their robes and made them white in the blood of the Lamb" (MLT).

Wow, did you see that? I believe these are people who have come out of the winepress and who have been washed clean of evil and hypocrisy! What is really fascinating is that Strong's* *first* definition is "a pressing,"

---

* All screen captures throughout the rest of the book, unless otherwise noted, were taken from Strong's Concordance at http://studylight.org.

yet *not once* is it translated this way in modern Bibles (see image).

Strong's Number: 2347	θλῖψις
Original Word θλῖψις	**Word Origin** from (2346)
Transliterated Word Thlipsis	**Phonetic Spelling** thlip'-sis 🔊
Parts of Speech Noun Feminine	**TDNT** 3:139,334

Definition

1. a pressing, pressing together, pressure
2. metaph. oppression, affliction, tribulation, distress, straits

Translated Words

KJV (45) - affliction, 17; anguish, 1; burdened, 1; persecution, 1; to be afflicted + (1519), 1; tribulation, 21; trouble, 3;

NAS (45) - affliction, 14; afflictions, 6; anguish, 1; distress, 2; persecution, 1; tribulation, 16; tribulations, 4; trouble, 1;

There's an interesting quote by Papia, one of the Church leaders of the second century. In his *Expositions*, he mentions an oral tradition he allegedly received from the apostle John, regarding what Jesus taught about the expanding Kingdom on earth:

The days are coming when vines will come forth, each with ten thousand boughs; and on a single bough will be ten thousand branches. And indeed, on a single branch will be ten thousand shoots and on every shoot ten thousand clusters; and in every cluster will be ten thousand grapes, and every grape, when pressed, will yield twenty-five measures of wine. And when any of the saints grabs hold of a cluster, another [cluster] will cry out, "I am better, take me, bless the Lord through me" (quoted by Eusebius, Church History, 3.39.1, Fragment 1, 3).

Deuteronomy 16:9–15 depicts a Feast of Ingathering celebration for Israel when *everyone* will be gathered at the end of the harvest season—sons and daughters, servants, priests, strangers, orphans, and widows—to rejoice in the provision of the Lord as well as the work that was done to bring in the harvest. I fully believe this was prophetic of the end of the Judgment Age (8th Day), when everyone will be rejoicing over the bountiful, completed harvest of all people! I believe this Deuteronomy passage corresponds to many other passages, like Ephesians 1:9–10:

> In all wisdom and insight [God] made known to us the mystery of His will, according to His delight which He purposed in Him into an administration (a management of His household affairs) of the *filling of the seasons, that is, heading up all in Christ, both in the heavens and on the earth* (Eph. 1:9–10, MLT).

Even in Isaiah, we see the old order of violence and scattering in the world being turned into the harvesting and gathering theme:

> And they will hammer their *swords into plowshares* and their *spears into pruning hooks*. Nation will not lift up sword against nation, and never again will they learn war (Isaiah 2:4).

A plowshare is a tool used in tilling soil for crops. A pruning hook is used for pruning grape vines and harvesting them, as we see in Isaiah 18:5: "Afore the harvest, when the bud is perfect, and the sour grape is ripening in the flower, he shall both cut off the sprigs with pruning hooks, and take away and cut down the branches" (Isaiah 18:5, KJV). Once, verses like that had no significance to me, now they are an illuminating part of *The Story*!

Jubilee

Though it's a big, beautiful study in itself, it's worth briefly mentioning the Law of Jubilee. Throughout Israel's history, Jubilee happened every 49th* year. Here is the essence of the Law of Jubilee from Leviticus 25:8–13:

> You are also to count off seven Sabbaths of years for yourself…namely, forty-nine years. You shall then sound a ram's horn abroad on the tenth day of the seventh month; on the Day of Atonement (a few days before Feast of Ingathering) you shall sound a

---

* As previously mentioned, there's modern debate among Jews as to whether this event happened on the 49th or 50th year. This might be because Jubilee began a few days after the Jewish New Year every 49th year, but continued throughout the coming year, which could be considered the 50th year.

horn all through your land. You shall thus consecrate the fiftieth year *and proclaim a release through the land to all its inhabitants.* It shall be a Jubilee for you, and each of you shall return to his own property, *and each of you shall return to his family.*

So then, Jubilee was a great time of celebrating. Even more than what is described here, all debts were cancelled, slaves went free, and people were restored to their families and to their own land that they may have had to sell off because of debt or misfortune. Jubilee was not just a fun idea of liberation for the people of Bible times. Certainly it was a prophetic picture of a future reality for all mankind when the last great Jubilee celebration occurs at the end of the Judgment Age. What will all the dancing, laughing, and partying be about? Every kind of debt—to God or man—has been satisfied once and for all. Slaves of sin have been freed forever. Everyone has been fully reunited to their loved ones and families. What a time of rejoicing! In his book, *The Law of Jubilee,* Stephen Jones says:

> Even as Jesus Christ is the central Person of all history, the law of Jubilee is the most fundamental law of all creation. The law of Jubilee is the basis of forgiveness and grace. It is the purpose and goal of the law itself. It compels a climax of earth history and a full end of the dominion of darkness and sin.[57]

Good Fruit is Coming

There's a story of a man who wanted his four sons to learn not to judge things too quickly, so he sent them each, in turn, on a quest to go and observe a certain tree located a distance from home. The first son went in winter, the second in spring, the third in summer, and the fourth in fall. When they had all gone and returned, he called them together to describe what they had seen. As you would expect, they were all in disagreement.

The first son said that the tree looked dead for it was ugly, bent, and barren. The second son said it was covered with green buds and full of promise. The third son said it was laden with such fragrant blossoms that it was the most beautiful tree he'd ever seen. The last son reported that the tree was laden with ripe fruit, full of life and fulfillment!

The man then explained to his sons that they were all right, because they had each seen only one season in the tree's life. He told them that you can't judge a tree—or a person—by only one season. The essence of who they are—where they've come from, what they're learning in the process, and the resulting success, pleasure, joy, and love resulting from that life—can only be measured at the end...when all its seasons are complete.

Is it any wonder the Bible parallels people to trees? I think we've been too quick to judge people based on only one season of their lives. Just like in nature, every tree's growing season is different. For most people who have ever lived, their growing season has either not begun, or it's only in the budding stages. But in some future point in time, everyone will have had the time and opportunity to yield a bountiful crop!

CHAPTER EIGHTEEN

NECESSARY EVIL?

What do we do with the problem of evil? How much power does the dark side really exert over our lives? And in light of the pervasive teaching of eternal separation from God—where evil appears to reign victorious as God loses most of creation from His grip—what possible hope do people in our world have who, by no choice of their own, are its most unfortunate victims? These kinds of crucial questions demand satisfactory answers—if we are ever to deem the character of God worthy of our trust.

Some people are going to read this chapter and perhaps come away feeling more hopeful and illuminated than before. Others are going to read what I have to say and, because of certain filters or distorted beliefs, will perhaps feel angry and even more distrustful of God than before. It is not my intention to cause further damage to anyone's perceptions of God, but I am compelled to share what I now see as the bigger picture—the redemptive and even *ultimately benevolent* purpose of evil in this lifetime.

To start, we're going to explore the problem of evil from a completely different angle. I have come to regard the problem of evil like a tension in a compelling novel, juxtaposed to the ultimate, euphoric resolution. In any good novel, the reader longs to find resolve, but has to wait until the final chapter to see how it is accomplished. In our *Story,* I believe God's expression of love is exponentially expanded, not diminished, through the *necessity of evil*. Evil does not reign supreme or have the final say, but is only a limited, temporary *tool* or a means to an end of a great, full circle, happily ever after.

God Authors (Makes or Generates) Evil

Gak! This suggestion a popular sermon does not make. Undoubtedly, this would not be a popular suggestion in most of today's theological circles. In the minds of most Christians, if you're going to profess that God wants and desperately hopes for all people to be saved, yet His hands are ultimately tied because He's constrained by man's free will, how can we then blame the source of evil upon Him? In such a belief system, evil maintains the upper hand, cannot possibly be God's responsibility, and is ultimately out of His control. Whether we realize it or not, our belief in the ultimate free will of man and the resulting victory cry of evil has reduced our God to a groveling wimp who can do nothing more than work up a little damage control. But that's not accurate. The truth is—as nothing exists outside of God—evil *must be* His doing and He's definitely no wimp (nor vindictive monster). He boldly states to Isaiah (45:7):

> "I form the light, and *create darkness*: I make peace, *and create evil*: I the LORD do all these things" (KJV).

Some people (and many modern translations) will try to explain away this verse, saying that what it really means is that God *allows* evil, not that He actually *creates* it. The Hebrew word used here for *create* (bara) is the same word used in Genesis 1:1, so following their logic we'd have to say that, "in the beginning, God *allowed* the heavens and the earth." Most people who reject the notion that God will save all, and who believe in hell, are still unyielding at this point because they can't reconcile a God who would actually create evil and then let it win out over most of His creation forever. Well, yeah! Can't say I blame them.

Now consider the word, *evil*. The Hebrew word for evil is "ra" and is defined by Strong's (#7451) as "bad, evil." There are many other places throughout Scripture where God takes responsibility for and uses evil: He sends evil spirits to torment people (1 Sam. 16:14–15); He deceives some people in order to purposely lead them astray (1 Kings 22: 20–23, 2 Thess. 2:11); and He sends evil (ra) or disaster upon people (Jer. 6:19).

Many Christians have a hard time accepting these verses at face value because, for centuries, many theologians have distorted Scripture and misinterpreted the character, purpose, and plan of God. They have failed to teach that evil is only a short-term tool for serving a greater purpose of contrasting what is good (to teach us that which we could learn no other way), and revealing God's mercy and His unceasing plan of good for all people. Stumped so far? Keep reading!

God Uses and Coexists With Evil

I have always been taught that God cannot be in the presence of evil nor tolerate it, which is silly really, since He inhabits plenty of Christians in seasons of rebellion and sin. Besides, if God were unable to be in the presence of evil, He would have to completely remove Himself from His creation, since it is permeated by evil, like yeast in dough.

The Bible paints a completely different picture than the recognized view. God interacts and works directly *with* and *through* forces, both evil and good, to accomplish His plans. Perhaps one of the most well-known passages occurs in Job when Satan asks God if he might test Job. They civilly discuss the matter and God gives him permission to test "the most righteous man on the earth" of his day, with many "evils" or calamities.

In 1 Samuel 16, God sends an evil spirit to torment Saul. What is especially interesting about this dynamic is that Saul is "God's anointed," yet the evil spirit tormenting Saul, directed at David, is also God's anointed. This evil spirit in Saul, sent by God, becomes a refining force in David's life, preparing him for leadership as a king. If we believe in a "Plan A" only, we must accept that God anointed Saul, knowing he would give him over to the dark side, for the very purpose of grooming David to be a righteous king through oppression and opposition.

Have you ever noticed that, like David, those most used by God seem to have some of the most pronounced oppression and trials to overcome? These very people are often criticized by their contemporaries as having some hidden sin that God is dealing with. Otherwise, people reason, *why would God let them suffer so*? But looking through history at people like David, Joseph, Job, and Paul, we find a different view of the purpose of suffering and oppression.

In 1 Kings 22, we read something astounding. Beginning in verse 19, "I saw the LORD sitting on His throne, and all the host of heaven standing by Him on His right and on His left." In other parts of Scripture, we find the hosts of heaven on His *left* to be evil spirit-messengers, while the ones on His right are good spirit-messengers. So all of the heavenly hosts are with Him, both evil and good, ready to serve His purpose of deceiving King Ahab in battle. God then asks who will deceive King Ahab for Him, and the text reads (vs. 21–23):

> Then a spirit came forward and stood before the LORD and said, "I will entice him." The LORD said to him, "How?" And he said, "I will go out and be a deceiving spirit in the mouth of all his prophets." Then [God] said, "You are to entice him and also prevail. Go and do so." Now therefore, behold, *the LORD has put a deceiving spirit in the*

mouth of all these your prophets; and the LORD has proclaimed disaster (evil) against you.

Now that we've entertained the notion that God creates, uses, and coexists with evil, let's chip away at the underlying purpose of evil in order to discover just how much power it really has.

Evil is Confined, Temporary, and Purposeful

If you are on your way to discarding the notion of hell, perhaps the above verses actually bring a measure of comfort. I know they do for me. Learning that God is not stumped, trumped, or surprised by evil, that He is actively using it and fully aware of it, and that it does not exist outside His space or confines has continued to give me great comfort and reassurance ever since my realization of it. I've finally connected with the hope and reassurance that the universe is not spinning out of control in the way I had once thought, and that God truly is more powerful and supreme than those in my Christian roots have given Him credit for, out of their misguided, exaggerated reverence for and fear of evil.

So what good could possibly come from evil? What benevolent purpose could it possibly serve in the scope of God's plan? Consider this perspective from the Ancient Hebrew Research Center:

> The Hebrew word for evil in Isaiah 45:7 is "ra" and literally means "bad" and is used consistently as the opposite of "good" (tov in Hebrew). While this sounds odd to most Christians, God did create bad as well as good, just like He also created dark as well as light.
>
> Our western perspective of good and bad is not the same as the eastern/Hebrew perspective. We see everything as good or bad, desiring good and rejecting bad. The eastern mind sees both [forces] as positive and negative. If your life were filled only with good you would not know it, as you can only know good if it is contrasted with bad. If you love ice cream and were able to eat ice cream, and your whole life never tasting anything else, you would not know ice cream tasted good because you had never tasted anything bad. All things have a negative and a positive. One cannot exist without the other. We usually see light as good and darkness as bad. *But if I filled your room with pure light you would be blind, and if I filled your room with pure*

darkness you would again be blind. In order to see, you must have a balance between light and darkness. In order to have a healthy life you must have a balance between good and bad.[58]

Some ancient rabbis claimed that the first thing God does in Genesis is to distinguish between light and dark, good and evil, and throughout the rest of Scripture, He teaches people how to do the same. My friend who is a painter says that if you want to bring light or anything else out in a painting, you put the opposite color next to it. It's the same on the canvass of *His Story*. Evil has a critical role in our universe of revealing to us what is good and noble and just. Without it, you and I could not be able to distinguish what is good. In other words...

- You would not know warmth without cold.

- You would not know light without darkness.

- You would not know relief without pain.

- You would not know satisfaction without hunger.

- You would not know fairness without injustice.

- You would not know mercy without deserved punishment.

- You would not know love without hate or indifference.

- You would not know what you had been saved from without experiencing the depths of your fallen state in this mortal life.

- You would not know life without death.

- You would not come to know the character of God without experiencing what is not the character of God — whether through His adversary, or perhaps through your belief in the once misleading doctrine of hell.

Evil's purpose only makes sense if you understand it in the context of a Father's bigger plan to reveal His character of love and goodness to His children. It was never meant to be a triumphant end of *The Story* but to reveal that which we can learn no other way so that, as we come to spiritual maturity, we might experience true joy, liberation, and be filled to the brim with gratitude. Otherwise, all that we learn about God and His character would be mechanical, flat, and sterile at best.

The Story

Jesus was a storyteller. Almost everything He taught, he illustrated through stories and pictures. It seems to me that the human heart and mind are innately captivated and taught by story. From birth, the love of story is woven into our very DNA. Perhaps this is because the Father is also a great storyteller — a novelist — at heart.

As you may have gathered by now, I regard this *Story* we're living like a great novel. The plot develops through specific characters coming on the scene as they are written in, each playing a unique and crucial role. Indispensable elements include the villain and his accomplices, the Hero and His accomplices, romance, suspense, conflict, unresolved tension, and a grand finale with a happily ever after for all the characters.

Ultimately there is a purpose in this *Story*, laid out for us from the very beginning. There were two trees in the Garden of Eden — the Tree of the *Knowledge of Good AND Evil*, and the Tree of Life. Before we can partake of and fully appreciate the Tree of Life, we must explore the Tree of Knowledge of Good and Evil. After the knowledge of good and evil has run its course, teaching its lessons to humanity, the Tree of Life takes center stage and provides the happily ever after for all. The Tree of Life wins!

Take note of the beauty in the full-circle ending. The Tree of Life opens *The Story* in Genesis 2, and the Tree of Life closes it in Revelation 22.

> On either side of the river was the Tree of Life, bearing twelve kinds of fruit, yielding its fruit every month; and the leaves of the tree were for the healing of the nations. *There will no longer be any curse...* (Rev. 22:2–3).

In this happily ever after scene, I believe the Tree of Life is Jesus, the leaves of the tree are those working with Him to bring His healing to the nations.* Each month they are bearing fruit, bringing in the harvest of the rest of mankind into "the city" (Kingdom of God) to wash their robes. Throughout *The Story*, we see humanity making a full circle journey from Life, to death and separation, back to Life.

I realize that, while this is a good start of an explanation of evil, it does not soften the blow for those living in the worst of conditions or

---

* Both symbols similar to, "I am the Vine, you are the branches..." (John 15:5).

oppression now. I still have my own unanswered questions about why some people have it so hard in this life and it often doesn't seem fair, even in light of the end of *The Story*. I have often asked God, "Why *this* way? Why so much hate, and suffering and evil, even in light of Your plan. Wasn't there another way?"

I can't say if it was God or not, but in my spirit, I have often sensed these words:

> "This is the way to the greatest joy for all. By the end of *The Story*, there will not be one complaint."

Though I can't possibly grasp the depth of this message now or sufficiently explain it in light of the suffering of the world, my grieving spirit has been put at modest ease for now because I believe the hope and promise of these words with all my heart.

If God creates and uses evil, as the Bible suggests, is there also sufficient evidence within Scripture that He is more powerful than evil? Is there evidence of His having complete, sovereign control over His creation in such a way that it cannot be interrupted, thwarted, usurped, or changed by the power of evil or human "free will?" Let's find out.

CHAPTER NINETEEN

WHAT GOD WANTS, GOD GETS

For years, my husband was moderately frustrated with Christianity and the Bible. Since he spent most of his life as a sweet, compliant missionary kid, I don't think he would have readily admitted this out loud to very many people. But while we were dating, I remember him expressing to me that he struggled at a deep level with the character of God, as portrayed by his lifelong version of faith. When I asked him why, our conversation went something like this.

"It feels like we humans are really just puppets."

"What do you mean? Don't we have a choice to love God or not?"

"That's just it. I didn't even ask to be here and I have to make a choice. And if I choose wrong or don't choose at all, I'll forever be punished. And while it's great for me, since I happened to be born into a family that taught me about Jesus, what about all those billions of people who have never heard about Him? Or what about those who did hear but, out of no fault of their own, couldn't connect the dots to 'make a decision' for Him? They didn't ask to be here either, especially not in the condition they were born into, and now they're going to be penalized forever for not believing? Where's the love and mercy in that?"

As I look back, I believe God was planting seeds of doubt in my husband's heart to receive a truer understanding at a later time. Through the years of our marriage since, he has been the one to question things that didn't add up long before I did. In fact, I used to shoot down many of his honest questions with pat evangelical platitudes. But now I see that God initiated the process so that someday we would both be ready to search for more solid answers than the ones we'd been offered all our lives.

A Perception Overhaul

Nothing has impacted our lives with a sense of peace like the discovery of God's ALL-powerful, boundless, intentional, fully benevolent plan for His creation. Throughout my own previous journey, I proclaimed God was 'mighty to save,' like I was taught to do in song and church, but come to find out, it was merely half-hearted lip service. God was all-powerful *until* I got to the problem of evil and the obstacle of human will. In that old belief system, these two forces usurped God's ultimate power, will, and control over His creation. No wonder I was insecure and stressed out all the time. In the subconscious recesses of my mind, evil was winning the war. The hardness of the human heart and the power of free will were more prevailing and determinate than God's loving heart and will. Creation was spinning out of control and all God could do, I subconsciously thought, was to stand back with His hands tied, putting out fires and hoping He could stay on top of them enough to salvage something before the end. At last, He could contain the rest of all that evil in hell, after saving a precious few.

Now how could I—or why would I—trust my existence or future into the hands of a god like that? Such a god (and his world) was not safe! Such theology only bred serious control issues of trying to run my own life (and the lives of my kids) and to chart my own destiny. As mentioned earlier, the prevalent views of God in today's mainstream Church logically leads to the conclusion that He is either too mean or too weak to get what He wants, what He plans, and what He wills.

What does God want? He's made it clear throughout Scripture:

God wills that none should perish and all should repent (2 Peter 3:9, KJV).

God wills all people to be saved (1 Tim. 2:3-4, KJV).

God wills that NOT ONE would be lost—and that includes everyone (John 3:35; 6:39, KJV).

God wills that His Kingdom fill the earth, and that His will be done by all (Matt. 6:10; Dan. 2:35).

God has declared that every knee will bow to Him, and every tongue will confess Him as Lord and give Him praise (Rom. 14:11, Phil. 2:10).*

I think it's silly to suggest, as the skeptic would have you believe, that this praise is coerced or that people would actually praise God on their way to hell. Praise is joyful worship and adoration. False worship would be nothing more than hypocrisy, something God rejects:

"Rightly did Isaiah prophesy of you hypocrites, as it is written: 'This people honors me with their lips, but their heart is far away from

---

* Isaiah 45:23 also says that "every tongue will swear allegiance to God."

me. But in vain do they worship me, teaching as doctrines the precepts of men.'" (Mark 7:6-7).

God only accepts true worship and praise overflowing from changed hearts filled with gratitude and belief. Notice also that "this people" (His people) are accused of teaching doctrines and precepts of men. It seems obvious to me that any doctrine that teaches anything less than God willing and attaining the salvation of all should be on that list.

What About Free Will?

In my opinion, one of the most damaging and senseless doctrines of the modern Church — after hell — is that of "unlimited free will." You will not find one ounce of support scripturally that people have "free will" in the way it's taught today. Free will implies that man can freely choose and alter his own destiny and that of others, even against the will, desire, and plan of God. This notion is about as possible as that of a two-year-old electing himself as President and setting up office. A two-year-old isn't even capable of knowing what his needs are, let alone the needs and best interest of a country. And even the President, who should have the most "free will" of anyone based on position, has very little control over the country or the world affairs (or often times even himself or his family).

Think about it, if free will truly exists the way we teach it, then we have many big problems on our hands. Other than what we have already mentioned of tying God's hands, it would also mean that people actually have the ability to ruin the ultimate destiny of others.

I fully agree that man does have a will and the ability to act on it. I also agree that the behaviors of others certainly affect us and can even appear for a season to have hindered our good. It's the "free" I take issue with. In order for people to be judged fairly in a world of genuine free will, a level playing field would be imperative for all humanity. In other words, we could not be judged fairly unless we all had the same choices available to us.

For instance, did you choose your nationality, gender, personality, skin color, genes, birth date and place, family, or parents? Isn't your supposed free will influenced by your culture, peers, religious affiliation, health, education, experiences, and life circumstances? Do people choose to get cancer, get hit by a drunk driver, exist in continual starvation and poverty, get abused by parents, die before they feel ready, or even be born? Does an orphan choose to grow up in a Hindu society, abandoned and mistreated by everyone, only to die without ever experiencing love, comfort, contentment, or hearing the name of Jesus? Does a happy, well-adjusted person who has no immediate unmet needs choose to grow up in a loving, nurturing family? Free will is nothing more than an illusion. There is no *free* in free will. Even the reason that we love God is completely outside of ourselves. His love is the first cause from which our love springs.

We love Him, *because* He first loved us (I John 4:19, KJV).

In church circles where people are claiming they "chose Jesus" or "came to Christ" (presumably of their own free will), the Scriptures paint a different picture. "You did not choose Me, but I chose you" (John 15:16). Our real first choice actually begins *after* our eyes have been opened and our heart has received a deposit of belief through an encounter with Jesus.

Because of the Creator's determined plan that trumps the will of the inferior creature, even the bad intentions and behaviors of others will most certainly be limited and worked out for our good. Sovereign will is one of the most comforting realizations I've ever had. If good hasn't resulted yet, it's only because the Story hasn't played out long enough.

One of my favorite biblical examples is OT Joseph. Sold against his "free will" by his ill-intentioned, murderous brothers, Joseph, the special son of his father headed into Egypt in chains of slavery. Goodbye childhood dreams. Goodbye goals and plans. And that was just the beginning of a long line of people who had it out for him, even though he did nothing to deserve their treacherous treatment. Many years later, after watching how his life unfolded, what was Joseph's response to those times when his life was seemingly ruined at the hands of others?

As for you [my brothers], you meant evil against me, but God meant it for good in order to bring about this present result, to preserve many people's lives (Gen. 50:20).

So where does man's will end and the sovereign will of God begin? Just how much power does man have to seize control over his own life or the lives of others? Here is where a Hebrew perspective on Scripture will once again bring great illumination.

In the beginning of *The Story*, in Genesis 1:26–28, God established something called the "Dominion Mandate."* This Mandate loaned mankind a big property to exercise authority over — the earth! In the days of Adam and the OT, the earth meant "dry land," (as opposed to seas) and people received literal pieces of that earth, called "allotments" to take care of as part of the Dominion Mandate. Only the priests who served in God's Temple courts did not receive allotments of literal land, because the Lord was their allotment or inheritance.

Applying our Hebrew understanding of repeated patterns on different levels, the Dominion Mandate was also a symbolic allotment of authority that each person has been given on this earth to impact or effect change on their environment and the lives of others. Though mistakenly referred to as "one's free will," it is actually more like "one's fenced yard."

In a very simplistic explanation, think of it like this. God is a landowner, but He needs people to tend it, so He doles out allotments or parcels of His land. To one person he gives a tiny little garden plot for growing a few veggies (think of an orphan or poor person with little influence or control over their circumstances). Another gets a couple acres and can cultivate crops and build a house. But then another gets a 500-acre orchard with ten different kinds of fruit to cultivate for profit, and dozens of workers to supervise (think a governing official or the pastor of a large church). As you can see, each of these has a quite different amount of God-given control and influence over their environment.

To each land tenant, God imparts a different set of instructions on how He wants it taken care of, giving each tenant a *limited* choice of complying with the requests or not. But in no way can the tenant venture off his God-assigned parcel to take over other land. He or she is confined to take care of the plot (dominion) that has been given. This dominion will affect those in close proximity or under the "employment" of the landowner, but it cannot go one step beyond. Consider the following verses:

Matt. 25:14-15: "For it is just like a man about to go on a journey, who called his own servants and entrusted his possessions to them. To one he gave five talents (the big orchard), to another, two (couple of acres), and to

---

* There is a movement in our day by the name of "Dominion Mandate." This is not the same as what I am presenting here. This is the Hebrew perspective on one's control or power over his or her environment or God-given sphere of influence.

another, one (small garden plot), *each according to his own power;* and he
went on his journey" (MLT).

Luke 12:48: "From everyone who has been given much [dominion],
much will be required; and to whom they entrusted much, of him they will
ask all the more."

Jeremiah 27:5: "I have made the earth with man...by My great strength,
and by My stretched-out arm, and I have given it to whom it hath been
right in Mine eyes" (YLT).

John 19:11: "Jesus answered [Pontius Pilate], 'You would have no
power over me if it were not given to you from above'" (NIV).

Daniel 4:35: "But He does according to His will in the host of heaven
and among the inhabitants of earth; and no one can ward off His hand or
say to Him, 'What have You done?'"

This is a very simple overview of a foundational Hebrew teaching of
Scripture. In *The Story*, each person is given a predetermined scope of
dominion or influence with which they either reveal the glory of God in a
positive way, or they provide the contrast in a negative way. Either way,
they can reach no further than their allotted influence.

Pharaoh was granted the power to impact millions of lives in a
negative way, but so was Moses in a positive way. Both of them operated
under the sovereign control of God to accomplish a part of His plan that
will ultimately work to the good of all, not the damnation of most. Though
everything written in this part of *The Story* is not good, God promises that
everything will work together for good eventually. This is the whole point
of Romans 9:14-24. Paul points out that God is truly fair because He will
ultimately have mercy on those who are intentionally put in roles as
adversaries, acting out evil by design for a temporary purpose. Remember,
you can't have a hero in the story without a villain:

> What shall we say then? *There is no injustice with God, is there? May
> it never be!* ...For the Scripture says to Pharaoh, "For this very purpose
> I raised you up, *to demonstrate my power in you*, and that my name
> might be proclaimed throughout the whole earth." So then He has
> mercy on whom He desires, and He hardens whom He desires. You

---

* Though most versions render this word "ability," the Greek word is "dunamis"
which literally means *strength* or *power*. Out of 116 NT uses, it is translated as power
95 times, and the other 11 times randomly as *miracles, wealth,* and *ability*.

will say to me then, *"Why does He still find fault? For who resists His will?"* On the contrary, who are you, O man, who answers back to God? The thing molded will not say to the molder, "Why did you make me like this," will it? Or does not the potter have a right over the clay, *to make from the same lump one vessel for honorable use and another for dishonor?* What if God, although willing to demonstrate His wrath and to make His power known, *endured with much patience vessels of wrath prepared for destruction?* And He did so to make known the riches of His glory* upon vessels of mercy, which He prepared beforehand for glory, even us, whom He also called, not from among Jews only, but also from among Gentiles (non-Jews).

Right there Paul explains that it is the contrast of roles in *The Story* that reveals God's glory, but He also makes it clear throughout all his letters that God will not be unjust about it—the "vessels of dishonor" will also be saved.† The "vessels of honor" only receive their calling and awakening ahead of the rest, but they will also be given the joy and responsibility of "overcoming" the resistance others with loving service in coming ages.

The most important point to glean from all of this is that God is not sleeping, tied up, caught off guard, or incapacitated in the face of evil. He has taken responsibility for evil as a *temporary tool* for a greater good and He is completely sovereign over it. Evil will not reign victorious in the end. Until a person grasps and internalizes this, there will be no rational or satisfactory way for evil to be explained or made sense of. "Have you not heard? Long ago I did it, from ancient times I planned it" (Isaiah 37:26).

Author and artist Joni Eareckson Tada, paralyzed from the neck down ever since an accident in her teens in the 70s, once said:

One day God will close the curtain on evil and, with it, all suffering and sorrow. Until then, I'll keep remembering something Steve Estes once told me as he rested his hand on my wheelchair: "God permits what He hates, to accomplish what He loves." I can

---

* This Greek word is "apoleia," from *apollumi*, meaning a temporary loss or destruction. See the section, "Common Misunderstandings of Scripture" to find more insight on this Greek word.

† Rom. 5:18, 8:32, 11:15, 14:10–12; 1 Cor. 3:15, 15:22–23, 15:54; 2 Cor. 5:14–19; Gal. 3:8; Eph. 1:9–11; Phil. 2:9–11; Col. 1:15–20; 1 Tim. 2:3–6, 4:9–11; Titus 2:11; Heb. 2:8.

smile knowing God is accomplishing what He loves in my life—Christ in me, the hope of glory.[59]

I also love how the apostle Paul says it in the more literal rendition of 2 Corinthians 4:17: "For the momentary lightness of our affliction is bringing forth an age-enduring weight of glory to us beyond measure" (MLT).

Earlier, I mentioned the friend of mine who has collected forty-some pages of verses on God's absolute sovereign power and control over His creation—both the good and the evil. If you still believe in God damning most of His creatures forever, these verses rather paint Him as a power-hungry monster instead of a loving, sovereign God who will overcome evil with good. This is probably why the modern teachings of Christianity seem to ignore so many verses where God takes credit for everything, both good and bad. They don't have a satisfying answer for how God could possibly be good while hiding truth from the very people He's going to hold responsible and send to hell.

However, if you believe in God reconciling all people by the end of the ages, as presented in Scripture, then these verses suddenly bring great illumination and comfort in knowing that *nothing* happens outside of God's ultimate plan of good for all His creation. There is nothing my kids, my family, my enemies, my friends, I, or anyone else can do that is not part of God's overarching plan for the good of them and for me. Let the comfort of this wash over you in that, every intention, allowance, and act of God is completely good in His final chapter, and that you and I can let go and let God run the universe without living in fear or insecurity. Check out some of these OT verses:

Deut. 32:39: "See now that I, I am He, and there is no god besides Me; It is I who put to death and give life. I have wounded and it is I who heal, and there is no one who can deliver from My hand."

Job 23:13: "He stands alone, and who can oppose Him? He does whatever He pleases" (NIV).

Job 42:2: "I know that You can do all things; no plan of Yours can be thwarted."

Psalm 135:6: "Whatever the LORD pleases, He does, in heaven and in earth, in the seas and in all deeps."

Proverbs 16:4, 9, 33; 19:21: "The Lord has made everything for His own purpose, even the wicked for the day of evil. ...The mind of man plans his way, but the Lord directs his steps. ...The lot is cast into the lap, but its every decision is from the Lord. ...Many plans are in a man's heart, but the counsel of the LORD will stand."

Eccl. 7:13–14: "Consider the work of God, for who is able to straighten what He has bent? In the day of prosperity be happy, but in the day of adversity consider—God has made the one as well as the other."

Isaiah 14: 24, 26–27: "Thus says the LORD of Hosts, 'In which manner I have said, so it will be; and in which manner I have deliberated, so it shall remain... *This is the plan which the LORD planned for all the inhabitable world.* And this is the high hand upon all the nations. For what the holy God planned, who shall efface? And who shall turn his high hand?'" (Septuagint).

Isaiah 42:24–25: "Who handed Jacob over to become loot, and Israel to the plunderers? Was it not the LORD, against whom we have sinned? For they would not follow his ways; they did not obey his law. So he poured out on them his burning anger, the violence of war. It enveloped them in flames,* yet they did not understand; it consumed them, but they did not take it to heart" (NIV).

Isaiah 54:16: "... And I [God] have created the destroyer to ruin."

Jer. 5:22: "The waves may toss and roar, but they can never pass the boundaries I set" (NLT).

Jer. 18:11: ... "Behold, I frame evil against you: and devise a device against you..." (KJV).

Lam. 3:37–38: "Who is there who speaks and it comes to pass, unless the Lord has commanded it? Is it not from the mouth of the Most High that *the evil things and the good* go forth?"†

Would Free Will Choose God?

Human pride is startling. To think that we could or would make the first move toward God on our own is not taught anywhere in Scripture. We are invited, and the variable is in *when* we respond to that invitation,

---

* Notice that Israel is depicted in flames and being consumed by burning fire. As covered earlier, this is clearly the nonliteral process God uses for testing and refining throughout Scripture. Its ultimate end is for purifying and for good.

† NASB prints "both good and ill" but they use the more correct (from Hebrew), italicized text in the footnotes.

not *if*. Earlier I listed a few scriptures that showed the first move is God's, not ours (Psalm 53:2–3; Isaiah 53:6, 65:1).

Remember too that Israel did not—could not—make the first move to get out of Egypt. Every single Israelite was delivered out of Egypt by powerful acts of God when they were too weak and completely helpless to save themselves. In fact, four times in Exodus 13 the following words are repeated: "...for with a powerful hand the LORD brought you out of Egypt." Israel is a macrocosm—a pattern—for each of us. Every person who has ever lived is helplessly enslaved to sin and death with no hope of escape. It is truly a death sentence for *all*. But God revealed through Moses that He would send a Savior to rescue us with mighty acts, through no will or might of our own:

> "I am the LORD, and I will bring you out from under the burdens of the Egyptians (law, sin, and death), and I will deliver you from their bondage. I will also redeem you with an outstretched arm and with great judgments. Then I will take you for My people, and I will be your God; and you shall know that I am the LORD your God..." (Ex. 6:6–7).

In the NT Scriptures, the word "church" is literally translated, "called out."* In other words, the NT believers took up the baton of being the ones *spiritually* "called out of Egypt." That word should never have been translated to be associated with a building or institution, but rather a type of people who would be, like Israel, given faith in this age and follow in the footsteps of Christ for the benefit of the rest of humanity.

A great example of an individual being *called out* in his season—coming to belief by no willpower, free will, or even desire of his own—is the apostle Paul. There was no moment of self-induced inspiration or desire for this "chief of sinners," persecutor, murderer, and hater of those who followed Jesus. Paul was a prototype of all people in that he was sought out by God and given belief through an unexpected encounter with Jesus. Yet Paul says in his own words that he is "a pattern" for how it will happen to everyone when it is also "their season to grow" (1 Cor. 3:6) by the hand of God:

---

* The Greek word is "ekklesia." Ek (out) klesia (called).

I have gratitude to the One empowering me, Christ Jesus our Lord, that He leads me faithful, placing me into service even though I was formerly blasphemous, and a persecutor, and arrogant. *But I was shown mercy seeing that, being ignorant, I acted in unbelief;* but the grace of our Lord more than super-abounded with belief and love of the One in Christ Jesus. Trustworthy is the word and worthy of all acceptance; that Christ Jesus came into the world to deliver sinners, whom I am foremost. But because of this I was shown mercy, that in me, Jesus Christ should be displaying foremost all patience, *for setting a pattern* for the ones being about to believe upon him for eonian life. (1 Tim. 1:12–16, MLT).

Think about it. If Paul qualified for salvation in the midst of his unbelief, admittedly from ignorance, who in the world will fail to qualify? Paul knew about believers. He knew about Jesus. But he was ignorant of the truth because he had not encountered it personally until Jesus sought him out.

It is worth mentioning in order to understand some of his teachings that Paul also "qualified" throughout his remaining life as a "firstborn" or "chosen" (barley) son for his single-hearted, faithful obedience to the mission he was given. This is why Paul talked about such things as "finishing the race" and "not being disqualified" (for the blessing of the Mosaic Covenant), rather than making a case for him being afraid of "losing his salvation." Otherwise many things Paul said would indicate (and have been interpreted as) a salvation of works and a very conditional God. If you read Philippians 3, you can easily spot what I'm saying. Paul had his eye on qualifying for the rewards of the chosen in the first resurrection. Here's a little key in verse 11:

...in order that I may *attain* to the resurrection from the dead.

Why would Paul have to work to attain resurrection if he was saved — which he clearly was? As it happens, translators did not translate "resurrection" properly. The accurate translation is "out-resurrection," which is only used a couple other times in the NT in relation to Jesus's resurrection ahead of others. I believe this speaks of the *first resurrection* (mentioned in Hebrews and Revelation), which we already discussed in chapter 11.

Spiritually firstborn children emerge from among those who are "called out." It is not about chronological birth order, which was the pattern established in the OT when God frequently "chose" subsequent sons in a family to receive the firstborn birthright—the responsibility and blessing.

Firstborn sons—then and now—were given a high place of honor in Eastern cultures because they "opened the womb" (Ex. 13:2, Septuagint) for future offspring, a precursor for thriving bloodline and prosperity. They were also endowed with the birthright, which implicated that in the absence of the father (death or temporary separation), the firstborn son acted in the stead of the father with the same authority. He was considered to be the *same as the father*. Perhaps that will shed some light on some of Jesus's teachings, such as, "if you have seen me, you have seen the Father" (John 14:9).

Spiritually speaking, "firstborn sons and daughters," continue to open the spiritual womb for all humanity—the birthing canal of new life—and to shine a light on the path of salvation for the world. This is an amplification of what Jesus began on earth and I believe it will continue into coming ages.

Jesus left no doubt about finding all His lost sons and sheep (people like Paul, and you and me), and "dragging" them into the fold. In John 12:32, we read: "And I, if I am lifted up from the earth, *will draw all men to Myself.*" That pretty much covers everybody. But even more interesting is the Greek word for *draw*. It is "helkuo" and according to Strong's (#1670) means, "to drag or impel by inward power." This word is used elsewhere in the NT in reference to dragging a net of fish, implying a deliberate, compelling force, even if the fish are not all in agreement about being caught. Jesus is trying to get a message across here. Not only are we blind, and deaf, and dumb as sheep, we would never find our own way home and must be *dragged* home. If God is truly fair, He must drag all lost sheep home, not just a few, which is exactly what He promised to do.

Can Clay Act Independently of the Potter?

In his article, "The Potter has Power," Clyde Pilkington, Jr., shares:

In the Scriptures, Father is spoken of as a Potter, an analogy that places great emphasis upon His ever-present hand, and His well-designed plan in our lives. The Potter always has complete power over His clay. He designs and makes His clay-creation, according to His Own masterful plan. He is active in His craftsmanship, with hands-on skill.

In Jeremiah 18:1-6, God called Jeremiah "down to the Potter's house." It is critically important for the believer to "go down to the Potter's house." It is only here that we will ever gain the true reality of the divine perspective. When Jeremiah went down to the Potter's house, there he saw the Potter fashioning "a work on the wheels."

Of course Jeremiah could clearly see the clay for what it was — just passive material, soil from the earth, completely powerless over its own design and destiny. It was the Potter, and the Potter *alone*, Who was steady at His important work.

Whatever is made out of the clay on the Potter's wheel is totally the responsibility of the Potter. Clay does not have the power to make itself into anything. Nor does it have the power to resist the Potter's purposes.

After this, Jeremiah saw that the vessel was "marred." But do not miss this! It was "marred in the hand of the potter ..." Of course it was! The clay can't mar itself! If the clay vessel is "marred," it is the Potter's responsibility. He is the One Who mars the vessel; it is His doing. Jeremiah also saw a process of the Potter making the clay over again into another vessel. Clearly and simply, any vessel is what it is because of the Potter.*

We are in the hand of the Potter. He is making us. Regardless of the stage of the clay's formation on the wheel, it is always in the Potter's hand. What peace we have when we truly consider these words. It matters not what our lot in life may be; what our circumstances may be like — each of His vessels rests ever secure in His able hands.

Beloved of the Potter, do not be discouraged with His loving work of wisdom and do not fret. Trust Him implicitly. Patiently wait upon Him as He does His life-long work on you. You are His workmanship,

---

* Remember, a pot is never complete or fit for use until it's been put through fire.

and He alone is responsible. He is absolutely skillful and faithful and He will accomplish His work—you—to supreme perfection! His work is larger and grander than we can see from the vantage of the spinning wheel. You are who you are because God has made you that way. He is steadily and devotedly working, making you the vessel of His own choosing.[60]

In the "Love Never Fails for Any or All" (chapter 11), we looked at the laws of liability. Since God is the one liable for the marring of the clay in His hands, and since it is He who put the tree in the middle of the Garden and did not put a safety fence around it, by His own laws of liability He must take responsibility for reforming His clay vessels so that they might become beautiful and useful. It was His plan from the beginning to form man out of dust, add a little water, and voila—moldable (and mar-able) clay! Since then, He has been reforming and refining that clay, and someday, after being fired and purified, the clay will be transformed into permanent vessels fit for service in the Kingdom! Jeremiah says of that day, "I will give them a heart to know me, for I am the LORD. And they will be My people, and I will be their God, for they will return to Me with their whole heart" (Jer. 24:7).

All in God

Hopefully now you have a better view of God's loving control over His creation, and His purpose of evil. Perhaps this will instill a great newfound joy in your heart as you realize that in God's grand *Story*, nothing will be lost. Every day I am smitten and peacefully released from my life burdens by this wonderful truth, carrying within me a renewed joy that those who are dealt a bad lot in life will one day experience complete restoration through a new and better life.

I mentioned earlier that in ancient Jewish teachings, all people are considered to be "divine sparks out of the Fire (God)," inherently bearing His spiritual DNA. As trillions of cells make up a human body, each and every person ever born reveals a tiny aspect of God's being and nature. In the Jewish teaching, still evident in Scripture, everything is out of God, and God fills everything:

Eph. 4:6: "One God and Father of all, who is over all, and through all, and in all."

Rom. 11:36: "For from Him and through Him and to Him are all things."

Each of us is a drop in a vast ocean, expressing part of this living, dynamic Body of Living Water. When you realize that God fills everything and nothing is outside of Him, suddenly life around you becomes less dangerous, more hopeful, promising, and beautiful. The skies look bluer, the trees look greener, every single person you meet is more valued—even the filth and pollution is less oppressive, and darkness is less suffocating.

Thank goodness I don't have to try to play God anymore. I can completely trust Him with my kids, my marriage, my finances, my health, and my future. I can simply trust Him in all things because His unchangeable plan has already determined that everything will work out in the end. In other words, if it hasn't worked out yet, it's not the end.

We've almost made it through our journey of Hebrew perspectives on the Scriptures, but there are a couple more vital stops we need to make. We can't forget to address one of the biggest objections people bring up when you tell them hell is merely a man-made doctrine…

What about Lazarus and the rich man?

CHAPTER TWENTY

LAZARUS AND THE RICH MAN

One of the questions that's likely been niggling at you while reading this book is, *"What about Lazarus and the rich man?"* After first inquiring about Hitler, this is usually one of the next objections people raise while trying to dismantle (or defend) the notion of hell. In fact, this parable is the Bible passage most often used by pastors and other proponents to prove that Jesus taught of hell. Just like everyone else, I've always heard that this is a literal story about a man who traded heaven for hell over his love of riches, and yet there is nothing in the story to indicate his rejection of Jesus. Supposedly, it's a picture of some rich man down in hell, suffering unending torments, while Lazarus and Abraham are in paradise looking on at his suffering and unable to do anything about it.

There are actually several significant points in this Luke 16 passage that completely and utterly disprove that this is a literal account of someone down in the eternal fiery flames of hell.

Evidence for a Parable

Let's consider a few elements that make this story what it is — a *parable* with symbolic meaning.

1. It's included with other parables. This story (Luke 16:19-31) falls immediately after six consecutive *parables* and contains the same theme as the one just before it — unfaithful stewardship. Repetition of an underlying theme or message is a normal pattern for grouped parables, just as we saw earlier from Luke 15 in the three consecutive parables describing the fates for the lost sheep, the lost coin, and the lost son.

When I read this story of Lazarus, it seems obvious to me that the "voice" is that of storytelling. *"Now there was a rich man, and he habitually dressed in purple and fine linen, joyously living in splendor every day...."* It could have just as easily began, "Once upon a time..." Also, notice that the previous parable started much the same way, *"There was a rich man who had a manager..."*

2. *It was a crowd; hence it was a parable.* There are times when Jesus is *only* speaking to His disciples and then times when He is speaking to both His disciples and the crowds. Jesus is clearly speaking to a crowd here (Pharisees, sinners, tax collectors, and disciples), and the NT writers make the point: "All these things Jesus spoke to the crowds in parables, and *He did not speak to them without a parable*" (Matt. 13:34).

3. *According to Jesus, neither Abraham nor Lazarus could be "in heaven."* In John 3:13, Jesus said, "No one has ascended into heaven, but He who descended from heaven: the Son of Man." Jesus squarely shoots down any chance that anyone has gone into the heavenly realm yet, except Himself.* Some people try to make a case for an in-between state of consciousness, but in Acts 2:25-36, Peter addresses this very idea with the men of Jerusalem. He plainly states that David died, was buried, and is still dead to this day, awaiting the resurrection, and that only Jesus was resurrected to a conscious state.

4. *It contains significant historical elements.* As we've covered, the Jews had never been presented with the notion of hell or everlasting torment before, since neither the Greek nor the Hebrew OT Scriptures taught it. However, if we put on some Hebrew lenses, suddenly this passage is loaded with references to historical concepts that the Jewish people were quite familiar with—it would have made sense to them as a parable. Here are the noteworthy Jewish elements:

a. *The rich man:* He's dressed in purple and fine linen, and has five brothers. Throughout Scripture, purple and fine linen are signs of nobility, royalty, and priesthood. Who could be considered more royal stock than the Jews, descendants of their ancestor Judah? In Genesis 49:8-12, Jacob gives his blessing to his twelve sons, and he names Judah as the *ruler* over all twelve tribes, and Judah is the son designated to receive all the promises bestowed to Abraham:

> "Judah, your brothers shall praise you; your hand shall be on the neck of your enemies; your father's sons shall bow down to you. ...The scepter shall not depart from Judah, nor the ruler's staff from

---

* Cross reference Ecclesiastes 9:5; Psalm 6:5; 115:17 also show that they could not have been in conscious form in some paradise, a notion we will explore in chapter 21, "Redefining the Soul."

between his feet, until Shiloh comes, and to him shall be the obedience of the peoples."

As a result, the Jews (a.k.a. Judahites) were rich in prophetic promises, having received firsthand ruling authority (dominion) and Torah from God. And can you guess how many full brothers (sons of Leah) Judah had? Five!*

b. Lazarus: I used to think that the Lazarus in this story was perhaps the same Lazarus from the NT, but it never quite made sense because nothing about this story is connected to the description of the Lazarus that Jesus hung out with and raised from the dead—not to mention Lazarus was no longer dead. Plus, how many of the crowds do you think knew the NT Lazarus enough that he would make it into a crowd-teasing parable by name? Likely he was known by few. Then who was *this* Lazarus?

The name *Lazarus* is the Greek translation of the Hebrew name, Eliezer, and…what a coincidence! There just so happened to be an Eliezer who was the faithful financial manager and servant of Abraham's household in the OT (Gen. 15:2). Wow, what are the chances that Jesus would bring up both Abraham and an Eliezer in the same parable—unless He was speaking about *thee Abraham* and *thee Eliezer,* prominent figures of the OT, in order to speak to the Jews from out of the well-known traditions of their own history.

c. Eating crumbs: Lazarus was depicted as eating the crumbs that fell from the rich man's table. Do you really think a person could survive on crumbs…or might this convey something else? In another passage, Jesus portrayed the Gentiles eating the crumbs under the table of the Jews (Mark 7:24–30). In context, this meant getting the meager leftovers of the teachings of God from the Jews. Well guess what? Abraham's servant Eliezer was a Gentile! Already, quite a different story comes into view.

I believe the point of the crumbs in this parable was that Eliezer, representing the Gentiles (non-Jews), only received crumbs of truth from Judah's rich banqueting table because Judah was not faithful with God's household riches (teachings) as Eliezer had been with Abraham's household riches. The rich man actually called Abraham his "father" three times. Remember the catchy little tune from your childhood,

---

* Genesis 30:20.

"Father Abraham"? Well, Abraham really was a patriarch or earthly father of the Jews; he was the great grandfather of Judah. All Jews were of direct descent, so calling him "father" was appropriate. Abraham, in turn, calls the rich man "my son" in the parable.

d. *Hades.* The rich man and Lazarus both die. Note that NIV and KJV are the only two versions that report that the rich man goes to *hell*, while all the other versions call it Hades or the place of the dead (which is true to the Greek). In other words, the Greek word used here is different than *Gehenna*, the Greek word translated "hell" in the other gospel passages. Lazarus is then said to have gone "into Abraham's bosom." According to Wikipedia:

> The phrase "Bosom of Abraham" refers to the place of comfort in Sheol (Greek: Hades) where the Jews said the righteous dead (unconscious) awaited Judgment Day. The word found in the Greek text for "bosom" is *kolpos*, meaning "lap." This relates to the Second Temple period practice of reclining and eating meals in proximity to other guests, the closest of whom physically was said to lie on the bosom (chest) of the host. It was also considered by the Jews of old to be a mark of special honor and favor for one to be allowed to lie in the bosom of the master of the feast (John 13:23), and it is by this illustration that they pictured the next world. They conceived of the reward of the righteous dead as a sharing in a banquet given by Abraham, "the father of the faithful" (Matthew 8:11), and of the highest form of that reward as lying in "Abraham's Bosom." ...Abraham Geiger suggested that the *parable of Lazarus* in Luke 16 preserved a Jewish legend and that *Lazarus represented Abraham's servant Eliezer...*[61]

Conversations Between Heaven and Hell?

If Abraham and Lazarus were in heaven and the rich man was in hell, one must conclude that the redeemed will be in close proximity and communication with those in hell and that those in paradise will be watching the tortured, agonized faces of their loved ones as they writhe in unrelenting pain. Can you imagine the joy and happiness the saints will have while viewing those nearby in agony for all eternity? Perhaps, if this parable were taken literally and with a modern Christian flair, you would get to see your unsaved father, mother, sister, brother, son, daughter, wife, or husband experiencing the reality of an eternal fire without any relief in sight, while you bask in the comforts, relaxation, and happiness of Abraham's bosom.

And what does the rich man ask of Lazarus? It's not to drag him out of the fire, but simply to take a drop of cold water and put on his tongue. Now, if the rich man were in a place like the imagined hell, a drop of water wouldn't do a bit of good for him. The water, if literal, would turn into steam before it even felt wet. And have you ever asked yourself how a fire could burn somebody endlessly, without consuming them?

I can only speculate what the drop of water means, but possibly the rich man (Jews) are depicted as asking the faithful, believing Gentiles for just a taste of the reward they missed out on—a whole age of drinking in the Living Water for which they had waited for and thirsted for so long.

Judah: Heir of Abraham

The parable of Lazarus and the Rich Man seems to expound on the parable before it about an unfaithful steward of an estate who had mishandled his master's money (Luke 16:1-13). Using the relationship between Abraham and his faithful household steward, this parable was told to further illustrate the rewards for proper stewardship as well as consequences for unfaithful stewardship of a master's household. It was specifically aimed at the Jews of Jesus's day. Consider Genesis 15:2-4:

> Abram said, "O Lord GOD, what will You give me, since I am childless, and *the heir of my house is Eliezer of Damascus? ...Since You have given no offspring to me, one born in my house is my heir.'* Then behold, the word of the LORD came to him, saying, 'This man will not be your heir; but one who will come forth from your own body, he shall be your heir" (Genesis 15:2-4).

Since Abraham had no son of his own with Sarah (the wife of the promise), he figured that Eliezer would be the one to inherit his estate. So what was the big deal? Abraham was the Bill Gates of his day! And there's no doubt that Eliezer knew he was in line for the big bucks, property, livestock, and the like. Not only that, I'm sure Abraham and Eliezer were both well aware of the spiritual blessing on Abraham, to bless all families of the earth through a lineage of the future Messiah, another blessing that would be passed onto Abraham's heir. So what happens? Abe and Sarah have a baby just when they're about ready to move into the local nursing home, but that's not all. Abraham gives Eliezer an assignment that will result in his own disinheritance, and Eliezer faithfully and precisely carries out the orders of Abraham, regardless of his own personal loss.

Without going into too much detail, Eliezer's faithfulness to Abraham was in finding a wife for Isaac, which disinherits Eliezer because Isaac will have his own offspring. As a result, Eliezer received none of Abraham's estate; it was given to Isaac and his future family. That inheritance included wealth, prestige, power, kingship, priesthood, and the land of Canaan as an "everlasting" (age-enduring) possession. Because of finding a wife for Isaac, Eliezer and his offspring inherited nothing. Thus, the parable refers to Eliezer (Lazarus) as a "beggar" who possessed nothing of earthly value, waiting to be fed from Judah's table (the Jews).

A Great Gulf

The parable says that a "great chasm" separated Abraham and Eliezer from the Rich Man (Luke 16:26). What was this chasm? The Greek word suggests a deep ravine or valley, perhaps with cliffs on each side. Its two sides were also "afar off" from each other (verse 23) and from the description in the text, it was impassable. In his article, "The Real Meaning of Lazarus and the Rich Man," Ernest Martin gives his thoughts in understanding what this chasm referred to in Jewish minds of Jesus's day:

> In all other occasions of its grammatical use in the New Testament, the word "pass" was used to denote a passage over water. ... Let us now look at such a chasm from a Palestinian point of view. In that environment there is only one possible identification for the "great gulf" of the parable if it is to fit the meaning of the Greek chasm precisely. This would be the Great Rift Valley between the highlands of Trans-Jordan and the hill country of Ephraim in which the River Jordan flows. This fault line is the greatest and longest visible chasm on earth. And what a spectacular sight it is! As one looks over the chasm he sees impressive cliffs on each side, a desert in its wastelands, and the River Jordan meandering in the center.

Identifying the chasm of the parable with the Jordan rift unfolds a beautiful symbolic story well recognized in contemporary Jewish allegorical narratives of the time. In the center of this "gulf" was the River Jordan. It divided the original land of promise given to Abraham from ordinary Gentile lands. The west side of Jordan represented the area that the Bible considered the original Holy Land. As the angel said to Joshua: "Remove your sandals from your feet, for the place where you are standing is holy." And Joshua did so (Joshua 5:15). When the Israelites finally entered the chasm of the Jordan and crossed the river, they then considered themselves in the Holy Land — the land promised to Abraham and his seed![62]

What might all this mean symbolically? Crossing the Jordan was a symbol for death throughout Scripture, and entering the land of Canaan was a symbol of the rewards obtained in the next age ("Wedding Feast") for the faithful under the Mosaic Covenant, as I explained in chapter 16 on the Covenants. So it appears to me that this parable was a warning to Judah (Jews) of missing out on this Age of the Kingdom — which they believed was theirs by inheritance — due to bad stewardship of their spiritual blessings. Out of possessiveness and perhaps jealousy, they did not share their vast knowledge of the truth with the Gentiles, but forced them to live on a diet of crumbs. Contrary to the greed of the Jews, Eliezer is now depicted as enjoying the future comforts in Abraham's bosom, because he remained faithful with everything entrusted to him. Here is the final appraisal according to Ernest Martin:

> The only Gospel to carry the parable of Lazarus and the Rich Man was Luke who was the companion of Paul, the apostle to the Gentiles. It showed a specific message that Gentiles could now inherit the promises to Abraham, provided they were faithful as Eliezer had been. Yet Paul did not want the Gentiles to be conceited in their new relationship with God.

> "What then? Israel hath not obtained that which he seeks for... God hath given them the spirit of slumber, eyes that they should not see, ears that they should not hear; unto this day" (Rom. 11:8).

> But Paul goes on to say, "Have they stumbled that they should fall? God forbid" (verse 11). Now if the fall of them be the riches of the

world [all people], and the diminishing of them the riches of the Gentiles [like Lazarus-Eliezer]; how much more their fullness?" (verse 12). One of these days, according to Paul, "all Israel shall be saved" (verse 26). God will show mercy on the natural sons of Abraham as He has on faithful Gentile stewards.[63]

Now that we've unpacked the truer meaning of the parable of Lazarus, there's one more major error we need to clear up in our quest to shed light on the salvation of all. I'm pretty confident that learning this new perspective will do your soul some good!

CHAPTER TWENTY-ONE

REDEFINING THE SOUL

Ever notice all the talk about the *soul* in church?

"Your soul is in danger of eternal hellfire!"

"Believe in Jesus or you will lose your soul..."

There's an intangible, inexplicable sense about this word in modern Christian teachings. When asked, most Christians will hem haw, trying to explain the soul as something like this: "A person is both body and soul. The body is the physical flesh-and-blood temporary 'shell.' The soul is the nonmaterial, intangible, immortal aspect. At death the soul leaves the body, and lives on consciously forever in either heaven or hell."

I'm going to make the case that we've been wrong — dead wrong. This is another critical Bible word that I believe has been way misconstrued (and mistranslated) to mean something it does not. It has taken on a soul of its own, so to speak, and the result is that many a soul has been lost in wrong conclusions (not hell, thankfully)!

What is a *Soul*?

Translators have made an utter mess of the Greek and Hebrew words for *soul*, and as a result, have contributed to the huge distortion of this once simple word. The Hebrew and Greek words for *soul* are *nephesh* and *psuche* respectively, both nouns, yet this one little word has been unbelievably mistranslated as a myriad of other words. Here are but a few of many (taken directly from a Bible Concordance): *life, death, corpse, heart, endure, myself, desire, greedy, hunger, heartily, perfume, slave, strength, fish, thirst, throat, mind, suspense, thing* — oh yes, and *soul*. You'll notice that within the list of words, each of which have radically different meanings, are also verbs, adjectives, adverbs, and even pronouns!

What is the reason for such sloppy translation? Nephesh and psuche are translated correctly in all the passages where translators wish to convey the concept of the immortality of the soul and it's supposed potential for "everlasting destruction." However, passages that would nullify the notion of the soul's ethereal immortal nature are mistranslated and masked with an assortment of misleading words. Let's bring some clarity to the definition of soul using real Scripture:

> Gen. 2:7: And the LORD God formed man of the dust of the ground, and breathed into his nostrils the breath of life; and man *became* a living soul (nephesh) (KJV).

> 1 Cor. 15:45: So also it is written, "The first man, Adam, *became* a living soul* (psuche). The last Adam became a life-giving spirit."

According to the Scriptures, a person does not *have* a soul. Each person *is* a living soul. Your soul is the sum total of you—your body, mind, will, emotions, and spirit. No one part of it can be separated from the rest or it is no longer you. You were brought to life as a living soul.

I should briefly mention the concept of "spirit." Our spirit, as I understand it, is the breath† of God that brings us to life and sustains us until our physical death. Ecclesiastics 12:7 says that, at death, our spirit or breath goes back to God while our body goes back to the ground, awaiting resurrection. What happens to our "soul" at death? Well, since our soul is the total of us (body, intellect, will, emotions), it is basically put away until God resurrects us back to life all in one piece again.

Actually, any living creature—man or beast—that has *breath and blood* is called a *soul* in Scriptures, although you might not glean this from reading most modern translations. For instance, in Genesis 1:20 and 24, where God creates the sea and land animals, the Hebrew text reads, "Then God said, 'Let the waters teem with swarms of *living souls* (nephesh)...Let the earth bring forth *living souls* after their kind."

Feel free to look up the words in a concordance (or you can check the Darby Translation on Studylight.org—it translated this passage correctly).

Pretty nifty, huh? When such mistranslating happens in the *very first chapter of the Bible*, twisting such an important concept, it should make you

---

* 1 Cor. 15:45 is a direct quote from Genesis 2:7. I find it noteworthy that NASB translates this word (nephesh) "being" in Genesis 2:7 but (psuche) "soul" here in 1 Cor. 15:45. They do footnote it in Genesis 2:7 as "soul" though. Why not just print it correctly instead of footnoting it? Hey, while we're at it, why not translate it consistently everywhere?

† Both the Hebrew and Greek words for *spirit* (ruach and pneuma, respectively) mean *breath* or *wind*. The word "spirit" is actually a Latin word for the same.

wonder how many other significant things you read that have not been translated correctly and gotten your understanding off track. Certainly by now you have come to realize it happens frequently.

When Translators Lost Their *Souls*

The truthful meaning of *soul* has been almost completely concealed in modern Bibles. Consider the word translators most often substitute in place of soul, and that is *life*. Hebrew and Greek each have a specific word for *life* (chayay and zoe, respectively), so there was no need to "improve on" or interpret the original intent of the writers of Scripture. In fact, there are many verses where both of these words occur together, showing that they are not interchangeable. Looking again at the same two verses above:

> Gen. 2:7: And the LORD God formed man of the dust of the ground, and breathed into his nostrils the breath of life (chayay); and man *became* a living (chay) soul (nephesh) (KJV).

> 1 Cor. 15:45: So also it is written, "The first man, Adam, *became* a living (zoe) soul (psuche). The last Adam became a life (zoe)-giving spirit."

Now, using the word *life* in and of itself is not so bad or far off of the true meaning of soul, but the problem is the way nephesh and psuche have been calculatingly and intentionally mistranslated, misleading people to think that the soul is some immortal, intangible part of us that can be damned forever. Whenever a passage is about something that carries a negative connotation, such as being lost or destroyed, translators correctly use the word *soul*. Whenever a passage conveys mortal existence or carries a positive or neutral connotation, they swap soul for the word *life*. To help you understand the significance of this more clearly, I'm going to give several verse examples. The italicized and bolded word in each of these verses is *soul* in the original text, not *life*:

Gen. 9:5: "Surely I will require your *life*blood; from every beast I will require it. And from every man, from every man's brother I will require the *life* of man." In order to keep up the fallacy of the immortality of soul, translators would not be able to give an accurate rendering of this verse because in truth, God requires the death of every soul.

Exodus 4:19: "Now the LORD said to Moses in Midian, 'Go back to Egypt, for all the men who were seeking your *life* are dead.'"

Lev. 17:11: "For the *life* of the flesh is in the blood, and I have given it to you on the altar to make atonement for your *souls*; for it is the blood by reason of the *life* that makes atonement." Notice now *nephesh* occurs *three times* in this verse but is translated two different ways at whim, attempting to convey a completely skewed picture to the reader.

Lev. 17:14: "As for the *life* of all flesh, its blood is identified with its *life*."

Deut. 19:21: "Thus you shall not show pity: *life* for *life*, eye for eye, tooth for tooth, hand for hand, foot for foot."

Psalm 31:13: "For I have heard the slander of many, terror is on every side; while they took counsel together against me, they schemed to take away my *life*."

Matt. 2:20: "Get up, take the Child [Jesus] and His mother, and go into the land of Israel; for those who sought the Child's *life* are dead."

Matt. 6:25: "For this reason I say to you, do not be worried about your *life*, as to what you will eat or what you will drink; nor for your body, as to what you will put on. Is not (the) *life* more than food, and the body more than clothing?"

Matt. 10:28: "Do not fear those who kill the body but are unable to kill the *soul*; but rather fear Him who is able to destroy both *soul* and body in hell (Gehenna)."* *Why is soul suddenly translated correctly where it is speaking of being destroyed, the translator's slant suggesting in hell?*

Matt. 16:25–26: "For whoever wishes to save his *life* will lose it; but whoever loses his *life* for My sake will find it. For what will it profit a man if he gains the whole world and *forfeits* his *soul*? Or what will a man give in exchange for his *soul*?" Again, psuche is used by NT writers *four* times here, not two! We are told to intentionally lose (give up) our soul here in the Greek text, but this would not be good for Sunday morning theology. Also, the word chosen by translators, "forfeits," is a completely blatant, biased (aggravating) mistranslation (and lie). It is Strong's #2210, *zemioo*, and should be "does damage to" or "suffers loss to."†

---

* I believe this says that people can kill our body, but they cannot take away the essence of us — our choices, personality, will, etc. Only God can transform our will and old nature into loving people through the second death, required of everyone.

† See Strong's definition for zemioo: studylight.org/isb/view.cgi?number=2210.

Matt. 20:28: "...just as the Son of Man did not come to be served, but to serve, and to give His *life* a ransom for many."* Did you know that *Jesus gave His soul for you*? This would not be possible based on modern theological teachings that want you to think the soul is immortal and only dies when it is eternally damned.

How Greek Mythology Influenced *Soul*

Hopefully by now you see how important it is to scrutinize verses and concepts you have always taken for granted, and you realize also that you don't have to be a pastor or have a doctorate in theology to do so. And now perhaps you're still wondering where the whole teaching of the immortal, intangible soul came from, if not from the Bible. In his book, *The Subversion of Christianity*, French author Jacques Ellul explains:

> A familiar example of the mutation to which revelation was actually subjected is its contamination by the Greek idea of the immortality of the soul. I will briefly recall it. In Jewish thought death is total. There is no immortal soul, no division of body and soul. Paul's thinking is Jewish in this regard. ...The soul is as mortal as the body. But there is a resurrection. Out of the nothingness that human life becomes, God creates anew the being that was dead. There is a creation by grace; there is no immortal soul intrinsic to us. Greek philosophy, however, introduces among theologians the idea of the immortal soul. The belief was widespread in popular religion and it was integrated into Christianity. But it is a total perversion. Everything is not now dependent on the grace of God, and assurance of immortality comes to be evaluated by virtues and works. All Christian thinking is led astray by this initial mutation that comes through Greek philosophy and Near Eastern cults.

> An ardent work brings to light this type of deformation. Louis Rougier, in his *L'Astronomie et Religion en Occident* (Paris: PUF, 1980), shows how belief in the soul's celestial immortality arose in the second half of the fifth century B.C. on the basis of astronomy. Pythagorean astronomy radically transformed the idea of the destiny of the soul

---

* Try putting 1 Tim. 2:5–6 with this verse: "...Jesus gave Himself as a ransom for ALL, the testimony given in due season."

held by Mediterranean peoples. For the notion of a vital breath that dissipates at death, for belief in a survival of shades wandering about in the subterranean realm of the dead, it substitutes the notion of a soul of celestial substance exiled in this world. This idea completely contaminates biblical thinking, gradually replaces the affirmation of the resurrection, and transforms the kingdom of the dead into the kingdom of God.

Successive generations have reinterpreted Scripture and modeled it after their own cultures, thus moving society further from the truth of the original gospel. The Church also perverted the gospel message, for instead of simply doing away with pagan practice and belief, it reconstituted the sacred, set up its own religious forms, and thus resacralized the world.[64]

Historian and archeologist, Keith Stump, provides some additional information on where the idea of immortality of soul originated, even before the Greeks:

The idea of an "immortal soul" long predates the founding of today's major religions. The ancient Greek historian Herodotus (5th century B.C.) tells us in his *History* that the ancient Egyptians were the first to teach that the soul of man is separable from the body, and immortal. This Egyptian idea was centuries before Judaism, Hinduism, Buddhism, Christianity and Islam came onto the scene.

The pagan Greeks got the concept of an immortal soul from the Egyptians! The foremost advocate among the ancient Greeks of the idea of an "immortal soul" was the Athenian philosopher Plato (428–348 B.C.), the pupil of Socrates. ...It was Plato who popularized the immortal soul concept throughout the Greek world. [Ancient Greek and Roman writers] suggest that he may have simply popularized what he knew to be a fiction as a means of keeping the citizenry in line through the fear of mysterious "unseen things" beyond this life.

The immortal soul concept, in other words, was a necessary companion doctrine to the doctrine of the terrible torments of parts of Hades or hell. Such fearsome teachings, some philosophers thought, were necessary to scare the masses into being good citizens.

Plato and the Jews

The Jewish communities of antiquity were deeply influenced by Greek philosophical ideas. Many will suppose that the Platonic view of the soul imprisoned in the flesh would have been nothing new to the Jews. But notice the testimony of Jewish scholars themselves:

"The belief that the soul continues its existence after the dissolution of the body is...nowhere expressly taught in Holy Scripture. ...The belief in the immortality of the soul came to the Jews from contact with Greek thought and chiefly through the philosophy of Plato its principle exponent, who was led to it through Orphic and Eleusinian mysteries in which Babylonian and Egyptian views were strangely blended" (*The Jewish Encyclopedia* article, "Immortality of the Soul").

But what of the professing Christian world? Certainly here we should find the doctrine of an immortal soul independent of any Greek influence. Now consider this fact: Many of the early theologians and scholars of the professing Christian religion—including such men as Origen, Tertullian, and Augustine—were closely associated with Platonism.

Tertullian (A.D. 155–220), for example, wrote: "For some things are known even by nature: the immortality of the soul, for instance, is held by many...I may use, therefore, *the opinion of Plato*, when he declares: 'Every soul is immortal'" (*The Ante-Nicene Fathers, vol. III*).

Augustine of Hippo (A.D. 354–430)—held to be the greatest thinker of Christian antiquity—also taught the immaterial and spiritual nature of the human soul. But notice the source of his teachings. The *Encyclopedia Britannica* states, "[Augustine] fused the religion of the New Testament with the *Platonic tradition of Greek philosophy*."

Why should those early professing Christian scholars have resorted to the opinions of a pagan Greek philosopher? Could it be that the immortal soul doctrine is not clearly supported in Christian Scripture? Throughout the centuries of professing Christianity, innumerable sermons have been preached and countless pamphlets written purporting to prove the soul's immortality. Upon careful and open-minded examination, they are all found to be riddled with surprising error. ...The doctrine of the immortal soul is built on a foundation of biblical mistranslations, false premises, and sloppy scholarship. Few had the spiritual courage to take a fresh, unprejudiced look at the question and accept the true Bible teaching. For when the false doctrine of the immortal soul is toppled, along with it falls the equally pagan and false concept of heaven and hell—one of the cornerstones of traditional Christianity![65]

Every Soul Must Die

God declared that *every soul* must die (Gen. 9:4–5). In reality, this is the curse of Adam, not torturous, eternal separation from God or eternal death. Adam brought the death of soul, or the death of every living, breathing, warm-blooded person (and animal). And when you understand this, it is easy to see that the gift Jesus brought to all mankind is life back from the dead through resurrection.

So then as through one transgression there resulted condemnation to all men, even so through one act of righteousness there resulted justification of life to all men (Rom. 5:18).

We know love by this, that He laid down His *soul* for us; and we ought to lay down our *souls* for our brothers and sisters (1 John 3:16, MLT).

Once so muddled and misleading, now such a simple, beautiful truth.

We've made quite a journey together, but we're not quite finished yet! Now that we've come to the end of our Hebrew perspectives, I'd like to share some of my recent reflections with you—my own personal take on *The Story*. Through some unexpected life parallels, I feel like I've come to see a glimpse of the heavenly Parent's heart. These thoughts, however humanly flawed, have continued to favorably transform my view of God and life.

CHAPTER TWENTY-TWO

LEAVING THE CALF PATH FOR GOOD

"Jesus is as narrow as himself and as wide as the universe.
He is as exclusive as himself and as inclusive as containing
every single particle of creation." –Rob Bell in *Love Wins*

Why in the world would God write *The Story* this way? If what I've proposed is true, why would God let hell take center stage, allowing His character to be smeared and most of His children to be (seemingly) unnecessarily deceived and estranged for more than 1,500 years? Why not plainly make us all aware of His true character—how He fully intends to find and bring home every lost sheep safely on His shoulders? Though I don't fully understand the scope of it yet myself, I believe God gave me a little bit of insight into this mystery through my friend, "Abigail."

I met Abigail on a support website for parents of high conflict divorce. She's a very loving, devoted mom who would climb the highest, most rugged mountain, and sail the deepest, stormiest sea, to be with her children and make them feel secure in her love. But from the day she got divorced, Abigail's ex-husband, knowing how deeply she loves her kids, decided the best way to hurt Abigail would be to use the kids as weapons of warfare. And the best way to do that was to alienate them from her. He did this by telling them lies about her (directly or indirectly), keeping them away from her as much as possible with fun diversions and distractions, and setting her up to look bad in "no win" situations, so that her kids often began doubting her character and intentions. After awhile, Abigail realized, as many parents do, that her kids had become the rope in a game of tug-of-war. Only this did not feel anything like a game. It was the most painful situation she could ever imagine and often times she felt like her heart had been ripped to shreds.

Abigail tried not to "play the game" and tried in every way to nurture a loving relationship with her children, but deliberate character assassination over a long period of time with naïve, defenseless children proved very effective. After a few years of this kind of conflict, the lies began to win out and her kids gradually became alienated from her until there was hardly anything left of the natural mother-child bond. There is actually a term for this type of high conflict divorce in counseling circles, where one parent can't control his or her anger and involves the children in the resulting hate campaign. It's called, "Parental Alienation Syndrome."

As the children got a little older, Abigail distinctly received direction from God, telling her to "drop her end of the rope." This would normally make no sense to a devoted mother, but the direction came to Abigail very clearly through a passage in the Bible where she believed God explained *why* He wanted her to do such a counter-intuitive thing.

In 1 Kings 3:16–28, there's a story about two mothers—prostitutes actually—who each had babies. In the night, one mother accidentally rolled on top of her baby and killed him. When she figured out what had happened, she tried to steal the baby of the other mother. The two women came before King Solomon, fighting over the living baby, asking him to decide to which woman the living baby belonged. Wisely, he pulled out his sword and said each mother could take home half of the remaining baby, after he cut it in two. The real mother instantly, with no thought of her own impending loss, offered to let the other mother raise it so that the child could be kept whole and alive.

Abigail believed her message from this story was that it is the real mother who is willing to let her most precious babies go in order that they might be preserved whole. The fighting over her kids needed to stop. No longer should they be put in the middle, forced to choose between parents or forced to spend time with her, even though it was her "right." But also the message to Abigail was that letting go would not be the end of the story. In His time and in His way, the good King would return the intact, living children back to their rightful mother.

It was probably one of the hardest things she'd ever been asked to do in her life. But along the way, Abigail had learned that God could be trusted with that which was most precious to her. God loved her children more than she, and only He knew the end from the beginning. Courageously, Abigail dropped her end of the rope and let her babies go.

Instead of getting easier, it got harder. Her ex capitalized on the situation and she saw them less and less until they withdrew almost completely out of her life. Abigail knew that she could "make" her children come to her legally, but she also knew that ultimately, this would not win them to her. If anything, it would alienate them further as they perceived (with help) her trying to control them. The only thing she could do is *invite them*, over and over, waiting for her children to accept her love. Someday when they did come around, it would be because her real character won out, leading the children to desire a relationship with their mom out of a response to her love, not out of duty or force.

Whether we realize it or not, Abigail's story is really our story.

As children of God, we have experienced this cosmic game of tug-of-war going on between "two homes." In one home, there's the vindictive, deceitful "father of this world," who would like nothing more than to alienate the children from the healthy, devoted, loving Father. His hate campaign is waged through lies, distractions, distortions, and diversions. He frames the heavenly Parent to look bad as much as possible, by smearing His character and making the children believe that the heavenly Parent doesn't really want to be with them — *that He would throw away most of His children forever.*

The heavenly Parent, in all His wisdom, drops the rope.

It looks questionable.

It's totally counter-intuitive.

But this is not to the end of abandoning His children; it's for a much higher purpose. He knows that when you drop the rope in tug-of-war, the enemy falls down. The one who lies and alienates, eventually loses.

You see, God owns the playground, so in dropping the rope, nothing is ever really lost. On the contrary, everything is to be gained. Though there may be the appearance of a loss or defeat in allowing the alienation and the deception to go on for a time, it's a temporary letting go for a greater good.

God knows that in order for His children to come out of the fight whole, we need be to set free within our God-given bounds — free to discover the lies and their source, free to explore both sides of the tree of good and evil, free to come to the end of the rebellious and wandering behaviors we have adopted from lying parent, and free to respond to the *invitation* of relationship. He wants us to come to Him out of desire and longing, not duty and coercion. He wants us to love Him freely and, in the likeness of our real Father, to love all His children. This might be the closest we come to "free will," but it is never to the end of choosing destruction, but learning to choose love.

True love cannot be instructed, forced, or manipulated, but only invited, experienced, and nurtured. It's the only way that a true father-child relationship can thrive. Ultimately, "love" born of duty fails (which isn't really love), whereas love born of desire thrives and blooms.

And therein lies at least a little part of this *Story*. It is a great invitation, and a great homecoming, happily-ever-after Love Story between Father and Child.

> But while he was still a long way off, his father saw him and felt compassion for him, and ran and embraced him and kissed him. And the son said to him, "Father, I have sinned against heaven and in your sight; I am no longer worthy to be called your son."

> But the father said to his servants, "Quickly bring out the best robe and put it on him, and put a ring on his hand and sandals on his feet; and bring the fattened calf, kill it, and let us eat and celebrate; for this son of mine was dead and has come to life again; he was lost and has been found." And they began to celebrate (Luke 15:20–24).

This is no quick or easy journey for any of us. Not only do we have a fallen nature with all its insecurities and distortions from our life circumstances to contend with, but the lying, slanderous parent often times masquerades as the "an angel of light" in the form of "Disney dad."

In Revelation 12:9, we read that part of the lying parent's job description is deceiving "the whole world." None of this makes sense unless you understand *The Story*, and the necessity of the villain to call forth the absolute saving, healing, benevolent, valiant nature of the hero.

How does the lying parent successfully work most of his lies to dupe mankind? Revelation 13:6 tells us that Satan works especially through the other children still trapped in the adversarial home who have adopted the attitudes and behaviors of the lying parent, giving them authority to blaspheme God's name and character.

With a lot of help, namely from those who promote the doctrine of hell, Satan has completely hamstrung most of mankind's perception of the character of God throughout the centuries, painting Him as a power hungry, vengeful, unforgiving, hypocritical, task master. It is not unlike the power-crazed little old man behind the curtain in the Wizard of Oz, who uses scare tactics to get everybody to do what He wants, when all along he has no real power to do much of anything.

Since the days of the establishment of Israel about 3,500 years ago, Satan has largely used those who are called out to belief in this mortal lifetime to do the his dirty work in the smearing campaign. It's easy to point the finger at all the verses condemning Pharisees and apostate Israelites, but those people were only a blueprint of the rest of us who have largely followed the same pattern of behavior ever since, blaspheming God's character to the peoples of all nations. It was a brilliant plan, really—using those who thought they were above deception to be the primary vehicles of such. Was God sleeping when this happened?

No. It was written this way.

It is a lesson with a happily ever after for everyone.

It's a Divine Story where no one can take credit for being smarter, more important, or better than another, and where there is no loser.

My Story is Now His Story

In the spring of 2009 a very special opportunity took place. My Mom had battled cancer for six years and though I didn't know it yet, she was in her final two months of life when I was finally able to share these truths with her. When I first told her, she got the most memorable, hopeful gleam in her eye and said, "*Are you sure?*"

At the forefront of Mom's mind throughout her last days was my brother, a wayward child who, according to conservative Christian teaching, is going straight to hell. She hadn't spoken to him in ten years (he didn't even know she was sick), and it cut her deeply to think she would never ever see him again—never tell him how much she loved him with all the ocean of a mother's love. But now, for the first time since the discovery of her cancer, she had reason to hope again.

When I went through her things after her death, I found a pair of my brother's toddler clothes stashed in one of her top drawers where she probably looked at them frequently. This is what a loving parent does. This is the undying, unceasing, unconditional love that originates from a heavenly Parent's heart.

Something amazing happened to my Mom after she learned the truth. I never heard her talk about her faith to others, especially to her friends. I know that some of her friends were heavy on her heart as she faced her death, thinking she would never see them again. She probably felt a burden about making sure they didn't go to hell, but she wasn't the confrontational type and didn't want to corner them either. Based on their bad experience with certain Christians, some of her friends didn't want religion shoved down their throats, so she'd spent many years simply serving them and loving them by example.

After I shared the true Gospel with Mom, she was so consumed by the joy of it that she began sharing it with most everyone around her—her hospice nurse, her cleaning lady, and yes, even her friends. You see, that's the effect that the true Gospel—*the irresistible Gospel*—has on people. You can't wait to tell people about a love so powerful, so complete, and so pure that it offers value, hope, and purpose to every human being, with no strings attached.

The last morning of my Mom's earthly life, I was sitting by her bedside, holding her hand, and reading verses to her about God's ultimate, victorious love for *all* His children. In the middle of 1 Corinthians 15—a passage that had become her favorite—about the ultimate conquering of the grave, the resurrection from the dead, and God becoming "all in all," my Mom took her last, very peaceful breath. It was a beautiful, holy, heavenly-orchestrated moment. One day, all men and women of all time will stand before their Father in adoration, declaring their love and devotion to the God of love who had a plan all along to save them as His beloved children. In that day, He will freely live among us, and I believe we will be captivated forever with absolute, magical joy.

It's ironic that I once felt sorry for all those deceived people "out there," believing I had somehow escaped deception and that I was lucky enough to be raised in "the truth." I now realize that I was as deceived as anyone, if not moreso. What is a bit sad and humiliating is how many people in my life I must have pushed away with my spiritual pride, treating them like they were the ones who were deceived.

These days, I know that nobody has "arrived" at ultimate truth, because truth is a consistently deepening journey—an unveiling process during our entire lives—not a one point destination. It's a process that requires living by faith (discovery), not sight (doctrines). To be on the right path you have to be willing to admit that you don't have a lot of the answers, but you are willing to follow the Spirit in a living, progressing, dancing, dynamic relationship. To do this, I believe it is necessary to leave behind doctrines, dogmas, marginalizing orthodoxy, restrictive institutions, and the traditions of men, which all stagnate and ultimately "build one's house upon sand."

Today I have made the journey back to the faith of my daughter – the simple faith of a child. With what I've experienced of God's love on this liberating, joyful journey, I could never go back to the old calf paths. What the true Gospel has done for me is impossible to quantify, but for the first time in my life, I feel truly reborn. For the first time ever, I feel like a salesman who believes in my own products. There are no words to describe the utter happiness and purpose that has been unleashed inside me. As I see people in my everyday life now – at the grocery store, at work, on TV, at school – more than ever I see people who have unlimited value because they are all children of God, my brothers and sisters.

Rob Bell puts some of his similar joy in discovery into words:

> "When you've *experienced* the resurrected Jesus, the mystery hidden in the fabric of creation, you can't help but talk about him. You've tapped into the joy that fills the entire universe, and so naturally you want others to meet this God. This is a God worth telling people about. Witnessing, evangelizing, sharing your faith – when you realize that God has retold your story, you are free to passionately, urgently, compellingly tell the story because you've stepped into a whole new life and you're moved and inspired to share it. When your God is love, and you have experienced this love in flesh and blood, here and now, then you are free from guilt and fear and the terrifying, haunting, ominous voice that whispers over your shoulder, 'You're not doing enough.'

> "Jesus invites us into that relationship, the one at the center of the universe. He insists that he's one with God, that we can be one with him, and that life is a generous, abundant reality. This God whom Jesus spoke of has always been looking for partners, people who are passionate about participating in the ongoing creation of the world."[66]

This is the kind of Gospel – where no one is a throw away – that breeds life, and joy, and continuous wonder. This Gospel births a sincere, deep love for people, and the excitement to share the truly unconditional love of God with everyone. It is so gratifying to know that every single kind word or deed offered will someday result in the growing of a seedling or the bearing of fruit from a person created in the image of God. No effort will ever be wasted or insignificant. The joy and energy this realization has brought into my life is positively captivating and simply impossible to fully articulate.

In the midst of the questions in the dark of night, *"Why this way?"* These words echo song-like in my heart. "This is the way to the greatest joy for all."

> And I heard a loud voice from the throne, saying, "Behold, the tabernacle of God is among men, and He will dwell among them, and they shall be His people, and God Himself will be among them, and He will wipe away every tear from their eyes; and there will no longer be any death; there will no longer be any mourning, or crying, or pain; the first things have passed away. ...Behold, I am making *all things* new. ...Write, for these words are faithful and true."

> ...The Spirit and the bride say, "Come." And let the one who hears say, "Come." And let the one who is thirsty come; let the one who wishes take the water of life without cost (Rev. 21:3–5; 22:17).

Part 4
Resources

THE SCRIPTURES: FOR SCHOLARS OR COMMON PEOPLE?

"Now as they observed the confidence of Peter and John and
understood that they were uneducated and untrained men,
they were amazed, and began to recognize them
as having been with Jesus." –Acts 4:13

Can people without theological or Bible college degrees study the Scriptures responsibly?

With so many free Bible study tools online, it's easier than ever for people like you and me to take a studious, thoughtful approach to Scripture. Using these resources, practically *anyone* can learn basic study of Hebrew and Greek Scripture in order to begin identifying problematic translation issues and correcting them on their own. In fact, learning how to identify and improve many translation errors is so simple; a little kid could do it.

Now, I'm certainly not suggesting that there is no value in attending seminary or Bible College. But the bottom line is that there's no correlation between the ability to learn and discern "truth," and the number of degrees one holds. "Knowledge puffs up" and can potentially cloud one's ability or willingness to discern the simple, evident things of God. This was the idea behind the Protestant Reformation of the 1500s. It was, at least on one level, about putting the power for personal spiritual growth and interpretation back into the hands of the laity. If you ask me, we've regressed back into the pre-Reformation pattern of needing pastors and theologians to define truth for us, as if we can't go deeper ourselves.

We've now entered what my husband calls the "Digital Reformation." In the same way that the printing press gave power to the lay people during the Protestant Reformation, the Internet has done the same today, leveling the playing field with access to previously controlled information and allowing common folks like you and me to gain new insights into Scripture like we've not been able to do before. This allows us to intelligently question the calf paths of our Christian Orthodoxy heritage.

I believe simplicity is one of the reasons God chose Greek as one of the primary languages of the Scriptures, particularly the NT. Koine Greek was the simple, methodical language of the common people of the day. In fact, the Greek word, koine, means *common*! Here are some perspectives on this biblical language from online resources:

> **LearnBiblicalGreek.com:** ...studies of Greek papyri found in Egypt over the past one hundred years have shown that this language was the language of the everyday people... As Paul says, 'In the fullness of time God sent his son' (Gal 4:4), and part of that fullness was a universal language. No matter where Paul traveled he could be understood. God used the common language to communicate the Gospel. The Gospel does not belong to the erudite alone; it belongs to all people. It now becomes our task to learn this marvelous language to help us make the grace of God known to all people.[67]

> **Wikipedia:** Native to the southern Balkans, [Greek] has the longest documented history of any Indo-European language, spanning 34 centuries of written records. It has been spoken as the major language of the Ancient Classical World, and it then became the official language of the Eastern Roman or Byzantine Empire. Historical unity and continuing identity between the various stages of the Greek language is often emphasized. Although Greek has undergone morphological and phonological changes comparable to those seen in other languages, there has been no time in its history since classical antiquity where its cultural, literary, and orthographic tradition was interrupted to such an extent that one can easily speak of a new language emerging. Greek speakers today still tend to regard literary works of ancient Greek as part of their own rather than a foreign language. It is also often estimated that the historical changes have been relatively slight compared with some other languages. *Ancient Greek texts, especially from Biblical Koine onwards, are thus relatively easy to understand for educated modern speakers.*[68]

> **GreekLatinAudio.com:** *...Thus, one need not be a scholar, a linguist, a Greek grammarian, etc., to follow along.* It is absolutely unreasonable to think that God would impose such requirements on anyone who is seeking to get to the truth of the matter under consideration here (Matt. 18:1-6). Furthermore, inasmuch as God undertook very

personal and painful measures to open the way to accurate knowledge concerning Himself and His son Jesus Christ (John 17:3), one may safely presume that such knowledge is fully intended to be attainable and clearly understandable.[69]

Maybe now you're gaining confidence that Greek is simple enough for people like "us" (lay people) to study on our own. However, be forewarned that not everyone will agree. A friend of mine has been a Baptist pastor for many years. He's extremely well read and serious about Bible study, and he openly prides himself on the fact that pastors from all over the region, and perhaps in other parts of the country, call him for help in understanding difficult theological questions and concepts. It's completely understandable why it would be hard for a man of his spiritual stature and learnedness to thoughtfully consider scriptural perspectives from someone like me, with no formal training whatsoever. On more than one occasion, he has made it clear that my novice attempts at studying and piecing together scriptural meaning and intent is treading in dangerous waters and better left up to the theologians.

My friend just so happens to be a King-James-only pastor. He (along with a big chunk of Christianity) is convinced that the KJV is the *only* accurate translation. One time I told him that I could easily prove to him that KJV is not exempt from significant translation errors, simply by using a free online Greek Interlinear Bible.[*]

I found his reaction very telling in how the deception has been sustained for many hundreds of years, via theological institutions and traditions. He said to me, "*A Greek Interlinear?* We were taught in seminary never to use those."

"Why not," asked I?

"I don't know," said he.

I sent him some mistranslated words and passages that clearly change the early writers intent (also recognizable with a Strong's Concordance), to which he never responded. This was a start in showing me that those in seminaries and theological institutions often rely on tradition-based

---

[*] An *Interlinear Bible* is one that shows the Greek or Hebrew words with Strong's numbers above and the literal English words underneath. It's a very useful and powerful tool for recognizing errors and inconsistencies in the modern Bible versions. Find both Greek and Hebrew Interlinear Bibles at: scripture4all.org.

education and *commentary* on Scripture, instead of looking into the original language of the Scriptures for themselves. Even for us lay people, looking into these matters is much easier than it sounds. I may not be a Koine Greek expert, but as I mentioned earlier, it is a fairly simple language. With a little effort, anyone can begin simple word and concept recognition. It can actually be a lot of fun—like treasure hunting!

SIMPLE STEPS FOR IDENTIFYING MISTRANSLATIONS

It's time to explore some simple techniques that anyone can apply for uncovering mistranslations.

1. Compare Versions Side-By-Side for Contradictions and Inconsistencies.

Let's look at a few obvious version inconsistencies — some of which we've already explored.

Acts 17:31:

(NASB): "He has fixed a day in which He will judge the world in righteousness through a Man whom He has appointed, *having furnished proof* to all men by raising Him from the dead."

(KJV): "...whereof he *hath given* **assurance** *unto all men*..."

(CLT): "...*tendering faith* to all, raising Him from among the dead."

Here we see three different words used for what was to be given to all men — proof, assurance, and faith, yet none of them can be used interchangeably to convey similar meaning. We already learned in chapters 4 and 17 that the Greek word used here, *pistis*, is more accurately translated "obedient trust" and is appropriately translated "faith" 241 out of 243 times in the NT. I simply found this out by looking it up in the online Concordance at StudyLight.org.

Hebrews 1:2:

NASB: "in these last days has spoken to us in His Son, whom He appointed heir of all things, through whom also *He made the world.*"

NIV: "...through whom *he made the universe.*"

KJV: "...by whom also *he made the worlds*..." (huh?)

NLT: "... through the Son *he made the universe and everything in it.*"

YLT (Young's Literal): "...through whom also *He did make the ages*..."

Were those Greeks so confused that they don't know their *world* from their *universe* from their *ages*, or if they were supposed to be singular or plural? As you can guess, this isn't a Greek problem. If you look this up in a Greek Interlinear Bible online, or a concordance, you can get to the bottom of what was actually said and find out that the Greeks were not the confused ones. Young's Literal is the correct translation of the Greek.

Understand that these are just a few examples of many such occurrences throughout the modern, popular Bible versions. You may ask, "What difference does it make whether it was ages or worlds or universe?" First of all, it matters because honest, accurate translation demands it, and when translators pick and choose words at whim (like *soul* and *life*), you end up with distortions that lead to false conclusions and doctrines. If they consistently used the correct words, we could better understand the concepts and themes in Scripture intended by the writers. To do any less is bad scholarship, incorrect translating, and often times totally dishonest.

2. Compare Word Usage or Theme Inconsistencies.

With Greek being fairly consistent, one can discover concealed or changed meanings by using an online Lexicon (*biblehub.com/strongs.htm* or *biblestudytools.com/lexicons/greek/nas*). A Lexicon gives you the definition of a Greek or Hebrew word, as well as a list of most of the passages where it's used. Just plug in the Strong's number to pull up any single word used.

To most easily obtain the Strong's number and Lexicon definition together, follow these steps.

Step 1: Go to http://biblestudytools.com/nas/ (can also use KJV) and enter verse or chapter you want to study in search bar. It will look like this:

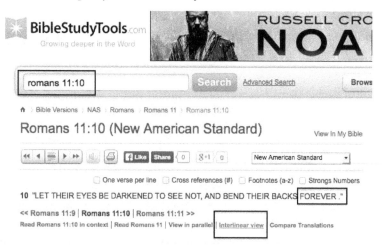

Step 2: Click on "Interlinear View," and you will see the Greek text below the verse. After awhile, you will begin recognizing certain words.

Step 3: Click on the highlighted word that you want to study to see what Greek word was used, the Strong's number, definition, and other verses where it is used (in the Lexicon). It will look like this:

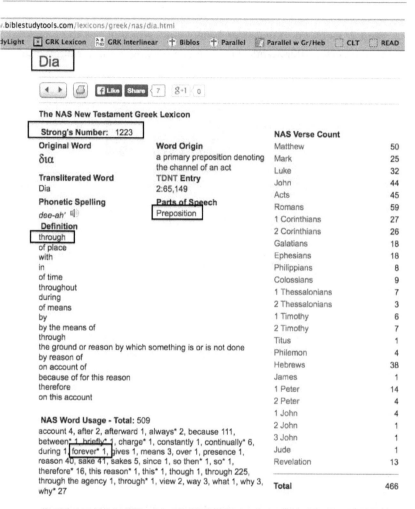

Notice that the Greek word translated *forever* here actually shows up as *through*. Hmmm. Looks suspicious. Perhaps we should visit the *Greek Interlinear Bible* for more clarity. You can find the Interlinear at http://scripture4all.org (select "Greek"), also listed in the resources section of this book. Here's what you find when you look up this passage:

11:10	CKOTICϴHTⲰCAN	OI	OΦϴAⲀMOI	AYTⲰN	TOY	MH	BAЄΠЄIN	KAI
	skotisthEtOsan	hoi	ophthalmoi	autOn	tou	mE	blepein	kai
	G4654	G3588	G3788	G846	G3588	G3361	G991	G2532
	v_ Aor Pas 3 Pl	t_ Nom Pl m	n_ Nom Pl m	pp Gen Pl m	t_ Gen Sg m	Part Neg	vn Pres Act	Conj
	LET-BE-BEING-DARKenED	THE	VIEWers	OF-them	OF-THE	NO	TO-BE-lookING	AND
	let-them-be-being-darkened !		eyes				to-be-observing	

TON	NⲰTON	AYTⲰN	ΔΙΑΠANTOC	CYΓKAMΨON
ton	nOton	autOn	diapantos	sugkampson
G3588	G3577	G846	G1275	G4781
t_ Acc Sg m	n_ Acc Sg m	pp Gen Pl m	Adv	v_ Aor Act 2 Sg
THE	BACK	OF-them	THRU-EVERY	TOGETHER-BOW
			continually	bow-together-you !

If you look back at the Greek words on the bottom line, you see "diapantos," Strong's #1275. The first thing I notice is that Biblestudytools.com assigned the wrong Strong's number (#1223), which only contains part of this compound word ("dia," which means *through*). This is probably because the word got divided into two words (dia pantos), as you might recognize in the Greek text. Either way, Strong's diapantos means, "through every" or "continually."

Interestingly, Biblestudytools.com only lists *diapantos* (#1275) as being used only once in NAS (1 Tim. 6:5, translated as "constant friction"), whereas it is listed seven times in KJV (five times as "always," two times as "continually"). To make matters more complicated, all eight occurrences should have been listed for both Bible versions!

But the point here is that *forever* and *constantly* or *continually* are completely different words and intentions, and this shows you just how slick the translations can be at tricking you into seeing the Bible through certain lenses, instead of the original writer's intent.

When there are dramatic differences in how a word is translated, a mistranslation should be suspect. As you get more familiar with the Greek, you find some interesting stuff. These days whenever I stumble across a contradiction, I go back to the Greek (or Hebrew) Interlinear Bible and usually can unravel the problem. Let's look at a few.

Hebrew word: Nephesh (noun)=soul. We covered this in chapter 21. Here are some of the many OT translations for one little word that should only be translated as "soul": any, appetite, beast, body, breath, creature, dead, desire, fish, ghost, heart, him, life, lust, man, mind, one, person, pleasure, self, thing, will, would have. *Now there's some bad translating!*

Greek word: Kairos (noun)=season. This one is a little tricky if using the Strong's Concordance because they have not defined it clearly or in the spirit it is meant. If you dig a little, you'll find that this word truly means "season." For instance, "idios kairos" is the Greek phrase for "due season." Perhaps translators didn't understand that the NT writers specifically intended to convey the OT concept of the harvest of people. Consider all the different translations of kairos: age (*aion*), epochs, occasion, time (*chronos*), times, opportune time, proper time, right time, opportunity, season, seasons, short, while.

If you put the word "season" in all eighty-six places where kairos occurs in the NT, it makes perfect sense in light of the harvest theme, taught throughout Scriptures. Consider the following verses:

"Allow both to grow together until the harvest; and in the *time* (kairos) of the harvest I will say to the reapers, 'First gather up the tares and bind them in bundles to burn them up; but gather the wheat into my barn'" (Matt. 13:30). Clearly, "season" is a much better fit than "time."

"Seeing at a distance a fig tree in leaf, He went to see if perhaps He would find anything on it; and when He came to it, He found nothing but leaves, for it was not the season (kairos) for figs" (Mark 11:13).

Greek word: Sozo (verb)= deliver, make whole, or heal. This is usually the word translated as "save" or "deliver," as in all verses pertaining to "salvation." As an example, the familiar verse Ephesians 2:8: "For by grace you have been saved (sozo) through faith; and that not of yourselves, it is the gift of God..."

But a deeper study will reveal that this word includes the idea of being made well or whole.* Using our Lexicon, here are some of the ways sozo (Strong's #4982) is used in the NT: bring safely, cured (sickness), get well, made well, preserved, recover, restore, save, saved. Consider:

"A woman who had been suffering from a hemorrhage for twelve years, came up behind Him and touched the fringe of His cloak; for she was saying to herself, 'If I only touch His garment, I will *get well* (sozo).' Jesus turning and seeing her said, 'Daughter, take courage; your faith has *made you well* (sozo).' At once the woman was *made well*" (Matt. 9:20–22).

"Receive your sight; your faith has made you well (sozo)" (Luke 18:42).

"My little daughter is at the point of death; please come and lay Your hands on her so that she will get well (sozo) and live" (Mark 5:23).

NAS footnotes "get well" as "be saved."

---

* http://ResourcesForChristians.net/node/83 offers perspectives on how *sozo* should also be conveyed as healing or making whole.

Just for fun, try looking up sozo in the Lexicon* for yourself so you can get some practice seeing how it is used in different passages. Can you imagine the implications if we were to include the fuller meaning of sozo with all the "saved" verses? It might look more like this:

Matt. 1:21 "She will give birth to a son, and you are to give him the name Jesus, because he will *[heal]* and deliver his people from their sins" (MLT).

Mark 6:56: "And wherever he went—into villages, towns or countryside—they placed the sick in the marketplaces. They begged him to let them touch even the edge of his cloak, and all who touched him were healed *[and made whole]*" (MLT).

A really important consideration of sozo conveyed in the Greek is that many of the verses about being "saved" are written in Greek in the *present-progressive verb tense*. This means that it is an ongoing action. Here are some examples:

John 10:9: "I am the door; if EVER anyone may be entering through me he shall be being saved (made whole) and shall be entering and shall be coming out and shall be finding pasture" (MLT).

Acts 2:21: "And it shall be [that] everyone who EVER should be calling on the name of [the] Lord shall be being saved (made well)" (MLT).

Acts 16:31: "Believe on the Lord Jesus Christ and you shall be being saved, you and your household" (MLT).

Rom. 10:9: "That if EVER you should be avowing with your mouth Jesus is Lord and should be believing in your heart that God rouses him out of the dead ones, you shall be being saved" (MLT).

Rom. 10:13: "For whoever should be calling the name of the Lord shall be being saved" (MLT).

1 Cor. 3:15: "If anyone's work shall be being burned up, he shall be being fined/penalized yet he shall be being saved yet as through fire" (MLT).

I capitalized the word "ever" in the above sentences because God is making His point: It is NEVER too late to be saved, delivered, and made whole. As a review, what are we being made whole, healed, delivered, and saved from? You are correct! It's not hell; it is *death*—the curse of Adam!

---

* http://www.biblestudytools.com/lexicons/greek/nas/

We are all in a process of being healed from death that we might come into imperishable life.

3. Look Up the Word in a Concordance.

This is helpful, but not fool proof. I usually use Strong's Concordance online (studylight.org—must use NASB or KJV to access—or biblehub.com) because it is quick and easy, but there are some definitions that have been added to or distorted to support faulty translations. Often though, it's very helpful in clarifying the meaning of certain words. Here's an example of a word that is defined fairly correct by Strong's, yet used by Bible translators to convey the harshest and least correct definition, *kolazo*.

Greek: Kolazo (verb)/ Kolasis (noun). Strong's definition:

> "to lop or prune, as trees and wings, to curb, check, restrain, to chastise, correct, punishment."

The essence of this word family is to prune and improve upon through correction; yet it is *only* translated as "punishment" (which I think was a later added bias to Strong's definition) in all four of its occurrences the NT (Matt. 25:46; Acts 4:21; 2 Peter 2:9, 1 John 4:18). Check out a more correct, literal translation of Matthew 25:46, a favorite of hell-preaching pastors, and you will see what I mean. When translated correctly, it loses the doom and gloom, revealing God's true character as the all wise Father with the perfect plan of good for His children:

"These will go away into eonian (age-abiding) *correction*, but the just ones into eonian life" (MLT).

4. Look for Changed Parts of Speech.

We've already discovered that often times when words are being mistranslated, nouns are swapped out for adverbs or adjectives, or other variations. This is a fundamental no-no when translating any language. There must be consistency, and if you find an adverb or adjective replacing a noun (or any other such substitution), be skeptical.

COMMON MISUNDERSTANDINGS OF SCRIPTURE

We've been playing the telephone game for more than 2,000 years, so it's no wonder that meanings have been altered by time and tradition. Though we've already covered many such words and concepts, we're going to look at a few additional common misconceptions and wrongful usages that could radically change—and hopefully enlighten—your perspectives.

Judgment (*Krisis*, Strong's #2920).

Many Christians seem to think that the Judgment is this one event when everyone is resurrected at the same time and either sentenced immediately to heaven or hell. This is confusing since most people also believe that those who have died are already in heaven or hell. So which is it?

First of all, it seems there are two resurrections separated by an unknown span of time, and it appears that the Judgment doesn't take place until the second resurrection (Rev. 20:1-6). Since Revelation is a highly symbolic book, 1,000 years could be literal or it could be figurative. Either way, not everyone appears to have the same future process.

Also, some people think the Judgment never ends, probably because every modern popular Bible translation renders Hebrews 6:2 as "eternal judgment." How could a Judgment, which is an event and not a condition, go on forever? This period could, however, take a long time, since it is depicted as lasting for an entire age. Consider two different translations:

NAS: "...and the resurrection of the dead and *eternal judgment*" (Heb. 6:2).

YLT: "of rising again also of the dead, and of *judgment age-during (age-lasting)...*"

If the Judgment lasts for an age, might it be more purposeful than we once thought? Earlier we saw the word "kolasis," meaning "correction" or "pruning." This word is often associated with the Judgment, and this is what the Judgment is all about—age lasting pruning and correction. As we mentioned before, the fact that some in the second resurrection of Matthew 25:46 spend it in "eonian life" is not cause for alarm and does not suggest that they do not have "everlasting life." The context is merely teaching that some are enjoying the age being more intimately connected to the Vine (Jesus), and others are not having such a good time while their willful old natures are being purified, refined, and "crucified with Christ." Remember, during any age that you are abiding in Christ, you are enjoying eonian life — even right now.

I might mention once more that my own personal viewpoint is that fair, life-changing judgment cannot plausibly take place by external, heavy-handed force, but rather I think this will be an age where people are having an internal experience of their hearts being softened (recreated), the resulting remorse over past wrongs to others, and the desire and effort to mend what has been broken. This is not unlike the process that happens for the earlier harvest of people now, who have been given new hearts in this age and who devote their lives to the good of others.

Lose/Destroy/Perish. (*Apollumi*, Strong's #622).

As far as I have found, all of the NT and Greek OT (Septuagint) verses that have to do with the destruction of people (some evil, some not) use some form of the Greek word, "apollumi" or "ollumi." Many verses use this word while speaking simply of the death of mortals, and many others seem to convey utter and final (eternal) destruction in hell.

So what does *apollumi* mean exactly? The best way to find out is to compare all the various ways it's used. Consider the following verses (uses of *apollumi* italicized):

Matt. 2:13: "Now when they had gone, behold, an angel of the Lord appeared to Joseph in a dream and said, 'Get up! Take the Child and His mother and flee to Egypt, and remain there until I tell you; for Herod is going to search for the Child [Jesus] to *destroy* Him.'"

Matt. 8:24–25: "And behold, there arose a great storm on the sea, so that the boat was being covered with the waves; but Jesus Himself was asleep. And they came to Him and woke Him, saying, 'Save us, Lord; we are *perishing*!'"

Matt. 10:28: "Do not fear those who kill the body but are unable to kill the soul; but rather fear Him who is able to *destroy* both soul and body in hell (Gehenna)."

Matt. 10:39: "He who has found his soul will *lose* it, and he who has *lost* his soul for My sake will find it" (MLT).

Matt. 27:20: "But the chief priests and the elders persuaded the crowds to ask for Barabbas and to put Jesus to *death*."

Luke 15:4: "What man among you, if he has a hundred sheep and has *lost* one of them, does not leave the ninety-nine in the open pasture and go after the one which is *lost* until he finds it?"

Luke 15:24: " '...for this son of mine was dead and has come to life again; he was *lost* and has been found.' And they began to celebrate."

Luke 17:29: "...but on the day that Lot went out from Sodom it rained fire and brimstone from heaven and *destroyed* them all."

Luke 19:10: "For the Son of Man has come to seek and to save that which was *lost*."

1 Cor. 15:18: "Then those also who have fallen asleep in Christ (died) have *perished*."

What can we conclude? First of all, you can clearly see that apollumi can't be used to convey utter, final destruction in most of these verses, but only temporary loss. *Apollumi* comes from two root words, "apo" and "ollumi." According to Strong's Concordance, *Apo* means "of separation" or "away." *Ollumi* is from the root word "olethros" which translates roughly in ancient Greek to "destruction," but often with a positive connotation, *as in the destruction required for and preceding renewal.*[70]

According to Wikipedia:

> A more enlightened translating of this word (olethros) in these verses** would be *punishment* – the kind of punishment that relieves one of guilt for a debt paid in full, enabling one to go on to share in the LORD's everlasting grace, continually receiving discipline as one of His beloved sons.[71]

A good example of this idea is demonstrated in Scripture is 1 Corinthians 5:5: "I have decided to deliver such a one to Satan for the

---

* **The Greek *olethros* is found in 1 Cor. 5:5; 1 Thess. 5:3; 2 Thess. 1:9; and 1 Tim. 6:9.

destruction (olethros) of his flesh, so that his spirit may be saved in the day of the Lord Jesus."

In his section on Word Studies from the NT, Marvin Vincent writes of olethros:

> But olethros does not always mean destruction or extinction. Take the kindred verb *apollumi,* to destroy or put an end to, or in the middle voice, to be lost, to perish. Peter says "...the world being deluged with water, perished" (*apoleto,* 2 Pet. 3:6); *but the world did not become extinct, it was renewed.* In Heb. 1:11–12, quoted from Ps. 102, we read concerning the heavens and the earth... "They shall perish (*apolountai*)...like and old garment they will also be changed (*allagesontai*)." The perishing is only preparatory to change and renewal. Compare Isa. 51:6,16; 66:22; 2 Pet. 3:13; Rev. 21:1.[72]

Understood correctly, *apollumi* never implies a total, permanent loss, death, or destruction of anything. In fact, throughout the NT, people or things that have been "*apollumi-ed*" are found, saved, and restored. It's a temporary putting away of the old through a process of finding that which is lost, correction, renewal, and restoration. Isn't that wonderful news?

Christ (*Christos*, Strong's #5547).

This word isn't a mistaken translation, but merely a misleading word because it's *not* translated. Many people actually think that it's part of Jesus' name. Christ, from the Greek word "Christos," should be translated as "anointed." *Iesous Christo* should be fully translated, *Jesus Anointed*. It's noteworthy that most English versions translate this word (anointed) whenever it's not referring to Jesus.

Church (*Ekklesia*, Strong's #1577).

The word "church" dates back before the 12th century A.D. and, according to Merriam-Webster, is defined as: "*a building* for public and especially Christian worship." As far as the word or concept of "church" in the Scriptures, it's not found anywhere. The Greek word translated as "church" is "ekklesia" which literally translates as, "out-called." Just for fun, try substituting "out-called" for *church* in the NT and see how it reads. This is a carry over of the theme in the OT for the ones called out of Egypt for deliverance ahead of the rest in this mortal lifetime. "The rest" would be delivered later. Modern believers are a continuation of the out-called. Andy Zoppelt, a participant in the Home Church movement and producer of TheRealChurch.com says:

> The changing of one word can literally change the world. Our word "Church" is one of those words that has impacted the world and has subverted the purpose for which it was intended. Because the translators used the word "church," meaning a building, instead of a more accurate word reflecting a functioning body, it has affected our whole approach to the meaning of the body of Christ. We have been given a word from the translators that has nothing to do with the original Greek word ekklesia. ...The [early] Catholic Church and the Church of England both used the word "church" and its meaning as a building to hold the people in subjection to their control. Without a building they would have lost their power over the people. Even today, without a building the clergy system would fall. This system of clergy/laity and the use of a building is what we have come to know as the "institutional" church system. This system was totally foreign to the vocabulary and the life of the disciples of Jesus, who built and depended on the move of the Holy Spirit through all the people being built together.[73]

Blasphemy (*Blasphemia*, Strong's #989).

What is blasphemy? I believe it's akin to knowing by experience the power or reality of the Spirit in one's life (having been called out) but choosing to deny or reject it. One of Strong's definitions is, "literally, slow (sluggish) to call something *good* (that *really is good*)." Perhaps 2 Tim. 3:5 takes a stab at it with, "holding to a form of godliness, although they have denied its power."

Many people believe that blasphemy against the Spirit is an "unforgiveable sin." If one reads Mark or Luke in a modern translation, it's easy to see where this notion comes from.

"Truly I say to you, all sins shall be forgiven the sons of men, and whatever blasphemies they utter; but whoever blasphemes against the Holy Spirit *never has forgiveness, but is guilty of an eternal sin...*" (Mark 3:28–29).

But then we read Matthew 12:32, quoting Jesus: "...whoever speaks against the Holy Spirit, *it shall not be forgiven him, either in this age or in the age to come*" (Matt. 12:31-32).

Why such a disparity between the two? Not being forgiven for this age (right now) or the age to come (a finite period of time) is quite different than *never* being forgiven. The key is the Greek word used for "eternal" in this case. It's that word "aionios" again. Read Mark 3:28-29 in Young's Literal (YLT):

"...but whoever may speak evil in regard to the Holy Spirit hath not forgiveness — to the age, but is in danger of age-during judgment" (YLT).

So you see, blasphemy against the Spirit can be forgiven, not in this age nor apparently the next, but I believe it will be forgiven during the Judgment Age, and most certainly before the last Jubilee!

Satan (*Satan*, Strong's Hebrew #7854).

Like the word *Christ*, his Hebrew word for *adversary* is not mistranslated, but is another word that is *not* translated. Most people think *satan* is a proper name, but actually, the primary adversary is never named in the Bible. KJV pins the name "Lucifer" on the adversary in Isaiah 14, but at closer inspection this is a complete mistranslation, which is why no other Bible versions use it.

Since *satan* only means "adversary," it is used to describe anyone who opposes (1 Sam 29:4 actually translates it as "adversary"), and is even used at times to describe the work or position of God in people's lives: "But God was angry because [Balaam] was going, and the angel of the LORD took his stand in the way as an adversary (satan) against him" (Num. 22:22). What is interesting to me is that, when speaking of The (supposed) Adversary, it is left untranslated (and capitalized) as *Satan*, but when speaking of any other opposition, it is translated as adversary. Again, that has misled most Christians to think that satan is a name.

Righteous (*Dikaios*, Strong's #1342).

Most modern translations place major emphasis on being "righteous" in the sense of being morally good. Certainly the Bible teaches us to be "good" people, but the problem is that this word has been misconstrued, placing over-importance on a concept that was not the intent of Jesus or the writer's of the Scriptures.

The word often translated as "righteous" (and all forms) is actually from the Greek word "dikaios," and is better translated as "just" (adjective) or "justice" (noun), with the intent of fair treatment of others.

We can see this in comparing different forms of dikaios. For instance, the Greek word for "judgment" (in the sense of arbitration) is "dikazo," and the word for "judge" is dikastes." Dikaios offers a sense of justice and fairness, especially in administering Law.

In many places, translators left this word with its proper translation:

"For Christ also died for sins once for all, the just (dikaios) for the unjust (adikaios), so that He might bring us to God..." (1 Pet. 3:18, KJV).

"Masters, grant to your slaves justice (dikaios) and equality..." (Col. 4:1).

But in most other places, you will see them translate the word as "righteous."

"...unless your righteousness (dikaios) surpasses that of the scribes and Pharisees, you will not enter the kingdom of heaven" (Matt. 5:20).

This verse has always been a stumper, especially since the Pharisees appeared to be very righteous in their outward adherence to the Law. Did that mean the rest of us have to be religiously and morally perfect? Well, had translators translated it correctly, the verse (and Bible for that matter) would make more sense. If you go to Matthew 23 and read Jesus' vehement slams against the Pharisees, it's all in the context of their injustice as administers of the intent of the Torah. They were practically faultless in following purity rules and rituals, but they had no application or intent of restoring justice to those who were oppressed and who relied on their merciful leadership.

So why the mistranslation? In his book, *The Jesus Secret*, Michael Wood reveals that Bible translators have fully known that dikaios means "justice" or "equitable treatment" of others since the discovery of the Greek papyri* at the turn of the century. However, the original KJV rendered it "righteous" in the 1600s, and for the sake of 300 years of tradition whereby complete theological doctrines had already been built

---

* See "dikaios" in *The Vocabulary of the Greek Testament: Illustrated from the Papyri and Other Non-Literary Sources*, by James Hope Moulton and George Milligan, Hodder and Stoughton, 1914–1929, page 162. Available on Google Books.

around the Middle Ages emphasis on a strict, morally pious code of conduct, most contemporary theologians ignored the true meaning and left it "righteous." If you begin reading both the OT and the NT with this new realization and application, substituting just or justice whenever you see righteous or righteousness, the Bible makes a whole lot more sense!

Heaven (*Ouranos*, Strong's #3772).

This is such a hard one to shake, but we have been led to believe that when we die, we go off to heaven, leaving earth behind. The Scriptures actually appear to teach the opposite—that we were made for earth, and our purpose is to bring heaven here—both now and later. This isn't to say that we won't someday have access to other realms and dimensions, but Scriptures seem to say that our earth will be renewed and restored, a fit home for God's imperishable people.

In keeping with the last word we looked at, *dikaios*, a major theme throughout the Bible is of people bringing a Kingdom to earth with a new system of justice, fairness, uncorrupted rule, and inclusion of all or becoming One. This is the intent throughout the Bible—restoring justice to the poor, needy, orphans, widows, and oppressed. So don't pack your bags just yet—it looks like you're going to be staying right here for a long while.

You've Got Questions For Me?

Bible Version? If all Bible versions are inaccurate, then which one should I use?

The key to any diet is variety and trying to consume "organic" as much as possible. I personally use NAS and the Septuagint as my primary study texts, but I frequently compare both to the KJV, Concordant Literal, and Interlinear Bibles when doing verse or word studies. And even then, I frequently look up words in the Concordance and Lexicon. Though it sounds like a lot of work, getting to the original intent is truly a treasure hunt and can be fun if that's the kind of thing you're into (if not, just read books by those of us who are). The most important consideration is acquiring a good foundation of God's plan for mankind through Hebrew lenses and then considering everything through those lenses. If something doesn't fit, study it out. God repeated throughout Scripture that we are to take anything only upon "the testimony of two or three witnesses." To me, the witnesses mean different authors and different sections—the Law, the Prophets, and the NT. Every single teaching in the NT should refer to an OT teaching, picture (type or symbol), or prophetic utterance. It's not an exact science and care must be taken not to be dogmatic while piecing together Scriptural teachings and themes because insight develops over time and maturing relationship with God.

Orthodoxy? How come most theologians and pastors believe in hell if it's not true?

First of all, there is "safety in numbers." Many theologians, and pastors don't want to step out of the safe zone long enough to question tradition or to change what they have personally taught and invested in for decades. As soon as they question or deviate from accepted doctrine and church tradition, they risk losing position (job), credibility, financial stability, popularity, and pride. This is exactly the same scenario that happened during the Protestant Reformation in the 16th century when the religious majority held firmly to their established doctrines. I'm sure many mainstream clergy then were confronted with more observable truths, but the cost of challenging the Church was often too great (i.e. burning at the stake) and that's why it took many years for the Reformation to unfold.

Being educated, studious, brilliant, or even super spiritual is no sure bet of being "right," because even the smartest scientists and theologians have opposing beliefs and views of their contemporaries on nearly every issues. Brilliant theologians with decades of education can't agree on many critical doctrines, which is why you have at least 21,000 "Christian" denominations.* Many of them would stake their lives on some of their core beliefs, no matter how misguided. Remember, even the most learned, studious, successful, and intelligent (don't forget religious) of Jesus's day did not see accurately either (not to mention, Jesus said God hides truth from the "wise and learned" (Matt. 11:25).

If you study history, "Christian orthodoxy" has always been embarrassingly divided and observably off-base on many issues. What makes you think we somehow got it together and have the full truth now? Understand, I'm not about to claim that I'm right and everybody else is wrong. I'm not even dogmatically saying that everything I've written in this book is correct—only time will tell. But things I'm learning now make a lot more sense and fit much better with the character of God than what I was ever taught by conservative evangelical Christianity. I'm only sharing another side of the story, and you can decide for yourself.

Established Doctrine? What about Church doctrines established for at least 1,500 years?

First, theologians don't agree on many things, even on critical Bible teachings that form their church doctrines. Can they *all* be right? Why should I trust that they came to the right conclusion about hell if there is much more evidence to the contrary? And what is so holy and authoritative about orthodoxy? Throughout the Bible, a foundational teaching is that those called out to belief in the true God will follow His leading in Spirit, not established religion, institutions, orthodoxy, tradition, doctrines, or dogmas (Rev. 14:4). Truth is a journey, not a destination. It's an unveiling process, much like ascending a mountain pass. Each new vantage point has something to reveal that's greater in

---

* According to the *Dictionary of Christianity in America* [Protestant] (Downers Grove, IL: Intervarsity Press, 1990): "As of 1980 David B. Barrett identified 20,800 Christian denominations worldwide . . ." (*Denominationalism*, page 351).

scope than what was seen from an earlier vantage point. Just when you think you've seen about all there is to see, you find that there is a whole mountain range to be explored that was, a few minutes earlier, blocked from view. No one has all the truth, so be open to the possibility that you've been wrong or misinformed, at least on some things.

Everyone? If everyone's going to be reconciled to God, what's the point of Jesus dying on the cross? It seems like "salvation for all" cheapens grace and diminishes the power of the cross.

Explain how God saving all people diminishes the power of the cross? If you're a fireman and you are called to a hotel fire, would you be considered more successful and honored if you rescued only a few people from out of the burning building, or if you rescued them all to safety?

"But if everybody is going to be saved, then Christ died for no reason!"

Again, that's like saying, "the fire department showed up to save *some* people from the burning building, but if they were expected to save *everyone* from the burning building, they didn't need to show up." Jesus died on the cross to save everyone from death—Adam's curse.

Evangelizing? Why bother to share the Gospel?

The whole point of the Good News is to give people hope, purpose, and healing in their lives, *starting right now*, through a relationship with their Father. We should be impassioned to share how others can come to a saving, healing relationship with the true Jesus (the "Savior of the world"), and how their lives can be filled with purpose, passion, liberation, and the abiding life in Christ, the life-giving Vine. If sharing this with others is not our primary life goal anyhow (with or without a belief in hell), we are not being good stewards of the great gifts and abundance we have received. We will be like the servant who hid his talents and was severely chastised!

Why wouldn't you be more interested in and excited about sharing a message that yields 100% returns with no strings attached? Every single person you meet and with whom you plant seeds with will bear lasting fruit, becoming part of your story. Doesn't that sound more hopeful and motivating than the old "gospel," where most of your efforts were going to fall on rocky soil and bear little fruit or fail? Wouldn't you then desire to share more, not less? If we really get God's loving character, and we realize what He has done for us, we should want everyone else to know about Him too, even (especially) without the fear of hell!

Obedience? What's the point of obeying God if there's no hell? Why not just live however I want and use my "get out of hell free pass" later?

Are you only obeying God now to stay out of hell? That's exactly why the early Church conjured up this lie—to control and "motivate" indifferent or half-hearted people with fear. God sees our motives, and fear-based service is not worthy of reward or "eonian life." Besides, there are plenty of great reasons *not* to live a rebellious, self-serving lifestyle:

1. Rebellion against God and selfish living leads to death, whether literally or figuratively. Try it if you want. Go out and have an affair, cheat your employees out of their fair wages, point out all the "specks" in the eyes of your friends, acquire a drug addiction, eat yourself into oblivion, mistreat your kids, live completely for yourself, and then ask yourself in a couple years if your existence is characterized more by life or death.

2. There's still a period of judgment. If you thoughtfully consider the words of the NT writers, the Judgment seems to be primarily for "Christians" with this kind of attitude (a.k.a. hypocrites). Scriptures teach that the wrongs of injustice you commit in this lifetime and do not make right will be much more painful to reconcile later.

3. You get a chance of being invited to the Wedding Feast. Jesus seemed to teach of a period of rewards for overcomers—those who are willingly faithful and obedient (check out the eight promises to overcomers in Revelation chapters 2, 3, and 21:7).

4. Malachi 3:16–18 speaks completely to this mentality. God says if you love Him with a pure heart demonstrated by obedience that He will write your name in a book of remembrance and you will be considered a "special possession" of His. God says He will esteem you and spare you (from Judgment), regarding you as a true son or daughter.

5. You get to avoid regrets and experience life in the now. "The mind set on the flesh is *death* (now) but the mind set on the Spirit is *life and peace* (now)" (Rom. 8:6).

6. You reveal your true motives for obedience—loving and obeying your Father out of desire and gratitude, not fear or duty. This in and of itself yields a life of great joy, proven by all who have lived in a loving and obedient relationship with Him.

Duped? How could the whole world be duped? Practically all religions believe in hell.

Jesus said that the whole world would be deceived by the adversary (Rev. 12:9), and He inquired as to whether He would find belief when He returned to the earth (Luke 18:8). I believe there's a purpose in all of this for God to identify those who would steadfastly believe in His loving character, out of the midst of the many who are deceived and who do not truly believe in His supreme love and power (re: all the Israelites except Joshua and Caleb). Consider a couple powerful verses in the Septuagint that read a bit differently than other translations:

Isaiah 17:10: "Because you forsook the God your deliverer, and your God you remembered not. On account of this you shall plant an unbelieving plant, and an unbelieving seed. And in the day whenever you should plant, you shall be misled..." (Septuagint).

2 Cor. 4:4: The God of this age blinded the thoughts of the unbelieving, so as to not shine forth to them the illumination of the good news of the glory of the Christ, who is the image of the unseen God" (Septuagint). God is the God of all ages, not Satan (KJV would have you believe it's the "god of this world"), and He is the one who takes credit throughout Scripture for blinding people to truth. The "unbelieving" are not "the world," but those called out who have forsaken true belief in the power of their God.

One Chance? Doesn't the Bible say we only get one chance to put our faith in Christ before we die?

No, there is nowhere in accurately translated Scripture that indicate there is only one chance to believe in our mortal lifetime, or else. On the contrary, God repeats over and over that *if ever* a person comes to Him, His mercy never fails (it's new *every morning*), and it triumphs over judgment. And even for those facing judgment, show me where in the Greek or Hebrew text that the Judgment (or results of it) is eternal.

The Book of Life?

Many people read about the book of life and assume it's some permanent, heavenly document written in ink by the hand of God. They also believe that all professing believers are included in the book of life. However, with a little research, one could certainly make an argument that this is a changing document and that it doesn't necessarily include all believers. Consider a few of the verses:

Ex. 32:32–33: "[Moses said] 'But now, if You will, forgive their sin – and if not, please blot me out from Your book which You have written!' The LORD said to Moses, 'Whoever has sinned against Me, I will blot him out of My book.'"

Psalm 69:28: "May they (certain 'believers') be blotted out of the book of life and may they not be recorded with the righteous (just)."

Mal. 3:13–16 (to professing believers): "Your words have been arrogant against Me," says the LORD. "Yet you say, 'What have we spoken against You?' You have said, 'It is vain to serve God; and what profit is it that we have kept His charge, and that we have walked in mourning before the LORD of hosts? So now we call the arrogant blessed; not only are the doers of lawlessness built up but they also test God and escape.' Then those who feared the LORD spoke to one another, and the LORD gave attention and heard it, and a book of remembrance was written before Him for those who fear the LORD and who esteem His name.*

Rev. 3:4–5: "But you have a few people in Sardis who have not soiled their garments; and they will walk with Me in white, for they are worthy. He who overcomes will thus be clothed in white garments; and I will not erase his name from the book of life, and I will confess his name before My Father and before His angels."

One must be careful when contemplating verses about the book of life because some of them have been twisted to convey permanence. For instance, Revelation 21:27 in NAS says: "…and nothing unclean, and no one who practices abomination and lying, shall *ever* come into [the City], but only those whose names are written in the Lamb's book of life." The way this verse is written, it sounds like anyone who isn't in the book of life can never get into the New Jerusalem. But compare this to a more literal rendition of the Greek:

"And in no way should anything common, and committing an abomination, and a lie enter into her (the New Jerusalem); only the ones being written in the scroll of the life of the Lamb."

---

* I've learned from Hebrew perspectives that one's "name" represents his or her character. Do our current beliefs about hell esteem God's character or diminish it?

Notice that this is in a present progressive tense, not a past tense. It indicates to me that people are in the process of being written into God's book of life, rather than having been written in there since the beginning of time, as most theologians would suggest.

This verse goes along nicely with Revelation 22:14–17 where the liars and murderers are depicted outside the City, but being invited into the City by "the Spirit and the Bride" to wash themselves in the River of Life (Jesus) and eat from the Tree of Life (Jesus). When they have "washed their robes" (reconciled with God through the blood of the Lamb), they are written into the book of life and invited into citizenship in the City.

Hell to Heaven 15:1? Isn't the New Testament rife with references to hell and eternal punishment?

I've heard pastors declare this from the pulpit, and even one of my pastor friends who preaches to large audiences all across the U.S. once told me that hell is mentioned fifteen times for every reference to heaven. Huh?

If we're going to compare apples to apples, the word "heaven" is mentioned 212 times compared to "hell," at around thirteen times, depending on the version. Conceptually, the NT uses the word "gospel" (Good News) ninety-four times and not once does it have to do with punishment. Don't you find it strange that Paul, the apostle to the non-Jews, never once mentions everlasting punishment or hell to his non-Jew audience? If hell is the worst thing that could happen to a person, shouldn't he have at least mentioned it, especially when he had the perfect opportunity with those unsaved, pagan Greeks who knew nothing about God in Acts 17? Shouldn't the OT be full of hell references? But hell isn't mentioned even once in the OT.

Hell Required? Free will requires hell, in that God will not force people to love and accept Him.

Using this logic, say you are the loving, devoted parent of a willfully disobedient five-year-old. You have clearly told this child not to go in the street by your home, and the child is clearly old enough to understand and obey. But one day you see the child looking to see if anyone is watching, and then you see him heading toward the street, unaware of an approaching car that is hidden from his limited view. You think to yourself, "I have the power to save my child, but I will not force him to obey. His free will demands that I let him get run over by his own choosing, limited in his understanding though he is."

If we're going to call it "free will," then the same person who chose not to love God (though they were blind to Him) should also be able to use their free will to not be sent to hell. If their will were truly free, they should then be able to exercise it not to go to hell and God would have to comply.

Regardless, I don't believe anyone is going to be forced to love God. In future ages, distortions will be removed and people will realize that they only rejected false perceptions of God and not God Himself. At that time, they will be invited into the Father-child relationship they always longed for, and they will desire to be His children and to love Him.

Eternal Fire? Doesn't Jude say that Sodom will be punished with eternal fire?

In Jude verses 6–7 we read in modern Bibles that Sodom and Gomorrah will undergo punishment of "eternal fire." We already have learned that "eternal" couldn't actually mean eternal here, since no Greek or Hebrew word for eternal was ever used in the Scriptures. But let's look at another angle as to why this can't be true.

Have you ever read Ezekiel 16:55? Ezekiel was written about 1,500 years *after* Sodom and Gomorrah were completely destroyed, yet Ezekiel says, "And your sister Sodom and her daughters shall be restored as they were from the beginning" (Septuagint).

On more than one occasion Jesus said, speaking to His own people, "It will be more tolerable for Sodom on the day of Judgment than for you..." The only way this could be possible is if there are different degrees of judgment, implying that it is not endless, which Ezekiel clearly declares. In fact, Ez. 16 is all about the anger of God against Jerusalem and her unfaithfulness and how, by comparison, Sodom was more restorable. However, at the very end of the chapter, it spells out even a good end for Jerusalem after Judgment:

"'And I will reestablish my covenant with you, and you shall know that I am the Lord so that you should remember and should be ashamed, and may no more be able to open your mouth because of your dishonor, when I am reconciled to you for all that you have done,' says Adonai the Lord" (Ez. 16:62–63, Septuagint).

Justice? The only justice for rejecting God in this lifetime and dying in sin is eternal punishment; it is consistent with His character of love. He can't tolerate sin.

First of all, who says God can't tolerate sin? He lives in you 24/7, does He not? Are you exempt from sinning? Is He completely removed from His sinful creation, or is He in the midst of it? "There is...one God and Father of all who is over all and through all and in all" (Eph. 4:5-6).

Secondly, you're saying that someone like Gandhi, who impacted a whole nation toward love, justice, and tolerance, goes to hell because he wasn't a Christian, but many "Christian" men like John Calvin throughout history, who approved of or participated in the brutal execution of "heretics" gets a first row seat in heaven...and *that's justice*? Didn't Peter say, "*Love* covers a multitude of sins"? And what about the 9/11 firemen? Didn't Jesus say there is no greater love than to lay down one's life for his friends? Isn't the greatest commandment to love? If a person thinks that someone who loved so perfectly will go to hell just because they didn't say "the sinner's prayer," then their sense of justice and their understanding of God's character needs some adjustments.

Superiority? Are the "chosen" or "overcomers" who rule and reign with Christ in the coming ages better than everyone else?

Absolutely not! The whole reason they are chosen is because they are willingly learning to love sacrificially, serve, forgive, and demonstrate atypical trust in God during their mortal lives. Jesus said if you want to be great, you will be a servant; if you want to be first, you will become a slave. Ruling and reigning with Christ will surely be a joy but it will be a lot of sacrifice and hard work, teaching people how to love and forgive by example. The effort will be with the ultimate goal of bringing all mankind to the same level playing field of being coheirs with Christ. The goal will be total unity and brotherhood for all, not heavy handed dictatorship, jealousy, divisiveness, or superiority.

Matthew 25:41?* If punishment is temporary (eonian), doesn't that make life also temporary?

We have covered this extensively. Eonian life or eonian punishment (better translated as *correction*) means life or correction pertaining to a particular age. There are many, many verses that teach that when we believe in Christ in *any* age, we have life right then, pertaining to that age.

A closer look at the more literal rendition of passages like Matthew 25 show them in a new light: "Then shall the king say to those on his right hand, 'Come ye, the blessed of my Father, inherit the reign that hath been prepared for you from the foundation of the world' ... Then shall he say also to those on the left hand, 'Go ye from me, the cursed, to the fire, the age-during, that hath been prepared for the Devil and his messengers'" (Matt. 25:34, 41, YLT). And just to reemphasize what we have fully covered in chapter 7 and other places, I do not believe that this is a literal fire, but a purifying process, just as it wasn't literal fire that came down on the disciples at Pentecost, in Acts 2.

John 3:16? What is the choice being offered in verses like this, if not a decision for eternity?

If this verse hadn't been so mistranslated with a slant toward eternal torment, you might have seen the truth presented in the last question — abundant, eonian life is now. Check out how it reads in the *Concordant Literal Translation*:

"For thus God loves the world, so that He gives His only-begotten Son, that everyone who is believing in Him should not be perishing, but may be having life eonian" (CLT). Life right now, in this age!

Matthew 16:24–25? Doesn't the Bible say you can lose your soul?

Be sure to read chapter 21, "Redefining the Soul," for the answer to this question.

---

* For more on Matt. 25:41, see "Ellicott's Commentary on the Bible" in the Resources section and also chapter 14.

Romans 1:18-23? Doesn't Paul say that all people have had the opportunity to respond to God's invitation and are therefore without excuse?

I offer a great explanation for this verse in chapter 11 in the section, "Does everyone really get a fair chance now?"

Hitler? What about Hitler — are you saying he is going to be saved?

The most frequent question I get from Christians when sharing my views on God's plan to save all is "What about Hitler" (probably because they haven't yet thought of the next, more obvious question, "What about Satan")? You will find all my perspectives on Hitler and those like him in chapter 10 starting with the section, "Father Forgive Them," and reading through the end. But now that I mentioned it, *what about Satan?*

Satan? I can maybe deal with Hitler...but Satan? That's impossible!

My Bible says that, with God, all things are possible. When I was a little girl, I remember asking God, "What if I prayed for Satan? Couldn't he be saved too?" These are the innocent, believing questions of kids. There are several verses that indicate to me that Satan (Hebrew for "adversary"), a created being, is merely playing a part in The Story. When the adversarial duties are complete, why wouldn't even Satan also be reconciled and brought into harmony with God? I think if God leaves even one person or spirit unrestored and unreconciled in His creation, He has unfinished business and has not fulfilled His promises.

Col. 1:15-20: "He is the image of the invisible God, the firstborn of all creation. For by Him all were created, both in the heavens and on earth, visible and invisible, whether thrones or dominions or rulers or authorities — all have been created through Him and for Him. He is before all, and in Him all hold together. ...For it was the Father's good pleasure for all the fullness to dwell in Him, and through Him to reconcile all to Himself, having made peace through the blood of His cross; through Him, I say, whether on earth or in heaven" (MLT).

Acts 3:20-21: "...and that He may send Jesus, the Christ appointed for you, whom heaven must receive until the period of restoration of all things about which God spoke by the mouth of His holy prophets from ancient time."*

Rom. 16:20: "And the God of peace shall bruise the adversary under your feet quickly" (YLT). Notice that this speaks of the God of peace, not vengeance, and the adversary will be bruised. Other versions use the word "crush," which isn't a bad rendition either. The Greek word used here for "bruise" is suntribo (Strong's #4937), and carries the idea of being brought to brokenness.

What if You're Wrong? Isn't it better to choose the safe side? If you're wrong, perhaps you will go to hell for teaching such blasphemy and causing others to lose their souls.

In the worst-case scenario that I'm wrong, I can't imagine Jesus or my loving heavenly Father saying to me at the resurrection, "Well, Julie, I'm going to have to send you to hell because you thought my love was too complete and too victorious. You really gave me too much credit for my plan and my power. How could you have spread such false rumors about me, admirable as they were? Not to mention, once you really latched onto this notion of Me saving *all*, you started to love people too much!"

How ludicrous it is to me to even think of doubting God's all-inclusive plan and the scope of His love! I say, if people are only turning to God as a way out of hell, it's not a true conversion, but only lip service, and God detests lip service (Matt. 15:8).

---

* See also 1 Peter 3:18–20.

TALKING POINTS

Can God's love fail?

1 Corinthians 13:8; 1 John 4:8

Deception of the masses?

Jeremiah 8:7–9; Luke 18:8; Revelation 12:9

Hidden truth?

Matthew 13:11, 34; Luke 8:10

Why would God purposely blind people and then send them to hell?

Exodus 4:11; John 12:39–40

Did Jesus intentionally doom non-Jews to hell?

Matthew 10:5–6; Matthew 15:22–24

Will all rich people go to hell?

Matthew 19:24; Mark 10:23; James 1:1–5

What kind of person does God resist?

Is. 29:13–14; Luke 10:21–22; John 12:39–40; 1 Cor. 1:27–29 (see CLT)

Did Paul wish to be eternally separated from God in hell?

Romans 9:3

Why didn't Paul ever mention hell to the non-Jewish world?

Is fire (i.e. "lake of fire") a *literal* fire?

Deut. 4:20; Zeph. 3:8–9; Mark 9:49; Luke 3:16; 1 Cor. 3:15; Heb. 12:29

How can people be dead forever if death is destroyed?

Isaiah 25:8; 1 Corinthians 15:26; Revelation 20:14

Why doesn't the Bible ever mention being concerned about the spiritual well-being/eternity of the orphans and poor?

Deut. 24:19, 27:19; Isaiah 1:17; James 1:27

Did Jesus die in vain for the lost?

1 John 2:2

What happens to the wicked when death is destroyed?

Isaiah 25:8; 1 Cor. 15:26; Revelation 20:14

Does God do exactly as He wills and wishes on earth and in heaven?

Isaiah 46:10; Matthew 6:10

Can coercion produce glory or allegiance?

Isaiah 45:23–24; Matthew 15:7–8; Romans 14:11; Philippians 2:10–11

Can a wicked person declare Jesus as Lord or be inhabited by the Spirit?

1 Corinthians 12:3; Romans 10:9; Philippians 2:10

Who are the "all humans" distinguished from "especially believers?"

Galatians 6:10; 1 Timothy 4:10

Are there some who are not ever drawn to salvation?

John 12:32

How many people exercise their "free will" to choose God?

Psalm 53:1–3; John 6:44, 6:65

Did Paul exercise his free will to choose Jesus?

1 Timothy 1:13–16 (also see *Concordant Literal Translation*)

How many of those condemned in Adam are declared alive in Christ?

Romans 5:18; 1 Corinthians 15:22

If all die in Adam, and only a few are made alive in Christ, how can grace "much more" abound than sin?

Rom. 5:20

Which heavenly dominions and rulers are to be reconciled to God?

Colossians 1:16, 19–20

Does God really create and cause evil?

Job 31:23; Isaiah 45:7; Jeremiah 16:10 (refresh your perspective with chapter 18)

What is the "first" or "better" resurrection? Why is everyone not resurrected together?

Hebrews 11:35; Revelation 20:4–6

Will "heaven" be heaven if our loved ones are being tortured in our presence (and God's) forever?

Revelation 14:9–11

Is the Bible the *inerrant, authoritative* word of God, immune to mistranslations?

Jeremiah 8:8–9

How come KJV is the only popular version to include 54 references to hell (compare to 0 in *Young's Literal*)?

If everyone else is in hell in the coming ages, which "nations" are the godly ruling and reigning over with "a rod of iron?"

Revelation 2:26–28, quoted from Psalm 2:8–9

Pictured is the New Jerusalem. Who is *the Spirit*? Who is *the Bride*? Who is being invited to take of the water of life?

Revelation 22:14–15,17

If God is reconciling the universe, how can some be tormented forever?

Colossians 1:20

How can God gather all things together as one, while billions remain eternally estranged?

Ephesians 1:10

If God is Love and has all power, will He not find a way to save all?

1 Tim. 2:3–4; 1 Timothy 4:9–11

VERSES PROCLAIMING
GOD WILL SAVE ALL

There are perhaps hundreds of verses proclaiming God's plan to save all, but here are just a few of my favorites.

Genesis 12:3

2 Samuel 14:14

Psalm 22:27–29

Psalm 65:2

Psalm 86:9

Isaiah 25:6–8

Isaiah 45:22–23

Lamentations 3:31–32

Hosea 14:4

Zephaniah 3:8–9

Luke 2:10

Luke 9:55–56

Luke 23:34

John 12:32

John 12:47

John 17:2

Acts 3:20-21

Romans 5:6; 18–20

Romans 11:32–36

Romans 14:11

1 Corinthians 3:11–15

1 Corinthians 13:8

1 Corinthians 15:22–28

2 Cor. 5:18-19

Ephes. 4:5–6

Colossians 1:15–20

Colossians 3:11

I Timothy 2:5–6

Hebrews 8:11–12

James 2:13

1 John 2:2

Revelation 5:13

Revelation 15:4

FURTHER READING AND STUDY

Online Study Tools

- *Studylight.org.* You'll find multiple Bible translations for comparisons, Strong's Concordance for looking up Greek and Hebrew words, word definitions, and Strong's word numbers for conducting further studies in a *Lexicon.* Don't forget to check *Young's Literal Translation,* which includes the truer translations on ages (as opposed to forever) and zero hell references.

- *Netbible.*org. Another great new resource with many of the same features as studylight.org, and many more besides. Looking up words in Strong's Concordance is as easy as mousing over the word. You can also add your own notes to a chapter and print them up with the text.

- *Scripture4all.org (Greek & Hebrew Interlinear Bible).* One of the best study resources! Use this to read the more exact word-for-word translation of Scripture. It is one of my favorite study tools because a lot of the hard work is already done for you!

- *Biblehub.com.* Look up another variation of Strong's definitions by number (first you have to find the Strong's number on studylight.org or in an Interlinear Bible, then search for the number to look up the definition). Can also be used as a Lexicon (see explanation below) by clicking on "occurrences" below the definition.

- *Greek & Hebrew Lexicon.* Once you have your Strong's word number from the Studylight.org Concordance or Interlinear Bible, use this tool to find where the word is used in other places in Scripture. You can compare ways it is used to check for consistency as well as to look for themes. Often times translated words will take a significant departure from the definition of a word, alerting a possible translation error. One of my favorites is Biblestudytools.com/lexicons/greek/nas/ (change out "greek" with "hebrew" for OT Lexicon in the URL).

- *Strong's Dictionary.* This tool can give a fuller meaning to words: htmlbible.com/sacrednamebiblecom/kjvstrongs/STRINDEX.htm.

- *Greek Septuagint Bible Online (can be ordered in hard copy):* septuagint-interlinear-greek-bible.com. The Septuagint dates back a few hundred years B.C.E. and is the version quoted by the NT authors. Though not a perfect version, it is interlinear so word studies are easy to conduct. The hard copy includes a concordance so you can easily look up words as well as follow themes between Old and New Testaments. I love mine!

• *Concordant Literal Bible Version.* This is easier to read than the Interlinear and usually closer to the Greek manuscripts than the modern versions. Notice the absence of *hell* and *forever:* Concordant.org/version.

Books

• *The Inescapable Love of God,* Thomas Talbott (1999). Download an excerpt from ThomasTalbott.com. Available on Amazon.

• *The Jerome Conspiracy,* Michael Wood (2008). Available on Amazon.

• *Hope Beyond Hell: The Righteous Purpose of God's Judgment,* Gerry Beauchemin (2007). Available on Amazon.

• *At the End of the Ages: The Abolition of Hell,* Bob Evely (2002). Available on Amazon.

• *Christian Universalism: God's Good News For All People,* Eric Stetson (2008). Available on Amazon.

• *Spiritual Terrorism: Spiritual Abuse from the Womb to the Tomb,* Boyd Purcell (2008). Available on Amazon.

• *The One Purpose of God: An Answer to the Doctrine of Eternal Punishment,* Jan Bonda (1993). Available on Amazon.

• *Universalism: The Prevailing Doctrine of the Christian Church During its First Five Hundred Years,* J.W. Hanson (1899). Available on Amazon or free at Tentmaker.org/books/Prevailing.html.

• *Ancient History of Universalism,* Hosea Ballou II (1842). Available on Google Books.

• *History of Opinions on the Scriptural Doctrine of Retribution,* Edward Beecher (1878). Available at Tentmaker.org/books/Retribution/DoctrineOfRetribution.html.

• *The Golden Thread: God's Promise of Universal Salvation,* Ken Vincent (2005). Available on Amazon.

Free E-Books, Articles, and Websites

• *Creation's Jubilee*, Dr. Stephen Jones (Gods-Kingdom-Ministries.org/list.cfm). Learn the symbolism and interconnected themes of God's plan to save all in Old and New Testaments. Dr. Jones has a gift for bringing to light the hidden meanings in Scripture and has a plethora of books and articles that offer immense understanding.

• *The Seed in Every Man*, J. Preston Eby (Kingdombiblestudies.org/seed.htm). This e-book will help you see the incredible value and redeemability of *every* person! By the time you're done, you might even love Hitler.

• *"Whence Eternity? How Eternity Slipped In,"* Alexander Thomson (http://thetencommandmentsministry.us/ministry/free_bible/ whence_eternity).

• *The Unselfishness of God* (3 Deleted Chapters), Hannah Whitall Smith (tentmaker.org/books/unselfishness-of-god.htm).

• *Savior-Of-All.com.* Ken Eckerty is a balanced, thoughtful, gentle teacher with many amazing insights for teaching the truth about God's plan to save all.

• *Tentmaker.org.* This is a great resource site for debunking hell from just about every angle and from many different writers. There's something for every palate.

• *ElShaddaiMinistries.us.* Get started on the correct foundation by learning valuable perspectives through the Hebrew DVD Feasts series offered on this website.

• *Ancient-hebrew.org/index.html.* Tap into the Ancient Hebrew Research Center for even more enlightening perspectives.

• *Brianmclaren.net/archives/blog/hell-yes.html.* "Brian D. McLaren is an author, speaker, activist, and public theologian. A former college English teacher and pastor, he is an ecumenical global networker among innovative Christian leaders."

• *RecoveringEvangelical.com.* "A movement that represents a growing number of young evangelicals, post-evangelicals, and others in our generation who resonate with the transformational vision of Jesus of Nazareth."

Documentaries (streaming available on Netflix)

- Hellbound? (Directed by Kevin Miller)

- God in America (6 part series)

- Constantine's Sword

- Empires: Martin Luther

Modern, Well-Known Commentaries on *Aion* and its Derivatives

- *Ellicott's Commentary on the Whole Bible.* Matt. 25:46: Everlasting punishment—life eternal. The two adjectives represent the same Greek word (aionion) aionios; it must be admitted (1) that the Greek word which is rendered "eternal" does not, in itself, involve endlessness, but rather, duration, whether through an age or succession of ages, and that it is therefore applied in the N.T. to periods of time that have had both a beginning and an ending (Rom. 16:25), where the Greek is "from aeonian times;" our version giving "since the world began." (Comp. 2 Tim. 1:9; Tit. 1:3)—strictly speaking, therefore, the word, as such, apart from its association with any qualifying substantive, implies a vast undefined duration, rather than one in the full sense of the word "infinite."

- *The Interpreter's Dictionary of the Bible, Vol. IV* (Page 643): Time: The Old Testament and the New Testament are not acquainted with the conception of eternity as timelessness. The Old Testament has not developed a special term for "eternity." The word aion originally meant "vital force; life;" then "age; lifetime." It is, however, also used generally of a (limited or unlimited) long space of time. The use of the word aion is determined very much by the Old Testament and the LXX. Aion means "long distant uninterrupted time" in the past (Luke 1:10), as well as in the future (John 4:14).

- *Lange's Commentary American Edition, Vol. V* (Page 48): On Ecclesiastes 1:4: The preacher, in contending with the universalist, or restorationist, would commit an error, and, it may be, suffer a failure in his argument, should he lay the whole stress of it on the etymological or historical significance of the words, aion, aionios, and attempt to prove that, of themselves, they necessarily carry the meaning of endless duration.

- *The Parkhurst Lexicon*: Olam (aeon) seems to be used much more for an indefinite than for an infinite time.

• *God's Methods With Men* (Page 185 – 186), G. Campbell Morgan (Moody Bible Institute): Let me say to Bible students that we must be very careful how we use the word "eternity." We have fallen into great error in our constant usage of that word. There is no word in the whole Book of God corresponding with our [word] "eternal," which as commonly used among us, means absolutely without end.

• *An Exegetical Commentary on the Gospel of Matthew* (Page 351 – 352), Dr. Alford Plumer: It is often pointed out that "eternal" (aionios) in "eternal punishment" must have the same meaning as in "eternal life." No doubt, but that does not give us the right to say that "eternal" in both cases means "endless."

• *Word Studies of the New Testament, Vol. IV* (Page 59), Dr. (Prof.) Marvin Vincent: The adjective aionios in like manner carries the idea of time. Neither the noun nor the adjective in themselves carries the sense of "endless" or "everlasting." Aionios means enduring through or pertaining to a period of time. Out of the 150 instances in the LXX (Septuagint), four-fifths imply limited duration. (Page 291, about 2 Tim. 1:9): "Before the world began" (pro chronon aionion) Lit. Before eternal times. If it is insisted that aionion means everlasting, this statement is absurd. It is impossible that anything should take place before everlasting times.

• *The Berean Expositor, An Alphabetical Analysis, Vol. I* (Page 52), Charles H. Welch, editor: What we have to learn is that the Bible does not speak of eternity. It is not written to tell us of eternity. Such a consideration is entirely outside the scope of revelation. (Page 279): Eternity is not a biblical theme.

• *The New Testament in Modern Speech* (Page 657), Dr. R.F. Weymouth: Eternal: Greek: "aeonion," i.e., "of the ages." Etymologically this adjective, like others similarly formed, does not signify "during," but "belonging to" the aeons or ages.

THANK YOU!

This book project was truly a supported effort by many hard-working friends and loved ones.

I'd like to especially thank "the herechicks," who helped make the message of this book possible, literally through years of research as we pieced this message together, one day, one verse, one book, one website at a time: Darcy Mae Englert and Barbie ("Kins") Riley.

Also a big and very special thank you to others who helped with the proofreading process: Giea (Pet) Kennedy, George Waye, and Christian Luca. And to William "Bill" Lenhart for the generous time spent on compiling the index for the revised edition!

Big time kudos to the two greatest daughters E-V-E-R, Dani and Jessi. You have both been an inspiration and crucial part of searching out this message on behalf of my mother-heart.

And of course, a ginormous thanks to my BFF and husband Shucks for all your design artistry, hard work, creative inspiration, crucial suggestions, and meticulous edits. How this book and message has radically changed our lives for the better. Thanks for sharing this amazing heretic journey with me!

ENDNOTES

1 Stephen M. Wylen, *The Seventy Faces of Torah: The Jewish Way of Reading the Sacred Scriptures* (Paulist Press, May 2005), 12.

2 William C. Symonds, with Brian Grow in Atlanta and John Cady in New York, "Earthly Empires: How Evangelical Churches are Borrowing from the Business Playbook," Business Week Online: http://www.businessweek.com/magazine/content/05_21/b3934001_mz 001.htm (May 23, 2005).

3 "Church Stewardship & Tithing Report," http://churchtithesandofferings.com/blog/giving-statistics/ (accessed June 28, 2010).

4 Ken Walker, "TULIP Blooming: Southern Baptist seminaries Re-introduce Calvinism to a Wary Denomination," Christianity Today Online: http://www.christianitytoday.com/ct/2008/february/8.19.html (January 17, 2008).

5 "Gehenna," New World Encyclopedia: http://www.newworldencyclopedia.org/entry/Gehenna (accessed January 5, 2011).

6 Tracy Rich, "Olam Ha-Ba: The Afterlife," JewFAQ: www.jewfaq.org/olamhaba.htm#Gan (accessed January 3, 2011).

7 "Problem of Hell," Wikipedia: *http://en.wikipedia.org/wiki/Problem_of_hell* (accessed May 11, 2010).

8 Ibid (Wikipedia).

9 Tracy Rich, "Olam Ha-Ba: The Afterlife," JewFAQ: www.jewfaq.org/olamhaba.htm#Gan (accessed January 5, 2011).

10 Rabbi Joseph Telushkin, "Afterlife," Jewish Virtual Library: http://www.jewishvirtuallibrary.org/jsource/Judaism/afterlife.html (accessed May 21, 2010).

[11] "Orthodox," Merriam-Webster, Inc.: http://www.merriam-webster.com/dictionary/orthodox (accessed April 28, 2011).

[12] Dr. Ken R. Vincent, Ed.D., "The Salvation Conspiracy: How Hell Became Eternal," http://www.christianuniversalist.org/articles/salvationconspiracy.html (accessed July 1, 2010).

[13] J.W. Hanson, D.D., *Universalism: The Prevailing Doctrine of the Christian Church During its First Five Hundred Years,* (Boston and Chicago: Universalist Publishing House, 1899), & *The Bible Hell,* (1888).

[14] Dr. Ken R. Vincent, Ed.D., "The Salvation Conspiracy: How Hell Became Eternal," http://www.christianuniversalist.org/articles/salvationconspiracy.html (accessed July 1, 2010).

[15] Frederick D. Farrar, D.D. F.R.S., Chaplain in Ordinary to the Queen, *Lives of the Fathers: Sketches of Church History in Biography* (London: Adam and Charles Black, 1907).

[16] Samuel G. Dawson and Patsy Rae Dawson, *The Teaching of Jesus From Mount Sinai to Gehenna: A Faithful Rabbi Urgently Warns Rebellious Israel* (SGD Press, June 26, 2009).

[17] "Vulgate," Wikipedia: http://en.wikipedia.org/wiki/Vulgate (accessed June 1, 2011).

[18] Alexander Thomson, "Whence Eternity? How Eternity Slipped In," http://thetencommandmentsministry.us/ministry/free_bible/whence_eternity (accessed June 1, 2011).

[19] David Daniell, *The Bible in English: its history and influence* (New Haven, Conn: Yale University Press, 2003), 439.

[20] Bart D. Ehrman, *Jesus Interrupted* (New York: HarperCollins Publishers, 2009), 272.

[21] Ibid (Ehrman), 17.

[22] Ibid (Ehrman), 276.

23 Thomas Talbott, *The Inescapable Love of God* (Universal Publishers, October 1, 1999), 164.

24 James Strong, Strong's Exhaustive Concordance of the Bible Online: http://strongsnumbers.com/.

25 Kent Whitaker, *Murder by Family: The Incredible True Story of a Son's Treachery and a Father's Forgiveness* (Howard Books, May 12, 2009).

26 Belinda Elliott, "Forgiving a Murderer (When He's Your Son)," Christian Broadcasting Network: http://www.cbn.com/entertainment/books/ElliottB_ForgiveMurder.aspx (accessed May 14, 2010).

27 Stephen M. Wylen, *The Seventy Faces of Torah: The Jewish Way of Reading the Sacred Scriptures* (Paulist Press, May 2005), 19.

28 Thomas Whittemore, *The Plain Guide to Universalism* (Boston: 1843, accessed online through Googlebooks.com, December 19, 2010).

29 Thomas Talbott, *The Inescapable Love of God* (Universal Publishers, October 1, 1999), 160.

30 Cary Sheih, "The Survival Story of Cary Sheih," NewYork-Stories.com: http://www.newyork-stories.com/cpo/911/detail.php?nr=145&kategorie=911 (accessed March 2008).

31 Julie Ferwerda, *One Million Arrows: Raising Your Children to Change the World* (Vagabond Group, September 1, 2009), 2–3.

32 Rob Bell, *Love Wins: A Book About Heaven, Hell, and the Fate of Every Person Who Ever Lived* (HarperOne, March 15, 2011), 173–175.

33 Jerome Milton, from a keynote address at the Tough Ministries Conference, The Woodlands, TX, November 2009.

34 Ken Eckerty, "Ultimate Responsibility: Man's 'Free' Will and God's Absolute Sovereignty," http://www.savior-of-all.com/freewill.html#reject (accessed May 21, 2010).

[35] "Martin Luther: Anti-Judaism," Wikipedia: http://en.wikipedia.org/wiki/Martin_Luther#Anti-Judaism_and_antisemitism (accessed May 11, 2010).

[36] "Religion: Luther is to Blame," Time Magazine Online: http://www.time.com/time/magazine/article/0,9171,803412,00.html (accessed May 11, 2010).

[37] "Adolf Hitler," Wikipedia: http://en.wikipedia.org/wiki/Adolf_Hitler#Childhood (accessed May 20, 2010).

[38] V.E. Jacobson, "Fifteen Bombs that Sank My Theological Ship," http://www.godfire.net/fifteen_bombs.htm (accessed November 21, 2010).

[39] Dr. Stephen Jones, *Creation's Jubilee*, God's Kingdom Ministries: http://www.gods-kingdom-ministries.org/BOOKS/creations/Chapter2.cfm (accessed November 24, 2010).

[40] Thomas Talbott, *The Inescapable Love of God* (Universal Publishers, October 1, 1999), 140–152.

[41] Barb Riley, Written Not With Ink: http://written-not-with-ink.blogspot.com/2010/10/responding-to-light.html (accessed October, 19 2011).

[42] Stephen Jones, "Free Will," God's Kingdom Ministries: http://www.gods-kingdom-ministries.org/free_will_-_chapter_2.htm (accessed May 20, 2010).

[43] Rabbi David Aaron, *The Secret Life of God: Discovering the Divine Within You* (Boston & London: Shambhala Publications, 2004), 106.

[44] Rob Bell, *Velvet Elvis* (Zondervan, June 27, 2006).

[45] Jacob Beaver, "Love is Offensive as Hell," http://b-logismos.blogspot.com/2011/04/love-is-offensive-as-hell-very-honest.html (accessed April 28, 2011).

[46] Rob Bell, *Velvet Elvis* (Zondervan, June 27, 2006).

47 J.W. Hanson, D.D., *Universalism: The Prevailing Doctrine of the Christian Church During its First Five Hundred Years,* (Boston and Chicago: Universalist Publishing House, 1899).

48 Ibid (Hanson).

49 Dr. Stephen Jones, *Creation's Jubilee,* God's Kingdom Ministries: http://www.gods-kingdom-ministries.org/BOOKS/creations/Chapter2.cfm (accessed May 15, 2010).

50 Jeff A. Benner, "What Does Eternity Mean in Hebrew," Ancient Hebrew Research Center: http://www.ancient-hebrew.org/1_faqs.html (accessed July 3, 2010).

51 "Eternal," Online Etymology Dictionary: http://www.etymonline.com/index.php?term=eternal (accessed February 6, 2011).

52 "Hebrew Roots," Wikibooks: http://en.wikibooks.org/wiki/Hebrew_Roots/Holy_Days/ Tabernacles/Tabernacles/Shemini_Atzeret_and_Simcha_Torah (accessed October 17, 2010).

53 Chuck and Nancy Missler, "The Kingdom, the Power, and the Glory," *The News Journal of Koinonia House* (January 2010, Volume 20, No. 1).

54 Renald Showers, "Millennial Views," http://www.docstoc.com/docs/8893328/MILLENNIAL-VIEWS (accessed August 30, 2010).

55 Dr. Stephen Jones, "Applying the Law with Impartiality," God's Kingdom Ministries: www.gods-kingdom-ministries.org/weblog/WebPosting.cfm?LogID=2166 (accessed August 31, 2010).

56 "Sukkot," Wikipedia: http://en.wikipedia.org/wiki/Sukkot (accessed November 25, 2010).

57 Dr. Stephen Jones, "The Law of Jubilee," God's Kingdom Ministries: http://www.gods-kingdom-ministries.org/CreationsJub/CJch07.html (accessed August 31, 2010).

[58] Jeff A. Benner, "Did God Create Evil?" Ancient Hebrew Research Center: www.ancient-hebrew.org (accessed October 4, 2010).

[59] Joni Eareckson Tada, "Why Do God's Children Suffer?" www.answersingenesis.org/articles/am/v4/n3/children-suffer (accessed Oct. 6, 2010).

[60] Clyde Pilkington, Jr., "The Potter Has Power," Daily Email Goodies (March 19, 2010, Issue #2313).

[61] "Bosom of Abraham," Wikipedia: http://en.wikipedia.org/wiki/Bosom_of_Abraham (accessed September 1, 2010).

[62] Ernest Martin, "The Real Meaning of Lazarus and the Rich Man," http://www.askelm.com/doctrine/d030602.htm (1984, accessed October 3, 2010).

[63] Ibid (Martin).

[64] Jacques Ellul, *The Subversion of Christianity* (Wm. B. Eerdmans Publishing Company, October 1986).

[65] Keith Stump, "What is Man?" http://www.british-israel.ca/immortalsoul.htm (accessed October 22, 2010).

[66] Rob Bell, *Love Wins: A Book About Heaven, Hell, and the Fate of Every Person Who Ever Lived* (HarperOne, March 15, 2011), 181–182; 178.

[67] "History of the Greek Language," Learn Biblical Greek: http://www.learnbiblicalgreek.com/greek-alphabet/greek-language (accessed April 24, 2010).

[68] "Greek Language," Wikipedia: http://en.wikipedia.org/wiki/Greek_language (accessed April 24, 2010).

[69] "John 1:1: Is Christ the Logos of God?" http://www.greeklatinaudio.com/john11.htm (accessed April 25, 2010).

[70] Marvin R. Vincent, "Word Studies in the New Testament: Note on Olethron Aionion," Tentmaker: http://www.tentmaker.org/articles/aionole.htm (accessed May 14, 2010).

[71] "Olethros," Wikipedia: http://en.wikipedia.org/wiki/Olethros (accessed May 14, 2010).

[72] Marvin R. Vincent, "Word Studies in the New Testament: Note on Olethron Aionion," Tentmaker: http://www.tentmaker.org/articles/aionole.htm (accessed May 14, 2010).

[73] Andy Zoppelt, "The Origin of the Word 'Church,'" http://www.scribd.com/doc/14424778/The-Origin-Of-The-Word-CHURCH (accessed April 30, 2010).